UFO: A DEADLY CONCEALMENT

This book is dedicated to the millions of unsuspecting innocents who are unaware of the enormity of what is happening in the world in which we live

UFO
a deadly
concealment

THE OFFICIAL COVER-UP?

DEREK SHEFFIELD

BLANDFORD

A BLANDFORD BOOK

First published in the UK 1996 by Blandford

A Cassell Imprint

CASSELL PLC

Wellington House

125 Strand

London WC2R 0BB

Copyright © 1996 Derek Sheffield

Reprinted 1997

The right of Derek Sheffield to be identified as author of this work has been asserted by him in accordance with the provisions of the UK Copyright, Designs and Patents Act 1988

Distributed in the United States by Sterling Publishing Co., Inc. 387 Park Avenue South, New York, NY 10016-8810

British Library Cataloguing-in-Publication Data

A catalogue entry for this title is available from the British Library

ISBN 0 7137 2620 2

Typeset by Ben Cracknell Studios

Printed and bound in Great Britain by Biddles Ltd, Guildford and King's Lynn

Cover photograph copyright © E. Mossay-SOFAM-SOBEPS

Contents

Note

In the various letters and correspondence reproduced in this book, the use of *italic* type indicates emphasis added by the author. The text includes these letters in a typeset form for overall clarity and style.

Introduction

It was my original intention that this book would take the form of a file which documented my investigations into, and attempts to prove the existence of, unidentified objects in the sky over Belgium in 1989–90. I envisaged the document would develop as a logical sequence of events, recorded as my investigations proceeded. However, because of the complicated nature of the enquiry, and the anomalies of the many issues under investigation, and the multifarious routes I was forced to take, this proved impossible. As I was in contact with so many organizations and agencies at the same time, for the sake of coherence the later chapters of this book are compiled as individual files of correspondence with the various individuals and agencies concerned. Therefore, no chronological order is followed.

The first part of this document is a record of three events. The first (at Eupen in the Hautes Fagnes of eastern Belgium) took place on the night of 29 November, 1989. The phenomenon was seen by many witnesses from surrounding villages, and, although there was only a general correlation, was detected by radar.

The second (east of the province of Liège) took place on the night of 15 December 1989, in which the radar detections were identified as similar to the Eupen detections, and in which the Belgian Air Force, for the first time, attempted interceptions of the objects sighted, but without success.

The third (over Wavre, Tubize and Brussels) took place on the night of 30–31 March 1990. This involved an estimated 13,500 witnesses, 2,500 of whom provided written statements. Seventy-five of these were members of the Belgian police force. Five NADGE (NATO Air Defence Ground Environment) radar stations made positive detections which were not identified. As a result these were classified as hostile and the Belgian Air Force made many confirmed interceptions.

My first discovery of the Eupen and Wavre incidents came as a result of reports from two Continental newspapers. It was followed by a confirmation of the Liège detection from the Belgian Minister of Defence.

There follows a compilation of details from two sources from within the Belgian Air Force. It is a record of police and radar reports of the events in central Belgium on the night of 30–31 March 1990. Details are then given of a radio transmission between the pilot of one of the two F-16 interceptor aircraft involved and Glons CRC (NADGE radar control). Details are given of the performance figures of these objects.

As no credible answers to my questions were forthcoming from various sections of the British defence establishment (despite the assistance of some eminent people), I compiled a 40-page document asking for an inquiry to be instigated by the European Parliament.

This has been accepted by the Committee on Petitions of the European Parliament for discussion by the Committee on Energy, Research and Technology, as Petition no. 990/93.

The Belgian defence establishment, despite repeated requests, will not confirm whether they will co-operate with an inquiry.

The Committee on Energy, Research and Technology have been advised of this.

It was my original intention to prove the existence of material objects over Belgium in 1989–90. *It is important to understand that my investigations have proved the existence of such objects. The evidence uncovered leaves no doubt that objects of substance and opacity appeared over Belgium on those dates.*

When we consider the replies of the various defence establishments whose correspondence is reproduced in this book, *note* that it is alleged that no one knows what these phenomena are.

There is also a chain of events that, step by step, link the Belgian unidentified radar detections directly with the British Ministry of Defence in London.

I have presented all the facts in a true and honest way. it will be noticed that these are repeated many times, and there is a variance in information as the book progresses. This is because it was necessary to repeat the facts to the agencies involved in my endeavours to obtain answers to my questions, and because more information was uncovered as the investigation proceeded.

It is up to my readers to consider them, and to reach their own conclusions . . . .

CHAPTER ONE

Clandestine Organizations

I had been invited by some friends to spend the weekend of the New Year with them in Paris. It happened that the New Year in 1991 fell on a Friday. As the journey down – by ferry and road – had been somewhat torturous, I decided, on arrival, that a rest would be in order before venturing out to join in the revelry of the Parisians in the Champs-Elysées.

I duly sank into the luxury of a splendid bed and, sleeping the sleep of the just, arose late in the dusk of a winter's afternoon for a refreshing shower before meeting my friends in the lounge of the hotel.

I unpacked my suitcase, and after arranging my belongings in a variety of drawers I noted a copy of *Le Soir* on the top shelf of the wardrobe. It carried a headline concerning a strange object that had appeared over Brussels . . .

I had almost completed a book on philosophy which I had entitled *A Question of Reason*. I had, by just that process, reached the last chapter. The subject of this chapter was the appearance in the skies of an increasing number of strange phenomena. I had previously tried to seriously research this subject through a variety of channels, but all enquiries seemed to come to a dead end.

There were, of course, many books on the subject in public libraries. Most of these seemed to stretch credulity to its limits. I was not interested in the science fiction aspect – I was looking purely for factual evidence and a rational explanation for something whose existence I suspected to be fact.

I had, in the first instance, reasoned that if these alleged phenomena had any substance whatsoever, then – as radar will only detect the reflection of its own wavelength from an object of some substance and opacity – the first point at issue would be to enquire from a credible radar establishment, in

1

this case the Central Radar Establishment at West Drayton, whether they could be of some assistance to me in this matter.

I wrote to them on a Thursday and my letter, being first-class mail, would have arrived the following day. I actually *received* a reply from the Ministry of Defence in London on the following Monday – three days after posting my original letter to West Drayton. I have never known the GPO to move so quickly! This struck me as being most odd.

In substance, a Mr N. G. Pope, Secretariat (Air Staff) 2a Room 8245 of the Ministry of Defence, stated that any questions relating to radar systems should be directed to his department. He said that for security reasons he would not be able to go into much detail on the range and capability of radar equipment.

In reply to a question on radar reports of a vague rumour that I had heard of an incident in Belgium, Mr Pope stated that any radar reports that occurred beyond our national frontiers were a matter of national security. I pointed out that the distance from Dover to Brussels was only 130 miles and that I did not want information concerning radar detection of intercontinental missiles coming from Russia 2,000 miles away. Mr Pope declined to answer.

I was informed – in reply to a question about any on-board radar detection by civil airlines – that these tapes were usually wiped clean within a short period. Mr Pope stated that in any case, too long a time had elapsed (three years) for any records to show whether radar sightings had been observed from Belgium.

He then stated that although radar enquiries were handled by his department, they did not have any figures concerning these. It was obvious that I was not going to get very far with this line of enquiry, and, as any radar enquiries would have been redirected to the Ministry of Defence, I consequently abandoned any further attempts on the question of radar detection.

Mr Pope observed that it was not strictly true to state that radar would only detect something of substance; he said that there would always be spurious returns. In a later letter, however, he admitted that spurious returns could occur in the form of scatter – a reflection from inclined surfaces – but that any skilled radar operator could easily detect the difference between false returns and true ones.

I persisted, however, on the subject of unidentified phenomena reported to the Ministry of Defence.

Mr Pope's replies were a plethora of contradictions.

He said that the ministry does receive reports of these phenomena; the previous year (1992) they had received 147 of them.

A request for information on these resulted in a few sparse details – heavily censored – which revealed no details that could be checked.

I was surprised at the standard of investigation that the Ministry of Defence attributed to these reports; in the main they consisted of minimal enquiries that indicated only a token interest and a juvenile attitude that trivialized the whole business; indeed, in the one letter that I included in a report that I had yet to make, I deleted a reference by Mr Pope to a particular book that would have reduced the whole subject to one of science fiction. But that, of course, could have been the intention.

The Ministry of Defence issued all the usual explanations for this phenomenon: aircraft lights, lasers, searchlights, meteorites, Venus, satellite, debris, etc. They did, however, admit that there was a small percentage of reports that would seem to defy explanation. The ministry did not have any definitive views on these.

I suppose the observation that caused me most concern was the reply given to a question as to how these phenomena could be classed as not being a threat to national security when we did not know what they were. Their reply was:

Reports of lights or shapes in the sky – even if not positively identified – do not constitute evidence, therefore they cannot be judged to exist, and as such are not a matter of national security.

The perfect 'catch 22' answer to which there was no reply. There was, however, one thing wrong with it. It was two months since I had picked up that copy of *Le Soir* from the shelf of my Paris wardrobe, and at about the same time I had received a letter from Bruce Cathie – a senior New Zealand Airlines pilot of many years' experience, who had tried to investigate a similar matter in New Zealand some time before – predicting that the answers from the Ministry of Defence would be of this nature. He advised me, ominously, to be wary of any government department or establishment in any research into this phenomenon. He recommended that I carry out any investigations on my own, and warned me to be particularly wary of any groups officially recommended by government departments.

This caused me to regard any statements by the Ministry of Defence with some caution. Already, at this early stage, observations made by them were vague, obscure and suspect in content. I had a feeling of unease that a deception of some kind was taking place.

This feeling was compounded by the statement that, despite these phenomena being classified as non-existent, any enquiry to see past reports was covered by the Public Records Act, and subject to a 30-year ban on disclosure.

Mr William Waldegrave, a minister appointed to *ensure more open government*, replied in the same vein, endorsing observations by the Ministry of Defence that they were unable to shed any light on the Belgian phenomena. He also stated that records had been preserved since 1967 with a view to release in accordance with the provisions of the Public Records Acts. I did wonder what had happened to previous records on such a contentious subject before this date.

A heavy ministerial hand indeed, for phenomena that government departments deemed not to exist.

The situation was the same with the Central Intelligence Agency. Letters sent to the American Eighth Air Force at Fort Worth, Wright Patterson Air Force Base and Professor Carl Sagan at Cornell University are all co-ordinated and answered by the Central Intelligence Agency (CIA).

In spite of their obvious co-ordination involving my letters, they replied that there had been no organized Central Intelligence Agency effort to research, study or collect intelligence on these phenomena since the 1950s.

The CIA then, like the Ministry of Defence, refer any enquiries to the National Archives and Records Administration in Pennsylvania Avenue, Washington DC.

Indeed, a strange incident occurred when I sent a letter to President Carter (to be forwarded to his private address), care of The White House, Washington DC. It is well documented that Jimmy Carter, with several others, witnessed an aerial phenomenon that impressed the company at large to such an extent that Jimmy Carter – at that time a Senator – stated that if he ever came to power, he would make all information on these phenomena public. He never did. My enquiry was to ask him to confirm the incident and to ask why his undertaking had never been carried out. My letter never left the country. It was returned to me one month later – unfranked – opened along the bottom, not resealed, and put through my letter-box with no explanatory comment whatsoever. The Post Office sent their apologies. They did not offer to accept the letter for further delivery.

The coincidences are too obvious to ignore. Both the Ministry of Defence and the CIA have the same policy, and the same set of rules to obscure evidence; further enquiries are then referred to specific civilian groups recommended by these agencies. This same situation now applies to the Belgian Ministry of Defence, the Belgian Air Force and SOBEPS, a civilian group to which further enquiries are referred. This would seem to give some credibility to the statements made by Bruce Cathie, the New Zealand Airlines Captain.

The British Ministry of Defence state that all records prior to 1967 were routinely destroyed. Anything subsequent to that is subject to a secrecy ban of 30 years. Six negative reports only are held by the Public Record Office at Kew in Surrey and may be viewed on request.

The CIA state that their investigations were terminated in 1969 and that there has been no intelligence collected since the 1950s. Their reports are held by the National Archives and Records Administration in Washington and may be viewed for inspection and purchase.

Because the whole aspect of these phenomena in the United States of America has become, probably intentionally, associated with extreme radical speculations, the whole American scene becomes unbelievable and quite unacceptable.

Similar reports in the United Kingdom have been explained away by a supposedly honest media and Ministry of Defence as apparently credible weather balloons, cloud inversions, flocks of birds or satellites, and my own opinions were as sceptical of those of the average British man in the street.

That was until one evening in August 1962.

CHAPTER TWO

A Thing in the Sky

L ate in the evening in the latter part of the month of August in 1962, as dusk was beginning to descend and it was beginning to get too dark to see clearly, a friend had arrived at my house and thankfully had caused my wife and myself to stop work in the garden at the end of a very hard day.

We were walking back to the house to put various garden tools away when my wife remarked on a very bright star in the sky; it was indeed as bright as Sirius on a clear winter's night.

A strange thing, however, about this star was that as one looked very hard, it appeared to have a distinct shape; it was not a sharp point of light like a normal star, but had a very positive shape. My neighbour, who also happened to be finishing a garden chore, remarked that this star seemed to have an unusual appearance and said that he had recently purchased an exceptionally good pair of binoculars for bird-watching and would get them in order to study this strange object further. This he did, and expressed absolute amazement at the phenomenon that showed up with clarity with the magnification offered by the binoculars.

I found that only by lying on the ground was I able to focus the binoculars steadily enough to hold the subject still, and so study it in detail. We all viewed this object for a period of approximately 45 minutes, and I give the following description of what we all saw.

Through the binoculars I saw a star-like object in the shape of an absolutely perfect triangle. Although initially it appeared to shine very brightly, when studied it appeared almost translucent, and on the side facing the Earth (apparently the underside) it had two circular, convex appendages, one beneath the nose, and one exactly half-way along one side. These circular, cupola-like bulges cast long shadows along the underside of the object.

In the 45 minutes during which we observed this phenomenon, we had time to measure the angle that it formed with the horizontal at my house, then to drive along a straight road to our friends' house and measure the distance by the milometer in my car (2.3 miles) and then to measure the angle formed with the horizontal from our friends' house. We were then in a position, having two angles and the distance between them, to calculate the approximate altitude of our strange visitor – this we estimated to be 20 to 25 miles.

During the final 20 minutes of our observation, this luminous triangle imperceptibly rotated on its own axis, moving from a north-westerly to a westerly heading, and in so doing changed shape from being perfectly triangular to having a 'V' configuration. Our visitor, hastily completing some hurried calculations (he had an advanced degree in engineering), said that if the object was shining by the reflected light of the Sun, then he would expect it to disappear at some time between 8.45 pm and 9.00 pm. At precisely 8.50 pm the object began to fade, and by 9.00 pm it had completely vanished.

This whole episode was witnessed continually for over three-quarters of an hour by four absolutely normal people, who were not prone to any flights of fancy or imagination. In no way could this object be explained by any of the platitudinous statements normally released by the establishment. I have some experience in matters of aviation and have never seen any object in the heavens, whether the planet Venus, a high-altitude balloon, a high-flying aircraft, etc., that even remotely resembled this strange craft. A telephone call to the newspapers later that evening was met with the response that scores of telephone calls had been received from all over Surrey, Kent and Essex during the period of observation. Despite enquiries from the newspapers to the armed forces and defence establishments, there was nothing on record that could shed any light on this illuminated object in the evening sky.

The general opinion was that it was a complete and utter mystery and that nothing was known about it.

This incident caused me to wonder. I suppose that it caused some unease in my mind as to the explanations offered by the establishment, although I found it difficult to accept that, in company with three other witnesses, I could have apparently viewed some form of advanced extraterrestrial technology. Even so, the whole affair had sown in my mind the seeds of doubt; it now caused me to think.

This sighting formed the beginning of an appendix to my first book. It was while this was being compiled and I was experiencing the first problems in obtaining information that I received a reply from Bruce Cathie in New Zealand and looked at the copy of *Le Soir* in Paris.

CHAPTER THREE

Le Soir

My command of the French language is not particularly good. I can order a meal and ask the way, but that is about all.

But there are some words that I do understand. 'OVNI' is one of them; it means UFO.

I also understand 'La grande muette s'explique.' It means 'the long silence is explained'.

Both of these made up the headline of that issue of *Le Soir* and – together with a picture – stopped me dead in my tracks.

The picture was a photograph of an on-board radar screen of an F-16 interceptor aircraft, showing a lozenge-shaped image that appeared to be doing some extraordinary things.

On booking in at the hotel I had mentally heaved a sigh of relief when the clerk at the reception desk had spoken to me in perfect English; it was to him that I headed now. The reception area was relatively quiet at that time of the evening, and I asked him if he could possibly translate into English the content of the front page of the copy of *Le Soir* salvaged from the top shelf of my wardrobe. He was delighted to accommodate me. He said that it was not often that he was asked to read a newspaper as part of his job, and, pouring out two cups of strong coffee, sat and translated. To the best of my recollection his translation went as follows.

He said that the opening remark stated that the UFOs had resumed their place centre stage. I queried this, and he explained that there had been an almost continuous period of UFO sightings throughout eastern Belgium which had come to an end at about the end of November 1989. He said that they had resumed with the most impressive display of all on the night of 30 March 1990.

He said that the Belgian Air Force had remained silent on this incident for a period of three months, but had decided to release the information obtained from two F-16 interceptor aircraft involved in the incident operating from their base at Beauvechain (south-east of Leuven).

I said at this point that his story had amazed me. I said that at no time had there been any reports of any Belgian sightings in the British media. He expressed surprise and said that reports in the newspapers throughout Holland, Belgium, France and Germany had been almost continuous for several weeks prior to November 1989, but that everyone had been talking about the incident mentioned in the copy of *Le Soir*.

At this point in the conversation he mentioned that one of the hotel staff – a Dutch employee – had only that morning spoken of the incident and had a Dutch newspaper that carried even more detail than the copy of *Le Soir*. He said that he would call him to show me this newspaper and would be pleased to translate this in conjunction with this employee.

He continued by saying that apparently several police patrols had witnessed an enormous black triangle with many lights above the Ramillies region of Belgium. These had been confirmed by the radar stations at Glons and Sammerzake.

At this point two F-16 interceptor aircraft, guided by the Glons radar, had pursued this object for almost an hour. He said that while the pilots – in the darkness – had seen nothing, their on-board radar had detected a scan that, when they attempted to lock on to the target, behaved in a most erratic manner. It evidently changed course in a step-like series of movements, violently decreasing its altitude and varying its speed to an alarming degree.

I believe the change in altitude was from 10,000 feet to 5,000 feet in little more than 1 second, and its acceleration was confirmed as from 175 knots to over 1,000 knots in $\pm\frac{1}{2}$ second.

Evidently these speeds were attained without there being a sonic boom and the general opinion was that such performances were beyond the range of any known aircraft.

Colonel Wilfrid De Brouwer – head of the Operations Section of the Belgian Air Force – said that the phenomenon could not be either a laser, another aircraft, or any radar-jamming device. He mooted the possibility of an extremely

strong electromagnetic source, but said that this was specu-
lation, and had never been seen before.

Colonel De Brouwer said that the Air Force did not want
to be involved in observations concerning extraterrestrial
phenomena.

The Belgian Ministry of Defence initially stated that the
two F-16 aircraft involved did not collect any documented
information but later events – with the release of confirmed
on-board radar photographs – proved contrary to this
statement. The delay in the release of information was said by
the Belgian Ministry of Defence 'to be in order to study this
phenomenon with complete objectivity; observations could
then be made without influence of the media and the wave of
UFO sightings in the Belgian skies'.

The ban on this release of information was admitted by the
Belgian Air Force; it was explained as enabling them to
correlate certain details between all the facts and elements
present.

The reception clerk folded the newspaper and said,
'Evidently no conclusions could be made concerning the
nature of this phenomenon and the question has still to be
answered!'

At this point the Dutch employee arrived with a copy of a
newspaper called *Het Nieuwsblad*. The conversation now
became a complex three-way affair, with the reception clerk
translating all three languages.

Things became complicated, but a reasonable translation
would seem to have been 'that a question exists as to what
aerial phenomenon is capable of a descent rate of 10,000 feet
to 4,000 feet in 2 seconds. What aerial phenomenon is capable
of accelerating from 570 mph to 1,000 mph in an instant?'
These were some of the readings from the on-board radar of
the pursuing F-16 fighters – which the Belgian Air Force at
first denied but which were later admitted to by Colonel
Wilfrid De Brouwer, who confirmed the interceptions after
the detections were compared with those at Eupen by the
radar stations at Sammerzake and Glons, and found to be the
same.

It would seem that there were many sightings by state police patrols which had not been satisfactorily explained. Colonel De Brouwer stated that the radar station at Glons had been contacted continuously by the Belgian police. It was because of this – and the fact that visual sightings reported by the public had been confirmed by the police and the radar stations at Glons and Sammerzake – that a patrol of F-16s were scrambled in an attempt to identify and intercept the phenomenon. This event (on the night of 29 November 1989) was the first to be confirmed by the Belgian Air Force and the Belgian Ministry of Defence in which actual interceptor aircraft were used. The incident was explained as being caused by a powerful laser display from a night club at Halen in Limburg.

What has not been explained is that radar *will not, in any circumstances, detect any form of light.* Radar is the detection of an object of substance and opacity by the reflection of its own wavelength.

Apart from the fact that it is highly questionable whether any commercial laser of the type mentioned by the Belgian Ministry of Defence would have been visible at the distances involved, a laser projection, in order to be visible, would have needed a backdrop of clouds as a screen to be projected against. The night of 29 November 1989 was clear and completely cloudless.

A spokesman for the Belgian Air Force said that the interception presented no problem; there was always an interception unit on stand-by at Bevekom and it was a normal exercise like any other.

On the night of 30 March 1990, however, things came to a head. After many sightings by the public and confirmation by the police, both radar stations having confirmed this phenomenon, two F-16 aircraft (numbers 349 and 350) of the Belgian Air Force were scrambled shortly before midnight from the airfield at Bevekom. They were to intercept an unidentified flying object to the south of Brussels. These were flown by a captain and a flight lieutenant, both of whom were very experienced pilots.

Within a very short period they had detected the target on their on-board radars, but each time they attempted to lock on, in order to obtain more detailed information, the object accelerated erratically away at amazing speeds.

Over the town of Tubize, the object disappeared from the radar screens of the pursuing aircraft, and also from the screens of the radar stations at Sammerzake and Glons.

At their debriefing, both pilots said that they had never known a phenomenon like the one that they had pursued.

Colonel De Brouwer said that to judge by its violent evasive action, this object could not have been a conventional aircraft. He said that there were occasions when radar screens showed false returns (these were known to pilots as 'Angels'), but in this case there was nothing to indicate that this phenomenon was interference from thermal inversions, signals from other radar, or unusual electromagnetic waves. Indeed, when there is interference from a false echo, the pilot immediately receives a warning to switch to a different frequency. That did not happen in this instance.

The General Staff of the Air Force do not regard this incident as a confrontation with an unidentified flying object. They state that there was no visual observation by the pilots involved, although witnesses observed the F-16 aircraft apparently appear to fly *through* the larger triangular configuration of lights. It was admitted that the circumstances were not straightforward. It was after midnight, the pilots were in formation – at an altitude of 3,000 feet – and had to keep a sharp look out for each other to avoid collision. They flew to within 5 miles of their radar targets, and their on-board instruments were under constant supervision. It would seem that under these conditions it would have been impossible to have seen an illuminated target against the background lights of the city of Brussels.

Colonel De Brouwer has said that all theories are being considered as to what these objects are.

I was now puzzled and confused. While the attitude of the British Ministry of Defence has been that they were not prepared to discuss the subject of radar returns, they had positively stated that there had *never* been an instance where a solid object had been detected on radar, and had not been identified.

I had already had confirmation of a radar detection of an unidentified flying object, from the two newspapers in my Paris bedroom; indeed, I had even mentioned the Belgian radar detections to the Ministry of Defence in London. Their comment was that they *thought that a single report had been made of that incident*. I found it very difficult to accept that a detection that had occurred barely 130 miles away had not been reported to the main radar co-ordinating office of the Ministry of Defence.

CHAPTER FOUR

Eupen

Because the Ministry of Defence were acting in such an odd manner, and because their attitude to radar information was – as predicted by Bruce Cathie – a faceless form of non-cooperation, I decided that the subject of radar confirmation of observed, unidentified phenomena was obviously an extremely sensitive subject in the Ministry of Defence.

It would be reasonable to assume that, as they would not even impart the most basic of details, they had their own reasons for withholding information. I decided to pursue another line of enquiry.

I can appreciate that it is the duty of any defence organization to protect its own sovereign state; that is what defence ministries are all about, but what now concerned me was *what are we being protected from?* I appreciate that there are highly secret defence projects, the like of which we cannot begin to comprehend, and these, and the reasons for them, I understand. What causes me alarm is the clandestine nature of the Ministry of Defence and the Central Intelligence Agency when applied to the probable existence of an advanced extra-terrestrial phenomenon that has made its appearance in the skies above Earth.

It is this ominous reason for secrecy that concerns me.

It was this attitude, by these intelligence organizations, that made me decide to take my research to the place where it all happened: the small town of Eupen, in the Hautes Fagnes district of Belgium.

As darkness was beginning to descend on 29 November 1989, two sergeant-majors of the Belgian gendarmerie who were on patrol on the road from Eupen to Kittenis in the Hautes Fagnes region of Belgium noticed a phenomenon 200 metres away, to one side of the road. It was moving slowly and was some 300 metres above the field that bordered that side of the road. Both police officers noted that it appeared to be a dark, triangular platform with three powerful lights shining from its underside to the ground below. It also had a central red light that pulsated from red to orange.

The object turned towards them and passed over their vehicle illuminating the whole area and becoming more clearly triangular in shape as it did so. It appeared to be almost noiseless, emitting only a soft humming sound as it passed overhead.

It then proceeded towards Eupen (above the area of Van Hoek Street) and stopped motionless above the dam at Gileppe for a period of 45 minutes. It finally moved in the direction of Baelen and Spa where it disappeared.

The two police officers contacted the Belgian Air Force base at Bierset which, together with Glons and Butgenbach had detected scans on their radars. The bases at Aachen and Maastricht were notified, and an AWAC aircraft was vectored to the area from Gelsenkirchen.

This whole incident was to last for two and a half hours and was witnessed by 19 other gendarmes who were guests at a nearby social event. There were also witnesses from two areas of Liège, Eupen, Plombières, Kittenis, Baelin, Verviers, Jalhan, St Vith, Andrimont, Lontzen, Voeren and Herbesthal.

Reports were received by the gendarmerie from all these locations, as well as from eastern Belgium and areas in the bordering countries of Holland, Luxembourg and Germany.

Descriptions from witnesses all confirmed the varying, and constantly changing, format of this phenomenon.

Fifty-five minutes later, the same two police officers witnessed another triangular platform – only this time apparently much larger – appear from almost ground level from behind a clump of trees. It described a climbing turn, all the time rotating slowly in the horizontal plane, following the course of a nearby main road; it seemed to be maintaining a relatively slow speed, estimated at 65 kilometres per hour.

This was the first sighting of the Belgian phenomenon. It was important because it was seen by hundreds of witnesses.

These sightings were confirmed by the Belgian police and, *because radar will only detect an object of substance and opacity by the reflection of its own wavelength,* it was the first official confirmation of an unidentified flying object of opacity and substance, and the confirmation had been made by three main radar stations.

CHAPTER FIVE

Wavre

Before I begin a description of the incidents at Wavre, it would be prudent to include the briefest details of the events of 15 December 1989.

The reason for this is that it is part of important cumulative evidence. It was the first time that military aircraft were scrambled on an interception mission because of an unidentified radar detection. It was also the first time that actual confirmation was received of this action by the Belgian Ministry of Defence.

It would appear from a letter I received from Leo Delcroix, the Belgian Minister of Defence, that on 15 and 16 December, 1989 F-16 aircraft of the Belgian Air Force attempted VID (visual identification) interceptions on two occasions.

These attempts were again made as a result of observations by witnesses that were confirmed by the gendarmerie at Eupen.

After the observations had been confirmed by the radar stations at Sammerzake and Glons (Belgium) and Vedem (Germany), F-16 aircraft were alerted to intercept an unidentified intrusion into Belgian air space.

Nothing was seen by the pilots on either of these occasions. It was speculated that witnesses' observations and the radar detections were from a laser display from Halen in Limburg. This could not be the case: the distance from the laser source to Eupen is over 70 kilometres, too far for any cloud illuminations from a small commercial laser, and in any case the conditions that night were clear and completely cloudless.

It is also part of the Belgian confirmatory system that before any aircraft could be authorized to attempt VID interceptions, witnesses' observations *had* to be confirmed by the Belgian gendarmerie, which then *had* to be confirmed by

Belgian radar. On this occasion, confirmation was made by three radar stations – and radar will *not*, under any circumstances, detect any form of light.

The Belgian Minister of Defence stated that from a military point of view:

1. AWAC aircraft are under military control.
2. The presence of F-117 aircraft was denied by the US Air Force.
3. Teleguided military aircraft were not in use at that period.
4. Ultra-light aircraft produce a specific sound.

Taking these and all other hypotheses into account, the Minister said that apart from the general correlation of witnesses' statements and radar detections, while there did not seem to be any actual pattern to the events at Eupen, there were flying objects present, and the Minister did not know what they were.

I would add that, in his reply to my letter, the Belgian Minister of Defence had apparently missed the point. Although I was very appreciative to receive his information on the events at Eupen, I had also enquired about the attitude of his government to the incident three months later, on 30–31 March 1990, over Wavre (Brussels).

My original letter to the Belgian Minister of Defence was written in April 1993.

The Minister had to refer to his predecessor Guy Coëme, who was Minister of Defence at the time of the 1989–90 sightings. I received a reply several weeks later on 26 May 1993.

It was this reply that covered the incidents at Eupen on 29 November and 15–16 December 1989. *It did not include the event at Wavre (Brussels) of 30–31 March 1990.*

I wrote again on 4 June, requesting details of the Wavre events of the night of 30–31 March 1990. I have received a reply dated 15 July 1993 from General-Major Schellemans, on behalf of the Minister of Defence, Leo Delcroix. This was to be the first obstructive letter:

The Minister of Defence, Leo Delcroix, thanks you for your letter dated the 4th July 1993, and has read it with attention.
Your demand has been forwarded to the appropriate service for investigation and answer.
Yours sincerely
J. Schellemans, General-Major

To date – five months since my original enquiry on this question – there has been no reply to my request for details of the March 1990 sightings, nor an answer to my question of the attitude of the Belgian Government to these events.

I am beginning to form the opinion that someone in the Belgian Air Force made an unofficial public disclosure, without permission from members of the senior staff and is continuing to disclose information to me.

My assumption is based on the fact that immediately after the Wavre event, the Belgian Air Force issued a denial that it had ever happened.

After a three-month period of silence, during which public pressure began to build up, the Chief of Operations of the Belgian Air Force, Colonel Wilfrid De Brouwer, finally issued a statement. He admitted a spectacular confrontation between two F-16 aircraft and the phenomena witnessed several times previously.

I had by this time made contact with two members of the senior staff of the Belgian Air Force. I am not prepared to compromise them.

They said, in effect, that the reports given by radar operators and witnesses on the ground and in the air, are quite genuine.

Evidently, during and after November and December 1989, the appearance of strange phenomena had been noted over eastern Belgium. The Belgian Air Force have several radar observers who are regularly in contact with the Belgian police. Previously the Belgian Air Force had been unable to confirm any radar detections.

During the night of 30–31 March 1990, numerous reports were received from the Belgian police force and members of the public that a strange object had appeared in Belgian air space south of a line between Brussels and Tirlemont. My contacts advised me that up to this time no radar confirmation had been obtained from any interception by the Belgian Air Force.

It would appear that the Belgian Air Force had taken several hypotheses into consideration. These had been passed to the Belgian Minister of Defence. The B-12 or F-117 Stealth aircraft was considered, as were RPV and ULM aircraft (Remotely Piloted and Ultra Light Motorised aircraft). The early-warning AWACS (airborne warning and control system) aircraft were also considered. All these hypotheses were discounted and the Belgian Ministry of Defence was advised of this fact.

A private civilian organization known as Société Belge d'Étude des Phenomènes Spatiaux requested that the Belgian Ministry of Defence co-operate with them in investigating this phenomenon. The request was accepted and the Belgian Air Force allegedly assisted this group with their enquiries.

The following is a list of the events of the night of 30–31 March 1990. The times quoted are local.

30 March

23.00: A telephone call is received by the supervisor responsible (MC) for Glons CRC (Control Reporting Centre) from Mr A. Renkin (Gendarmerie MDL), who confirmed that he is observing three unusual lights from his home at Ramillies; they appear to be in the direction of Thorembais-Gembloux. They are considerably brighter than any star, are at the points of an equilateral triangle, and are stationary. They are constantly changing colour, from red to green and yellow.

23.05: Glons CRC asks Wavre gendarmerie to send a patrol to confirm.

23.10: A further telephone call from Mr Renkin with information that a new phenomenon in the form of three bright lights (with one far brighter than the other two) has appeared, and is moving towards the first triangle. Glons CRC observes, in the meantime, an unidentified radar contact about 5 km north of the Beauvechain airport. This contact is moving at approximately 25 knots towards the west.

23.28: A gendarmerie patrol including, among others, Captain Pinson arrives at the premises of Mr Renkin, and confirms his observation of the phenomenon. Captain Pinson describes the phenomenon as follows:

. . . the bright points have the dimensions of a big star. Their colour changes continually. Their prevailing colour is red, then it changes to blue, green, yellow and white, but not always in that order. The lights are very clear, as if they are signals. This enables them to be distinguished from stars.

23.30–23.45: Three new lights have appeared; these have moved closer to the original triangle. These in turn – after a series of erratic movements – form themselves into a triangle. Glons CRC now confirms that it has the phenomena on its radar.

23.49–23.59: Semmerzake TCC/RP (Traffic Control Centre/ Reporting Post) confirms in its turn that it has a clear radar contact in the same position as indicated by Glons CRC.

23.56: After prerequisite co-ordination with SOC II, and as all conditions have been met for QRA take-off, Glons CRC give scramble order to 1 J Wing.

23.45–00.15: The bright lights are still clearly observable from the ground. Their respective position does not change. The whole formation seems to move very slowly in comparison with the stars. The witnesses on the ground in visual contact notice that from time to time the phenomena seem to emit more intense, luminous signals. Two weaker luminous points of light are now observed moving towards Eghezee. These – as with the others – also move in short erratic movements.

31 March

00.05: Two F-16s, QRA of J Wing, AL 17 and AL 23, take off between 00.07 and 00.54 under the control of CRC. Nine interception flights have now been undertaken by fighter aircraft; these aircraft have had several brief radar contacts on targets designated by the CRC. In three cases the pilots managed to lock on to the target for a few seconds, but each time this resulted in violent evasive action by the target. At no time did the pilots have visual contact with the phenomenon.

00.13: First lock-on to the target designated by the CRC. Position: 'on the nose' 6 nautical miles, 9,000 feet, direction 250. Target speed changes within minimum time from 150 knots to 970 knots, with decrease in altitude from 9,000 feet to 5,000 feet, then up to 11,000 feet and, shortly after, down to ground level. This resulted in radar break-lock with the pilot losing contact. Glons radar comments that at the moment of break-lock the fighters are above the target position.

±00.19–00.30: Semmerzake TCC as well as Glons CTC loses contact with the target. Odd scans appear from time to time but the occasions are too few for proper contact to be established. Both pilots use VHF radio of civilian air traffic to co-ordinate their moves with the Brussels TMA. Radio contact is maintained with Glons CRC.

00.30: AL 17 has a radar contact at 5,000 feet – 20 nautical miles from Beauvechain (Nivelles) at position 255. The target moves at very high speed (740 knots). Radar lock-on lasts for 6 seconds and, as it is broken, a jamming signal appears on the on-board radarscope.

±00.30: Ground witnesses see the F-16 aircraft make three attempts at interception. On the third pass they appeared to go right through the centre of the large phenomenon originally seen. At the same time witnesses notice the disappearance of the small triangle. The brightest point (west) of the large triangle seems to move very fast, up and away from the observers. During this manoeuvre this point emits very bright, red signals in a repetitive fashion. The two remaining points of light of the original large triangle disappear shortly afterwards. The clear lights of the triangle above Eghezee are now no longer visible; only the western point of this triangle can still be seen.

00.32: The Glons and Semmerzake radars have a contact at 110, 6 nautical miles from Beauvechain which proceeds towards Bierset at 7,000 feet at high speed. Recorded speeds are from 478 to 690 knots. Contact is lost above Bierset. Maastricht CRC has had no contact with this sighting.

00.39–00.41: The Glons CRC mentions a possible contact 10 nautical miles from the interceptor aircraft at an altitude of 10,000 feet. The pilots pick up a radar contact at 7 nautical miles. Again an acceleration rate of the target is recorded at 100–600 knots. Lock-on is recorded for only a few seconds before the target is lost by both the pursuing aircraft and the CRC.

00.47: The Beauvechain RAPCON mentions a contact on its radar at 6,500 feet altitude 5 nautical miles away at bearing 160. Glons CRC also has a contact in the same position. This contact is observed for 9 minutes.

00.45–01.00: Further attempts are made to intercept this phenomenon but the aircraft register only a few very short radar contacts. Ground observers see the last phenomenon disappear towards Leuven to the north-north-west.

01.00: The phenomenon has now completely disappeared.

01.02: Aircraft AL 17 and AL 23 close the frequency to Glons CRC and return to their base.

01.06: The Jodoigne gendarmerie reports to Glons CRC that it has just observed the same phenomena as witnessed by Mr Renkin at 23.15.

01.10: Interceptor AL 17 reported as landed.

01.16: Interceptor AL 23 reported as landed.

01.18: Captain Pinson arrived at the Jodoigne gendarmerie and reports that he witnessed, directly above Jodoigne, four lights that formed the apexes of a square. He said that the phenomenon seen towards Orp-Jauche (south-west of Jodoigne) was the brightest and was yellow to red in colour. These luminous points of light move in quick, short movements.

±01.30: The phenomena lose their luminosity and seem to disappear in four different directions.

General Information

Weather Information

The conditions regarding the area concerned during the night of 30–31 March 1990 were as follows:

Visibility: 8–15 km with clear sky
Wind at 1,000 feet, 50–60 knots
Two slight temperature inversions, one at ground level and one at 3,000 feet.

These conditions were confirmed in Captain Pinson's report. He mentions that the stars were clearly visible.

Because of lack of equipment, ground observers were unable to take any photographs of the phenomena. These phenomena, however, when observed by telescope seemed sometimes to take the form of a sphere, part of which seemed very luminous, and sometimes appeared triangular. Captain Pinson gave a more detailed description in a separate report.

Observations

This was the first time that a positive radar contact of this phenomenon had been observed, and it had been separately detected by various sources belonging to the Belgian Air Force (CRC, TCC, RAPCON, EBBE, F-16 radar). There were also visual observations that confirmed the radar detections.

This could be explained by the fact that these sightings (30–31 March) were observed at an altitude of ±10,000 feet; in other instances visual observations were usually at low altitudes.

The visual evidence on which this report is based comes from reports of gendarmes on duty whose objectivity cannot be questioned.

The phenomena, as soon as radar lock-on was established (in 'target mode' after interception), drastically changed their parameters. The speeds measured and their altitude shifts exclude the hypothesis that they could have been any kind of aircraft. The slow speeds indicated would also exclude this possibility.

The fighter pilots did not have visual contact with these phenomena. This can be explained by the changes in luminosity of these phenomena, and their apparent ability to disappear when the F-16 aircraft arrived at their location.

The hypothesis that the phenomena were planets or had a meteorological origin is in contradiction to the radar observations; especially since the 10,000 feet altitude and the geometrical shape of these objects indicate a definite physical existence.

The first observation of the slow speed of these objects would indicate their direction and speed to be approximately the same as that of the wind at the time. Their drift differs by 30 degrees in wind direction (260 degrees instead of 230 degrees).

The hypothesis of sounding balloons is very improbable: the altitude of the objects detected on radar did not exceed 10,000 feet, whereas sounding balloons go to progressively higher altitudes. It is also difficult to explain how balloons could exhibit such colour changes, keep geometrically perfect formation, and stay at the same altitude for more than one hour.

In Belgium, during the radar observation, there was no meteorological inversion in progress; this and the hypothesis concerning balloons must be absolutely dismissed.

Although speeds greater than the speed of sound were measured several times, no sonic explosion was noticed.

There does not appear to be any explanation for this.

Although different witnesses on the ground pointed out eight points in the sky, radar stations registered only one contact at the same time. It could be that at a distance the same sighting was reported by several witnesses at the same time. There is no plausible explanation for this.

The theory of aerial images resulting from either holograms or lasers must also be discounted: holograms and lasers are phenomena of light and are not detectable by radar.

Any suggestion of a laser projection from Liège showing up on low clouds is not acceptable: apart from the fact that such projections would have been seen by the respective pilots involved, the distances of projection would be too great, and clouds or mist would be needed to form a screen on which the laser images could be projected. On this night, and at this time, there were no temperature inversions to speak of, and the sky was completely clear.

The above is a summary of the information received from two sources in the Belgian Air Force.

CHAPTER SIX

A Conversational Piece

The following is a record of a conversation between the fighter pilots of the Belgian Air Force F-16 interceptors and their NADGE radar control (CRC at Glons on the night of 30–31 March 1990.

The interception was designated QRA (1) SCRAMBLE.

22.07:	*Control*:	Loud and clear, how me?
	Pilot:	Reading you 5, flight level 90.
	Control:	Task VID check armament safe.
	Pilot:	Safe.
	Control:	For your info contact at your bearing 310, range is 15.
	Pilot:	310, 15, and confirm it's still on FL 90.
	Control:	Checking.
22.07.30:	*Pilot*:	Bravo reading you 5.
	Control:	Bravo 5 as well.
	Control:	No height on the contact for the moment.
	Pilot:	Both levelling off FL 90.
	Control:	Roger and both starboard 310.
	Pilot:	OK, SB 310.
	Control:	Last altitude on the contact is FL 210.
	Control:	Keep on turning, roll out 320.
	Pilot:	320.
22.08:	*Control*:	320, 17 miles. And for the moment maximum level 10,000.
	Pilot:	Steady 320.
	Control:	Roger 330, 5 to 10 right range is 15, possible altitude is 10,000 ft.
	Pilot:	Steady at 10,000. No contact.
22.09:	*Control*:	Contact 330, range 10. 11,000 ft. Starboard 330.
	Pilot:	Steady 330.

	Control:	330. 5 Right, Range IS 9.
	Pilot:	No contact, keep on talking.
	Control:	345 range 7. Reduce speed. Slow moving.
	Pilot:	Roger, slow moving.
	Control:	Still at 10,000 ft. Bearing 345 range 5.
	Pilot:	Confirm altitude.
22.10:	*Control*:	Last altitude 10,000 ft. Check 10 left range is 3, left side 2 miles. No altitude. Passing overhead.
	Pilot:	No contact.
	Control:	Just below you.
	Pilot:	Say again.
	Control:	Just below you. Both vector 090. Contact is 090 range 2. When steady check 090 range 3. Slow moving. Inside turn 4 nm [nautical miles], 060, 3.
	Pilot:	One blinking light just in front of you, do you see it, just below you. An orange one.
	Control:	Range is 3, 060, 3.
	Pilot:	. . . heading 180. Roger reversing 180 you have contact on me MEEL. Roger contact on you. If you reverse 180, on your nose 1 mile. It should be 1 o'clock for you. Blinking orange light. It's on the ground.
	Pilot:	Efflux, you still have contact.
	Control:	Contact for the moment 020, 15.
	Pilot:	Confirm 020.
	Control:	020, 5 miles.
	Pilot:	See the blinking light I mean . . . [garbled]. . . flash.
	Control:	030, 6 miles.
	Pilot:	Contact on the ground seems to be 1 light.
	Control:	Another contact now 360, 10 miles.
	Pilot:	360, 10.
22.13:	*Control*:	Altitude 11,000 ft, 350, 11 miles.

	Pilot:	I have a contact 9,000 heading 250 at 970 knots.
	Control:	Possibly your target.
	Pilot:	One contact on the nose 9,000 ft speed 310.
	Control:	Range is 6?
	Pilot:	Eddy do you confirm contact? I have the same in B15 now unreadable.
	Control:	Contact is 3 miles now. On the nose 3.
	Pilot:	Contact is coming in and out.
	Control:	Roger and now . . . 2 miles. Right inside turn, level 1 mile.
22.14:		Expedite right roll, roll out 130.
	Pilot:	[Garbled] 130.
	Control:	140 range 3.
	Pilot:	Confirm heading Efflux.
	Control:	130, 120 even, and continue roll out 180. He's now 170, 4. Check camera on. 160, 3.
	Pilot:	Camera on. I've a possible contact now at 550 knots in C. 6 alt 10,000.
	Control:	Just overhead.
22.15:	*Control*:	If possible take a maximum of pictures.
	Pilot:	May I suggest you keep the HUD, I keep . . .
	Control:	At your 6 o'clock 2.
	Pilot:	[Garbled]
	Pilot:	Efflux, give a new heading.
	Control:	Roll out 360, 360, 2 unreadable. Continue SB 030.
	Pilot:	030.
	Control:	He's now 050, 3. Altitude 105. Keep on turning towards 090.
	Pilot:	Steady 090.
	Control:	090 on the nose 2.
	Pilot:	One a/c passing below. Efflux is it possible?
	Control:	At what altitude?
	Pilot:	I see it Efflux.

	Control:	On the nose 2 miles.
	Pilot:	MEEL, you see it, just below me now. Efflux you have a new heading.
	Control:	South 2.
	Pilot:	Say altitude.
	Control:	FL 105. Snap 130. 130. 3, last alt reported 10,000 ft on the nose 2.
	Pilot:	Come in attack.
	Control:	Past the contact now. Altitude is 10,000 ft.
	Pilot:	I'm at 9,000 ft.
	Control:	Still no contact?
	Pilot:	Still no contact! Heading please.
	Control:	270, 2.
	Pilot:	Confirm. 260.
22.19:	*Control*:	270.
22.20:	*Pilot*:	Roll out 270. 10,000 ft.
	Control:	No more contact for the moment.
	Pilot:	MEEL you switch 135 05 go.
	Control:	Can you contact Brussels on 127.15.
	Pilot:	127, 15 go. Efflux confirm new heading.
22.21:	*Control*:	Keep on turning right 090.
	Pilot:	Turning left 090. Efflux steady east now.
	Control:	Roger, maintain.
	Pilot:	Positive contact as well.
	Control:	For the moment no more contact on scope.
22.22:	*Pilot*:	No contact on scope as well. Check fuel. [Garbled] Possible contact at 19 miles, 800 knots h 350 3,000. Efflux confirm one contact at 5 miles, left side, speed fast.
22.23:	*Control*:	No contact for the moment.
	Pilot:	4 miles to the left.
	Control:	Clear to investigate.
	Pilot:	Investigating. Rolling out now 034.
22.24:		Brussels is calling. No contact.
	Control:	Traffic approaching from 320 range 15,900 ft.

		Possible contact bearing 270 range 12. Starboard turn.
22.25:	*Pilot*:	Turning right 270.
	Control:	This contact appears to be civilian traffic.
	Pilot:	Say again, Efflux.
	Control:	Contact is civilian traffic.
22.26:	*Pilot*:	Rolling out 277.
	Control:	Roger, maintain. 17 from Efflux.
	Pilot:	Come in Efflux.
	Control:	Did you see the previous investigation . . .
	Pilot:	I had a kind of flashing light on the nose 5 miles.
	Control:	And was this light coming from the south?
	Pilot:	The light was steady.
	Control:	When did you pass over the light? Give me a top.
	Pilot:	Turning left to pass overhead at 10,000 ft and give you the co-ordinates. Just passing overhead the light.
	Control:	Roger.
	Pilot:	Co-ordinates: 50.32.08. 04.11.08. Reversing east. 10,000 ft.
	Pilot:	Reversing east, 10,000 ft.
	Control:	Roger.
	Control:	Possible contact bearing 020 12 miles.
	Pilot:	12 miles looking out.
	Control:	High speed roll out 040.
	Pilot:	040.
	Control:	Heading is 115 starboard 060.
	Pilot:	One contact on nose at 10 miles.
	Control:	That's the target. No altitude on him at the moment.
	Pilot:	Contact in C MEEL, at 5,000 ft. 740 knots. Good contact again.

		Investigating. One contact on nose 7 miles.
	Control:	Clear to investigate, check armament safe.
22.31:	*Pilot*:	Sweet and safe.
	Control:	Passing overhead BE for the moment.
	Pilot:	Lost contact now, he's moving very fast.
	Control:	That's affirm. High speed for the moment.
	Pilot:	One contact on the nose 6 miles, speed 100 knots.
	Control:	080, 10 miles. Heading is 120.
	Pilot:	120 confirm.
	Control:	Affirmative.
22.32:	*Control*:	Last alt reported 10,000 ft, 070 10 miles.
	Pilot:	070, 10 confirm. Rolling out 070. Altitude 7,000 ft.
		Lost contact, more info Efflux.
	Control:	Lost contact as well. It should be 090, 10.
		Roll out 100.
22.33:	*Pilot*:	100.
	Control:	Normally on the nose range 15, you have contact.
22.34:	*Pilot*:	No contact.
	Control:	095 range 18.17. Both starboard 310.
	Pilot:	SB 310. Fuel 044.
	Control:	Check playtime left.
	Pilot:	Playtime left 15 minutes.
	Pilot:	17 steady 310.
	Control:	Roger 17. Maintain heading for the moment.
		One civilian traffic 315 range is 12 at 5,000 ft in the TMA.
22.38:	*Pilot*:	Looking out. Contact at 6,000 ft slow moving at C.
	Control:	It's civilian traffic. Passing 2 o'clock 5 miles 5,000 ft, check 310. 12 miles possible contact.

22.39:	*Pilot*:	10 miles on the nose 10,000 ft. Contact.
	Control:	On the nose range 7.
22.40:	*Pilot*:	Got the same.
	Control:	Check camera on.
22.41:	*Pilot*:	Camera on.
	Control:	If possible take max of pictures.
	Pilot:	Very slow moving.
	Control:	Check alt of contact.
	Pilot:	I still have contact, 5 miles.
	Control:	No height.
	Pilot:	No height.
	Control:	3 o'clock 2 miles.
	Pilot:	3 o'clock 2 miles.
	Control:	Crossing left to right.
	Pilot:	Say again.
	Control:	Left side high.
	Pilot:	Looking out. I see one beacon on the nose.
22.42:	*Control*:	One civilian traffic west, 10 miles.
	Control:	Contact 100, SB, 100.
	Pilot:	Roger SB 100.
	Control:	Civilian traffic 300, 5 miles.
	Pilot:	Civilian traffic 300, 5 miles. Steady 120.
	Control:	Continue 100.
	Pilot:	100.
	Control:	Even 060 now. 060, 5.
	Pilot:	Steady 060.
	Control:	060, 3. You have contact?
	Pilot:	One contact but speed is changing from 100 to 600.
	Control:	I have the same contact.
	Pilot:	Slightly to right 4 miles.
	Control:	Affirmative. High moving.
	Pilot:	Steady east now.
	Control:	Roger.
	Pilot:	Lost contact.
	Control:	Both vector 180.
22.44:	*Pilot*:	Turning right south.

	Control:	Contact south higher.
	Pilot:	Looking out. Steady south.
	Control:	Nine o'clock 3, sorry 3 o'clock.
	Pilot:	Steady south no contact.
22.45:	Control:	Disregard, snap 360 now.
	Pilot:	360 to the left. Check fuel.
	Control:	Possible contact 350 range 10.
	Pilot:	350, 10.
22.46:	Control:	2 contacts civilian traffic same position 345, 9 17 left 330–left 330. Civilian traffic 340 range 7.
	Pilot:	Contact on traffic.
	Control:	At 5,000 ft other contact 325 is 7, no height.
	Pilot:	Contact on the radar now.
	Control:	Check camera on.
	Pilot:	Camera on – losing contact.
	Control:	He's now 345 range is 5.
	Pilot:	We have the same in B 8, 10,000 ft MEEL.
	Control:	350, 3.
	Pilot:	Radar contact.
22.47:	Control:	Contact slightly to your left, 8 miles, lost contact.
	Control:	He's at your 360 now. 360.
	Pilot:	Request turn north.
	Control:	Clear now.
	Pilot:	Steady north Efflux.
	Control:	Roger, no contact.
	Pilot:	Negative.
	Control:	Reverse south.

(Continued until 22.35, but nothing interesting. Light at co-ordinates 50.32.08/04.11.08 easily identified as light on top of chimney stack.)

The conversation between the pilot and Glons NADGE CRC radar between 22.14 and 22.19 is of particular relevance:

22.14:	Control:	Expedite right roll, roll out 130.

	Pilot:	[Garbled] 130.
	Control:	140 range 3.
	Pilot:	Confirm heading Efflux.
	Control:	130, 120 even, and continue roll out 180. He's now 170, 4. Check camera on. 160, 3.
	Pilot:	Camera on. I've a possible contact now at 550 knots in C. 6 alt 10,000.
	Control:	Just overhead.
22.15:	*Control*:	If possible take a maximum of pictures.
	Pilot:	May I suggest you keep the HUD, I keep . . .
	Control:	At your 6 o'clock 2.
	Pilot:	[Garbled]
	Pilot:	Efflux, give a new heading.
	Control:	Roll out 360, 360, 2 [garbled]. Continue SB 030.
	Pilot:	030.
	Control:	He's now 050, 3. Altitude 105. Keep on turning towards 090.
	Pilot:	Steady 090.
	Control:	090 on the nose 2.
	Pilot:	One a/c passing below. Efflux is it possible?
	Control:	At what altitude?
	Pilot:	I see it Efflux.
	Control:	On the nose 2 miles.
	Pilot:	MEEL, you see it, just below me now. Efflux you have a new heading.
	Control:	South 2.
	Pilot:	Say altitude.
	Control:	FL 105. Snap 130. 130. 3, last alt reported 10,000 ft on the nose 2.
	Pilot:	Come in attack.
	Control:	Past the contact now. Altitude is 10,000 ft.
	Pilot:	I'm at 9,000 ft.
	Control:	Still no contact?
	Pilot:	Still no contact! Heading please.

	Control:	270, 2.
	Pilot:	Confirm. 260.
22.19:	*Control*:	270.

This recorded transmission proves beyond any reasonable doubt that an unidentified flying object of opacity and substance was detected by Glons NADGE CRC radar, that it was declared hostile and that the Belgian Air Force military aircraft were guided to it on a VID interception. Its presence was witnessed and confirmed by the pilots of the interceptor aircraft who, by stating 'come in attack', confirmed the hostile classification of the target.

CHAPTER SEVEN

Radar Contacts

A video film of the various interceptions was recorded showing the on-board radar screen of one of the pursuing F-16 aircraft. The other aircraft did not operate its on-board video camera. The aircraft on which the video camera was functioning recorded 13 actual contacts; one of these was for 46 seconds. The actual contacts can be divided into five groups, separated by periods without contact.

Contacts	Duration (seconds)	Actual time	Date
1	3.4	22.13	30.03.90
2	2.3	00.13	31.03.91
3	19.9	00.15	
4	27.5	00.29	
5	8.0		
6	11.4		
7	9.3		
8	0.1		
9	45.9	00.39	
10	16.2		
11	11.4		
12	9.5		
13	11.2	00.46	

All positions and speeds are recorded. Descent rates indicated 1,000 knots and above. Indicated speeds in three figures only; for example, 200 knots could be 200 knots or 1,200 knots. Positions and speeds can be correlated; above 1,000 knots the last three digits are dubious.

The Belgian Air Force has released performance details of the phenomenon, taken from the video of the on-board radar of the pursuing aircraft. They make impressive reading.

Seconds after lock-on	Heading (degrees)		Speed (knots)	Altitude (feet)
00		200	150	7,000
01		200	150	7,000
02		200	150	7,000
03		200	150	7,000
04		200	150	6,000
05	Sharp	270	Acceleration 560	6,000
06	turn	270	= 22g 560	6,000
07		270	570	6,000
08		270	560	6,000
09		270	550	7,000
10		210	560	9,000
11		210	570	10,000
12		210	560	11,000
13		210	570	10,000
14		270	770	7,000
15		270	770	6,000
16		270	780	6,000
17		270	790	5,000
18		290	1,010	4,000
19		290	1,000	3,000
20		290	990	2,000
21		290	990	1,000
22		300	990	0,000
22.5		300	Break-lock 980	0,000

An altitude indicated as 5,000 feet would be somewhere between 4,500 feet and 5,500 feet. 0,000 feet indicated would mean between 0 feet and 500 feet. Zero is sea level; mean ground altitude in this area is ±200 feet; this means that 0,000 indicated is between 200 and 500 feet.

There was, in fact, another radar incident that occurred at the same time as these recorded detections.

The Belgian skies south-east of Brussels were densely populated during the night of 30–31 March 1990. There were at least between three and six bright lights that were changing colour. These were observed by gendarmes for two hours between 23.00 and 01.00 hours. There were two F-11 interceptor aircraft hunting true or false radar echoes from 00.00 to 01.00 hours local time.

At 00.28, Semmerzake radar detected an object 2,500 feet over the western part of the Brussels agglomeration moving eastwards towards Liège at a speed of 450 knots.

At 00.29 this object was detected by the radar at Glons.

From 00.29 to 00.33, both radars followed the object, which was following a straight course towards Liège, and increasing its speed and altitude. Semmerzake radar again detected it at 6,000 feet over Liège at 00.35 at a speed of 650 knots. It was last detected at 00.36 at a point east of Liège at an altitude of 12,000 feet.

Semmerzake radar is an array-type radar used for military air safety. Semmerzake is situated approximately west of Brussels. Glons Control Reporting Centre is part of the NATO Air Defence Ground Environment. It is one of the 80 NATO Control Reporting Centres situated throughout Europe. Glons radar is a multi-purpose impulsion-type radar. Its functions are:

1. To detect and follow every flight in Belgian air space.
2. To identify it as friend or foe.
3. If foe, to intercept and/or destroy according to alert status.

Glons is situated 6 miles north of Liège. The distance between Brussels and Liège is 60 miles.

There is another radar at Bertem; this is for civilian air traffic. The object passed 5 miles south of Bertem at 00.30 but was not detected by Bertem radar.

CONCLUSIONS

Civilian air traffic could not have been responsible. There is no aircraft used in civilian aviation that will show the speeds indicated at such low altitudes. All civil flights are known to military radar.

It could not have been a small private jet aircraft. There are no private jet aircraft capable of the speeds shown on the radar scans.

It was not one of the F-16 interceptors; these carried out a complicated search pattern that was well known to the air force and did not follow a straight course.

While this had all the characteristics of F-117 or TR-3A stealth aircraft (because it appeared to be detectable only from certain angles), the recorded performance figures are not attainable by any known military aircraft.

An anomaly was that Bertem radar, which was best situated to register a detection, did not do so. What also seems to confound the issue is the fact that Glons Control Reporting Centre – which is part of the NATO Air Defence Ground Environment radar system – ought to know of the movements of both civil and military aircraft. It would appear that at the time of the release of the first statement, in May 1990, Glons CRC was not aware of any unauthorized infringements of Belgian air space by unknown military aircraft that could have caused this radar detection.

Despite the evidence that the recorded performance figures show the impossibility of this being any known aircraft, the Belgian Air Force have stated that in certain situations it is possible to over-react and make mistakes. They say that this could well have been a military stealth aircraft.

It is interesting to note figures taken from the video of the on-board radar of the pursuing aircraft after lock-on was achieved. These show that after 5 seconds the object turned violently through 70 degrees, increased its speed from 150 to 560 knots, and lost 1,000 ft in altitude *all in less than one second*.

Two seconds later, its heading stayed constant but its speed increased and decreased regularly by ±10 knots; it also increased altitude by 1,000 ft in 2 seconds.

Three seconds after this it altered its heading by 60 degrees and, keeping its same pulsating ±10 knot variance, climbed 2,000 ft in 1 second.

One second later, still keeping the same pulsating speed and on the same course, it climbed another 2,000 feet in 1 second. It was now at a height of 11,000 ft.

Fourteen seconds from lock-on it again changed its heading by 60 degrees to its original course, and for 3 seconds accelerated from 570 to 790 knots, losing height progressively from 11,000 ft to 1,000 ft in 8 seconds.

At the 17-second point, changing its heading by another 20 degrees, it increased its speed to 1,010 knots.

In the last 5 seconds before break-lock it again changed its heading by another 10 degrees, dropped its speed to 980 knots and dropped its altitude to below 200 ft.

The total time of this pursuit was 22.5 seconds. In that 22.5 seconds there were 5 changes of direction, 14 changes of speed, and 14 changes in altitude. These are figures confirmed by Glons CRC.

CHAPTER EIGHT

An Odd Situation

I now found myself with a situation that was difficult to explain. The Ministry of Defence had stated quite categorically that they examined any radar report of any potential significance. They said that they did not have any figures concerning unidentified radar returns. Indeed, they said that there had not been instances where solid objects had been detected but not identified. They concluded by saying that any questions concerning radar returns should be directed to the Ministry of Defence, Secretariat (Air Staff) 2a, Room 8245, Main Building, Whitehall, London SW1A 2HB.

They also stated that they had no knowledge of the Belgian sightings, but, from what they were able to recall, although there were many visual sightings there was *only one reference to radar*. They stated that the definitive position on this would have to come from the Belgian government.

At that time I had just had a book on philosophy published entitled *A Question of Reason*. This questioned most of the current theories on the expanding universe, the existence of black holes, and more importantly, the theory of evolution.

The impossibility of the evolution of man on Earth, in the time scale thought to be available, led to the last chapter in that book. My discovery of the copy of *Le Soir* in a Paris hotel, and my knowledge of the appearance of the phenomenon above Brussels in 1989–90, led to another development that made me question further the motives of the Ministry of Defence.

A Question of Reason appeared to cause some interest amongst the media. Local newspapers and magazines gave it good reviews. I suppose that its ultimate accolade was a discussion on a book programme on local radio. This resulted in many letters from interested parties and a request from Radio Kent to appear live on their early morning show.

This I found awesome. To be confronted by a microphone and several thousand listeners – when an innocent swallow can sound like a clap of thunder and a gentle sneeze is able to deafen the whole of Kent – was an intimidating experience in the extreme.

Although my embarrassment on the replay was humbling, the effect of the broadcast was enlightening. I received telephone calls from all over Kent and as far away as Oxford and Woking. One of these – also confirmed in a letter – told me what I had already suspected. This (added to information already coming in from other sources) caused me to question the honesty of the Ministry of Defence and its dubious attitude to a matter of national security.

My correspondent, being a senior pilot of long standing with an international airline, stressed, first, that – because his airline was particularly sensitive to any media exposure on the incidents in question – he must request that neither his company nor his name be disclosed. I have respected his request and my reader must be assured that I have this letter on file and it is quite genuine. It reads as follows:

August 23rd 1993

Dear Mr Sheffield,

Many thanks for your letter of the 17th August. I have had a number of UFO sightings, two of which were radar confirmed.

The first was in the mid sixties. I was a co-pilot on a Vanguard over the Manchester area, flying south to London. Preston radar (as was) advised us of '*fast moving opposite direction traffic in our 12 o'clock "unknown"* –' In effect, right in the airway 'Amber-One.'

Almost immediately we three – Captain and two first officers – saw an archetypal disc-shaped craft, size 30–40 ft, travelling at a very high speed – in the order of 1,000 mph – on a reciprocal track, i.e. heading north. It was shining metallic in the bright sunlight and passed us about a quarter of a mile away and some hundreds of feet below.

I had a clear view of it from my position in the right-hand seat. There is no doubt in my mind that this was not an aeroplane; given the speed, a shock wave would have been certain, but there was none.

The second was around 9 pm on the 22nd March, 1967 over the bay of Biscay. Again all three of us observed two very bright (2 × Sirius) disks performing aerobatic manoeuvres at very high speed and, I would say, non-survivable angular accelerations, i.e. very high 'g' turns.

This display lasted for about ten minutes and Bordeaux radar confirmed 'Unknown traffic'.

Neither of these sightings have been or would have been reported officially.

I have no doubt that UFO and allied technology allows the occupants to choose when and where they enter and leave the radar and visible spectrum (or spectra); and on reflection, the display over the Bay of Biscay was exactly that - a show especially put on for us.

Given our rapid advances in stealth research and application, UFO's would obviously have achieved this capability long ago. It does seem though as if from time to time they become careless in the use of this invisibility facility.

If you wish for further information on my sightings, feel free to telephone at any time - it will be an answerphone if nobody is at home.

All the best for your Oxford conference,

Sincerely,

****** ******

It would be reasonable to assume that if there have been *two* occasions when one particular pilot has witnessed this phenomenon, then there must also have been other occasions when similar radar sightings by other airline pilots were reported to the Ministry of Defence. While these sightings were not reported officially by their respective aircrews, it would be reasonable to suppose that the radar stations involved would indeed have reported these highly irregular sightings to their respective radar co-ordinating centres. Since all radar sightings by NATO's 80 main radar centres throughout Europe are all co-ordinated, then the Ministry of Defence – Britain being part of NATO – would also be in full possession of these facts.

Bearing this in mind I found the denial by the Ministry of Defence – of any unidentified British radar sightings, and that in the Belgian sightings there was only one reference to radar – to be untrue, and, when the co-ordination of NATO radar reports is involved, *an obvious deception.*

Consider these facts, and their statement that:

Reports of lights or shapes in the sky cannot be classed as evidence – even if the sightings cannot be positively identified – and therefore cannot be judged to exist. *The fact that they do not exist, therefore, means that they cannot be considered a threat to national security.*

I found this to be very alarming, particularly in view of the reports that had been coming in to me from the Belgian Air Force, the Belgian Defence Minister and the Belgian Ministry of Defence. These reports confirmed mass sightings of this phenomenon by the population. Observations were made by telescope, TV, video, and the media. Written statements were given by 2,600 witnesses, 75 of whom were members of the Belgian gendarmerie. Completely authentic reports were given by one German and two Belgian radar stations. F-16 interceptor aircraft were scrambled and vectored on to their targets by radar – which they pursued for over an hour. Six interceptions were made. Confirmed videos were made at the radar base stations as well as the on-board radar on the pursuing aircraft.

It became quite obvious to me at this time that something indeed was going on. The attitude expressed by the department of Mr William Waldegrave (the minister appointed to ensure more open government) and the Ministry of Defence made it quite clear to me that any further enquiries on this subject would have been futile. I therefore resolved to pursue a completely different line of enquiry.

As the American and British government agencies, in any reference to this subject, were both obviously following the same obstructive policies of deception, media censorship, and ridicule, any future course would have to be in an area not corrupted by these policies.

The answer hit me like a bomb. It had been staring me in the face all the time. It was the event that had happened in our own backyard, and which (apart from a complete news blackout by the British media) had not apparently been affected by contact with either the American or British agencies. In short, the Belgian incidents at Eupen in 1989 and Wavre in 1990.

It was to the Belgians that I consequently went. My approach resulted in a veritable Pandora's box of information, which led me to compile a report entitled *A European Parliamentary Question: A Report on Unidentified Aerial Phenomena for Ratification by the European Parliament*. This report was simply a request to the European Parliament for an inquiry into the events at Eupen in November 1989 and Wavre (Brussels) in March 1990.

CHAPTER NINE

A European Parliamentary Question

Research produced extraordinary results, and my report began to take form. A problem, however, was how best to present an objective case in a fair and unbiased way, so that a congregation of honest councillors might make a learned judgement.

Once again the answer was in the question: it was to use literary licence and present a factual case in the form of a legal representation.

My report consisted of four parts. First came *The Postulation*, in which opinions are expressed – by the greatest academics of our time – on the probability of the development of highly developed extraterrestrial civilizations within our own Galaxy. This part then deals with the evolvement of intelligence and life, from the basic atom of hydrogen, to life (molecular constructions able to replicate themselves), not only on Earth, but elsewhere in the cosmos.

The report continues with *The Witnesses*. This section contains statements by the world's most intelligent and unimpeachable men. It contains their observations as to their beliefs in the existence of this phenomenon.

Part 3 is *The Testimony*. This questions the clandestine operations of the American Central Intelligence Agency and the British Ministry of Defence. It details (by a compilation of the reports given by many witnesses) the phenomena in question. It describes in detail the events at Eupen in November 1989 and at Wavre (Brussels) in March 1990, with comments by senior Belgian commanders and politicians. This section is completed with a list of supporting documents.

The last part is entitled *The Indictment*. This emphasizes the responsibilities of the European Parliament for the national security of the member states. This section gives a summary of the events that made up the Belgian incidents of 29–30 November 1989 and 30–31 March 1990. It suggests that an inquiry should be conducted into these events and the form that inquiry should take. It lists the witnesses who should be questioned and the documents that should be studied. It emphasizes the photographs that should be confirmed and studied: of the radar stations involved, of the video pictures of the on-board radar of the pursuit aircraft, and of still photographs when seen under a blue enhancement.

The Indictment then states:

> If – as a result of this inquiry – this phenomenon is thought to be of probable extraterrestrial origin, it is imperative in the interests of international security that this be recognized.
>
> It is therefore incumbent upon the European Parliament that this declaration should be made public.

A copy of this report, together with some of its supporting documents, now follows.

A EUROPEAN PARLIAMENTARY QUESTION

A REPORT ON UNIDENTIFIED AERIAL PHENOMENA FOR RATIFICATION BY THE EUROPEAN PARLIAMENT

Copyright Derek Sheffield, 1993

[Page numbers refer to document pages]

INDEX

* These are shown in the picture section.

PART 1. THE POSTULATION

Section 1. The Teeming Universe

Professor Sir Bernard Lovell, OBE, LLD, DSc, is a Fellow of the Royal Society of Great Britain, a Professor of Radio Astronomy at the University of Manchester and a Director of the Experimental Station at the Nuffield Radio Astronomy Laboratories at Jodrell Bank. He is probably the greatest astronomer in modern times.

In a very profound book *In the Centre of Immensities* he postulates on the improbability of the existence of the human race: *This generalised proposition – that processes of chance and natural law led to the emergence of living organisms from the relatively simple organic molecules in the primeval seas – is valid only if the probability of the right assembly of molecules occurring is finite within the time scale envisaged. Here is another great problem. In the example already given of a relatively small protein molecule with 100 amino acid residues, selection of this sequence of residues had to be made by chance from 10 to the power of 130 alternative choices; an indication of this amount is that there are 10 to the power of 78 hydrogen atoms in the whole of the observable universe! The operation of pure chance would mean that within the half billion to a billion year period the organic molecules in the primeval seas might have to undergo 10 to the power of 130 trial assemblies in order to hit upon the correct sequence. The probability of such a chance occurrence leading to the formation of one of the smallest protein molecules is unimaginably small. Within the conditions of time and space which we are considering, it is effectively zero!*

Professor Lovell then makes the assumption that

nevertheless, the presence of ourselves on Earth today is evidence that a sequence of similar events of almost zero probability did take place over 3 billion years ago.

Whilst this zero probability would apply to the time scale that exists with reference to the emergence of life on Earth, it assumes that the planet Earth is the only planetary body in the universe on which life has emerged.

It does not mean that we are here because that zero chance occurred. It is more rational to make the assumption that

(1)

because time is the limiting factor concerning the emergence of life on this planet, that this chance could – and indeed must – have occurred elsewhere in the Universe at an earlier time.

Harlow Shapley, Director of the Harvard Observatory, using the most rule of thumb calculation and generalising to a great extent, conservatively estimated that in our Galaxy, there must be at least one billion stars with a planet capable of supporting life.

Professor Lovell – using a finer method of theoretical calculation – reasoned that there are at least twenty billion stars with similar planets to Earth in our Galaxy alone. He stated that *The Astronomical answer from these theoretical considerations seems inescapable; there are billions of stars even in the observable Universe which could provide a suitable environment for a habitable planet.*

Professor Carl Sagan, Director of the Laboratory for Planetary Studies and Professor of Astronomy and Space Sciences at Cornell University, is probably the deepest thinking of all astronomers. He possesses a probing ability to venture into the realms of imagination and contention with refreshing brilliance.

In his book *Cosmos* – on the issue of habitable worlds – Carl Sagan uses a complicated formula to calculate his estimate on the number of worlds able to sustain a technological civilisation in our Galaxy; it involves the number of stars in our Galaxy, the fraction of stars that have planetary systems, the number of planets in a given system that are ecologically suitable for life, the fraction of otherwise suitable planets on which life actually arises, the fraction of inhabited planets on which an intelligent form evolves, the fraction of planets inhabited by intelligent beings on which a communicative technical civilisation develop, and the fraction of a planetary lifetime graced by a technical civilisation.

Using this complex formula he arrives at the conclusion that the number of technological civilisations existing within our own Galaxy may be numbered in millions.

He then comments that because there must be extraterrestrial life – because we are not able to imagine other life forms – then we will not be able to recognise the form that extraterrestrial life forms would take; he expands on this by saying that 'if we should receive a radio message from an extraterrestrial civilisation, how could it possibly be understood?

(2)

Extraterrestrial intelligence will be elegant, complex, internally consistent and utterly alien.'

Professor Sagan is on record as saying that *Civilisations hundreds or thousands of millions of years beyond us should have sciences and technologies so far beyond our present capabilities as to be indistinguishable from magic. It is not that what they can do violates the laws of physics; it is that we will not understand how they are able to use the laws of physics to do what they do.*

Philip Morrison and Giuseppe Coccini are scientists of Cornell University. On the question of the existence of intelligent life in the Universe, they approached the question in a novel and interesting way.

They postulated that disregarding all other speculations made by other scientists, our solar system with its central star and planet Earth is an example of a unit that has developed within our own Galaxy.

On this premise they reasoned that not only must there be many more similar solar systems, but that they could be considerably more technically advanced than we are.

They have suggested that attempts should be made to detect radio emissions emanating from the nearest star.

Professor Lovell – on the question of existence of highly technological extraterrestrial life forms – has stated that *Today there are responsible sections of the scientific community who do not question that elsewhere in the Universe there are planetary systems on which intelligent life has developed.*

He goes on to say that *certain observational developments have stimulated scientific interest in the possible existence of extraterrestrial life forms.*

The suggestion by Philip Morrison and Giuseppe Coccini – that attempts should be made to detect radio emissions from the nearest star – has been taken up by the United States Government; a £50,000,000 programme of exploration in the search for extraterrestrial life has been instigated that commenced in the last quarter of 1992.

It is engaged in the continuous and systematic study of over 14,000,000 radio frequencies in an attempt to discover any signs of advanced civilisations from outer space.

(3)

To summarise the propositions of the world's greatest astronomers and scientists:

- There is a zero probability that life evolved on this earth in the time scale that we have. (Lovell)
- Because life exists on this earth it must therefore have evolved elsewhere over a longer period of time. (Author)
- There can be no doubt that planets exist by the million in our Galaxy on which there are highly advanced extraterrestrial civilisations at the present time. (Lovell, Sagan, Morrison, Coccini)
- Advanced extraterrestrial civilisations would have technologies so in advance of ours that they would be beyond our understanding. (Sagan)
- *Certain observational developments* are leading to the possible existence of extraterrestrial life forms. (Lovell)

(4)

Section 2. Origins

As Professor Bernard Lovell has stated *The probability of a chance occurrence leading to the formation of one of the smallest protein molecules is unimaginably small. Within the boundary conditions of time and space which we are considering, the chance is effectively zero for the complex molecular structure of the human organism to have evolved.*

It is more logical to say, that given unlimited space and time, this event *must* have happened elsewhere in the universe.

The simple fact of the matter is, that pure space in its original form consists of nothing, and atoms of hydrogen.

Hydrogen atoms would appear to be the original and most simple of all atoms; they consist of one proton, about which a single electron is alleged to revolve at the speed of light.

Under certain completely natural conditions involving gravitational compression, heat, and time, hydrogen atoms will fuse together to form firstly deuterium, and then an atomic structure of a nucleus consisting of two protons and two neutrons, about which two electrons rotate at the speed of light. This is the atom of helium, and this is the process which fuels the engines of the Universe, the stars.

So it will be seen that the atom of hydrogen is able to change to a completely different element, the atom of helium.

This process continues by the same set of rules (a mixture of protons and an equal number of electrons) to make a total of 92 atomic elements. These are atomically different and form totally unrelated substances. Thus it will be seen that by a natural set of circumstances, the hydrogen atom is able to form all the other atomic elements that exist in the Universe.

Pure space originally consisted of nothing and hydrogen atoms, the situation now, however, within the observable Universe, is somewhat different. Space is now contaminated with the residues of evolving galaxies and supernovas. The size of a cloud of hydrogen atoms will ultimately determine its fate; stars form from hydrogen and are only a process of conversion from hydrogen to helium – the larger the cloud

(5)

57

the bigger the star – until the time will come when the actual size and pressures involved, start a process that is both rapid and spectacular.

The initial start is the normal conversion from hydrogen to helium; the compression of two neutrons and two protons. Because of the vast size and the pressures involved, the conversion proceeds at a rapidly increasing rate, running down from element to element, with the fusion of neutron and proton additions.

The release of the colossal amounts of energy that these fusions cause, results in vast amounts of the individual elements being ejected into surrounding space.

The result is – that as the detonation from element to element grows in intensity – so the run down is more rapid with the central core becoming more compact. Finally a point is reached when the detonation of almost all that is left – probably a core of iron formed by the conversion of silicon to iron – takes place.

This climax is the biggest bang in the heavens. A flare equal in brightness to millions of stars – and a temperature of 7,000,000,000 degrees – filling the universe with a contamination of all the residues of the elements, and the molecules necessary to re-create new planets and life.

(6)

Section 3. Intelligence and Life

The definition of intelligence is 'the faculty of reasoning'.

It could be said that the addition of two hydrogen atoms to one oxygen atom does in fact begin to show one of the first signs of this faculty. The mixture forms the simple molecule of 'water'.

Freeze a droplet of water and study the snowflake that forms; it will have five arms that radiate equally and precisely from a common centre, each arm will have a complex pattern that is exactly duplicated on all five arms. It is said that no two snowflakes have exactly the same pattern.

So we have firstly, a form of intelligence in that the families of identical atoms have affinity and congregate together to form an element of their own kind; and secondly a form of intelligence that is expressed in their ability to link easily with other selected atomic elements to form molecules of increasing complexity.

This complexity could be interpreted as the second basic form of intelligence.

Molecules would seem to be a formation that is based on a crystalline structure that has assumed a regular geometrical form.

The structure of the molecule water, a mixture of two of the simplest of atoms, is difficult to understand. A study of the apparent simplicity of an atom, however, will reveal deeper complications which make this structure easier to comprehend.

The inherent parts of an atom are divided into two families, Leptons, also known as neutrinos, which are a form of light and of which the electron is one, orbit within the atom at the speed of light. And Hadrons, which make up the nucleus. This is composed of protons and neutrons which in their turn are composed of things called quarks. These are now known to come in a variety of forms which all have different characteristics.

So, the original *simple* atom of hydrogen – once thought to consist of only three basic things – is found to be a structure that consists of many components that all have their own characteristics and behave in different ways.

(7)

It is now possible to begin to understand the complexity of a crystalline formation that has assumed a regular geometric form by an alliance of two atoms of hydrogen with one atom of oxygen.

Imagine the complexity of an atom of uranium. This has a nucleus of 92 protons and 92 neutrons, surrounded by 92 electrons all repelling each other and moving at the speed of light. Complicate this by the sub-division into quarks of its constituent parts, and you have the basis – when linked to many other atoms – of forming a molecule that contains all the complexity of its other atomic constituents.

Molecules then link with other molecules – communicating their vast crystalline information – until a structure is formed that is able to replicate, and form the beginning of the first cell of life.

The Human Cell

The molecule that makes up the human cell, is barely half the thickness of a human hair or one thousandth of an inch in diameter.

It has at its centre an object known as a nucleolus in which it collects things called ribosomes. These are used to convert amino acids into proteins. Surrounding this nucleolus is an area containing chromosomes. This is where the molecule DNA – the blueprint of life – is contained. It is said that if the lines of communication between the 46 strands of chromosomes were laid out as one, their combined length would be over two metres long!

The molecule DNA (deoxyribonucleic acid) is staggering in its complexity, it is shaped like a twisted ladder (double helix). There are said to be over 100 million twists, and each twist is said to consist of over one million atoms. Simple multiplication will show that a DNA molecule consists of over 100,000,000,000,000 atoms.

Each DNA molecule also has the remarkable ability of replicating itself.

(8)

Surrounding the nucleus, which contains the nucleolus, DNA, and chromosomes, is a coating that consists of a double envelope; this is responsible for conducting information from the nucleus to the rest of the cell.

Covering all is a thick layer of ribosomes, centrioles, golgi and mitochondria. These are factories for: converting amino acids into proteins, reproducing cells and distributing proteins, and for supplying power to the living cell.

The complete human cell is an intelligence unto itself. It controls the form that its host organism takes, and monitors all factors needed for the survival of the organism. It is in fact the progression of development from the atom to the molecule, to the living cell, and the human cell, and as the development of the crystalline intelligence of the atom is compounded into the construction of the complex intelligence of the molecule, so this molecular intelligence is transferred to – and results in – the construction of the human cell.

Because the human cell is the most intelligent of all, then the human cell must be the ultimate development in intelligence of all living cells.

It must then follow, that on this earth – because we are the most intelligent of all living species – then we must be the ultimate result of the accumulated intelligence in the development from the hydrogen atom to the human form.

Because it is impossible to create something out of nothing, and since space in its original form consisted of nothing and atoms of hydrogen, then the hydrogen atom must have always existed.

As the hydrogen atom is at the beginning of all things, it must therefore be the original creator.

(9)

Summary of Part 1

It would appear that according to the world's greatest astronomers, that highly advanced technological civilisations *must* exist in the Universe by the million.

That if there were visitations by extraterrestrial life forms, the mere fact that they were here, *must* mean that they would come from technological civilisations far more advanced than our own.

That a visitation made by any extraterrestrial entities would not be recognised, indeed their technologies and sciences would be so in advance of ours that they would be alien to us and beyond our understanding.

The probability of the development on Earth – in the time available – of even the smallest protein molecule is effectively zero.

The probability of the development on Earth of the most completed intelligence known – the complete human organism – in the time scale that we have is completely impossible.

The fact, however, that the human organism exists, can only mean that its development took place other than on this planet, at a much earlier period of time, and arrived here at some time in the past.

By a natural process involving compression, heat, and time, the atom of hydrogen – which in the first instance shows a form of intelligence by accumulating together with its own kind – is able to convert to 91 other atomic elements which all behave in the same way.

These 92 elements are able to join together in a multitude of combinations – passing on their own information – to form molecules which have the same ability to form together with their own kind.

Molecules are able to join other molecules, passing on their respective information, to form complex molecular forms that are able to replicate. This was the first appearance of life and the further development of reason.

These complex molecules are able to recreate and to reproduce to a specific pattern – the human form – which has life and intelligence.

(10)

These were the course of events that – over aeons of time – created intelligence, life and the human form.

They were also the course of events that produced the extraterrestrial civilisations that exist by the million throughout the universe.

(11)

PART 2. THE WITNESSES

Section 4. Unimpeachable Men

A Scientific Advisory Panel on unidentified flying objects was established by the Pentagon to confidentially analyse evidence of this phenomenon. The Central Intelligence Agency was directly concerned.

The report (known as the Robertson report) was released by the American Air Force Office of Public Information on 9 April, 1958. This was confirmed by Pearl Cohen of the Public Liaison Staff of the Central Intelligence Agency on 26 February, 1993.

A member of that panel was a Major Keyhoe.

The following is a statement made by the United States Air Force on Major Keyhoe. It is signed by Albert M. Chop of the Air Force Press Office and reads as follows:

We in the Air Force recognise Major Keyhoe as a responsible and accurate reporter. His long association and co-operation with the Air Force in our study of unidentified flying objects, qualifies him as a leading civilian authority on this investigation.

All the sighting reports and other information he has listed have been cleared and made available to Major Keyhoe from Air Intelligence Records at his request.

The Air Force Investigating Agency is aware of Major Keyhoe's conclusion that unidentified flying objects are from another planet. The Air Force has never denied that this possibility exists. Some of the personnel believe that there may be some strange natural phenomena completely unknown to us, but that if the apparently controlled manoeuvres reported by competent observers are correct, then the only remaining explanation is the interplanetary answer.

Allen Hynek is Director of the Lindheimer Research Centre at the Northeastern University of Illinois.

He criticised the United States Air Force statement that unidentified flying objects were not potentially dangerous; apart from the fact that *this was an admission of their existence*, the fact that they had not so far been hostile *did not* mean that this would also be the case in the future.

(12)

Admiral Calvin Bolster, Chief of the Office of Naval Research, ordered a thorough investigation of all sightings of unidentified flying objects within the Navy's sphere of influence (United States Navy Investigation, 1952). This resulted in the conclusion that: *UFOs were a real phenomenon and were unidentified, intelligently controlled, flying objects.*

Professor James E. MacDonald of the Institute of Atmospheric Physics at Arizona University, stated at an address to a United Nations Outer Affairs Group, that he was convinced that sightings of genuine unidentified flying objects were of extraterrestrial entities observing and investigating earth and its life forms.

Doctor Morris J. Jessop, Professor of Astrophysics at Michigan and Drake University postulated that from the different forms taken in a variety of sightings of unidentified flying objects that these objects were extraterrestrial visitors able to adapt to the circumstances and concepts of many different periods.

On 10 September, 1977, at 4.40 pm, Yuri Gromov, Director of Petrozavodsk Meteorological Station, in company with hundreds of other witnesses saw, over the western shore of Lake Onega near to the town of Petrozavodsk in western Russia, the appearance in the sky of a disc of gigantic size. It was reported to be some 100 metres in diameter and that five intense rays of light were emitted downward from the underside of this object. It remained stationary for 15 minutes and in that time holes were burnt in glass windows and paving slabs in the town of Petrozavodsk. Yuri Gromov observed that a small flying object left the large disc, and both then proceeded to disappear through the clouds.

U Thant, Secretary General of the United Nations, stated at a private meeting that *apart from the Vietnam war, unidentified flying objects were* the most important problem confronting the United Nations.

A committee formed in the Union of Soviet Socialist Republics in 1970 named the Stoljarov Committee, summarised their findings as follows: *There are so many well-documented sightings and radar traces, as to rule out the possibility of optical illusions,* they were clearly produced by concrete, real objects, the origin of which could only be explained by further systematic research. The committee recommended that Meteorological,

(13)

Astronomical, Geophysical and Hydrometeorological stations be commissioned to observe them. They stated that *The hypothesis that unidentified flying objects are of extraterrestrial origin was the one that best fitted the data already collected.*

President Harold F. Truman, on 4 April, 1950, stated at a press conference at Key West in Florida, that *unidentified flying objects did not originate in the United States of America nor any other terrestrial nation.*

This was in reply to the sightings – from 17 March to 20 March, 1950 – of over 500 unidentified flying objects over the nuclear restricted zone in New Mexico. This phenomenon was witnessed by the 50,000 inhabitants of Framlington in northern New Mexico.

On 21 December, 1989, Guy Coëme, Minister of Defence in the Belgian Government, stated to the Chamber of People's Representatives (Kamer van Volksvertegenwourdigers), in reply to the spate of sightings over Belgium and its capital that *The Government did not know what they were.*

Colonel W. De Brouwer of the Belgian Air Force stated that the Air Force had tracked an unidentified flying object on radar on 30 March 1990, and that it had accelerated from 175 mph to 1,125mph – and altered height by by more than two miles – in 15 seconds.

President Jimmy Carter, together with several witnesses, *observed an unidentified flying object and resolved that he would instigate an enquiry* – the results to be made public – when he was able to do so.

Presidents of the United States of America:

Truman, Reagan, Eisenhower, Carter, Johnson, John F. Kennedy. Former Vice President and Governor of New York, Nelson Rockefeller, Senator Robert Kennedy, Ex-presidential candidate Barry Goldwater and Haydon Burns, Governor of Florida *were all convinced of the existence of alien phenomena in the heavens above Earth.*

Jacques Vallee, astrophysicist and scientist, has said that by visual observation and their behaviour on radar, unidentified flying objects have the *ability to dematerialise.*

Sir Eric Geary, Prime Minister of Grenada; Robert Galley, French Minister for the Army; Admiral Lord Hill-Norton, former Chief

(14)

of Defence Staff of the Ministry of Defence; Air Chief Marshal Lord Dowding of the Royal Air Force; Admiral Delmer Fahrney, United States Navy; General Max Chassin of NATO Air Defence and Commanding General of the French Air Force, have all expressed their *explicit belief in the phenomena of unidentified flying objects.*

Professor Meesen, University Libre of Brussels; Doctor Felix Zigel, Moscow Institute of Aeronautics; Professor V.F. Kuprevich, Professor of the Soviet Academy of Sciences; Professor Ananof, Soviet Rocket expert; Professor Vladaroff, Moscow Academy for Space Research, are all *confirmed supporters in the existence of extraterrestrial visitors.*

Russian astronaut Valery Bykovski; American astronauts White, Boorman, Young, and Collins; Apollo 12 astronauts, Conrad, Gordon, and Bean; Mercury 7 and Apollo 9 astronaut, Scott Carpenter; Gemini 7 astronaut, James Lovell; Gemini 4 astronaut, James McDivitt; Apollo 11 astronauts, Neil Armstrong and Edwin Aldrin; and Discovery astronauts, Michael Coates, James Buchli, John Blaha, Robert Springer and James Baglian are alleged to have witnessed unidentified flying objects whilst on missions to the Moon and in Earth orbit, indeed a radio message to Goddard Space Flight Centre – the back-up centre for Houston – on 14 March, 1989, was picked up by several sources at 06.42 eastern standard time. It said: *Houston. This is Discovery. We still have alien spacecraft under observance.*

NASA pilot, Joseph Walker, whilst flying the Bell X15 supersonic aircraft in April, 1962, *reported and filmed five disc-shaped unidentified flying objects.* And later, in July, 1962, an unidentified flying object was observed by Major Robert White, whilst on test in a Bell X15 *at an altitude of fifty-eight miles.*

These pilots believe in the existence of *unidentified flying objects.*

These then are the witnesses to the appearance of *unidentified flying objects* in the heavens of earth.

Their credentials are impeccable and their credibilities unimpeachable. From the positions of the greatest political power in the most powerful country in the world, to Scientific Advisory panels and committees made up of the world's greatest scientists, astronomers and astrophysicists. Reports from directors of astronomical, geophysical and

(15)

hydrometeorological establishments, added to reports from eminent astrophysicists and a host of academic professors from the world's greatest universities, all reach the same conclusions.

Add to these the expressed beliefs of the most senior military commanders of the armies, navies and air forces, and the personal experience of senior test pilots and astronauts both American and Russian, and the result is, that beyond a shadow of doubt, *a phenomenon is taking place in the heavens of the earth, in the appearance of a form of extraterrestrial intelligence that is beyond our understanding.*

The world's greatest astronomers, Professor Carl Sagan and Professor Sir Bernard Lovell have both stated that highly-advanced civilisations *must* exist in the Universe by the million. Professor Lovell has said that we could not possibly have evolved on this Earth in the time scale that we have. Professor Sagan has said that advanced extraterrestrial civilisations would have technologies and sciences so in advance of ours that they would be *alien to us and beyond our understanding.*

It is also an obvious fact that any extraterrestrial civilisation able to traverse the distances between worlds, would of necessity be of superior intelligence to us, and have advanced technologies far beyond our understanding.

I have submitted the Postulation and the Witnesses.

Now I will provide the testimony.

(16)

PART 3. THE TESTIMONY

Section 5. The Belgian Affair

The whole story of the phenomena of unidentified flying objects in relation to the United States of America, is – and has been – one of utter confusion and deception.

To a lesser degree the same confusion and deception exists in Great Britain.

It would now seem, however, that a common policy is expressed by both countries in that all matters relating to this phenomenon involve national security and as such are held to be classified information.

After forty-five years of information and disinformation, the whole American scene must therefore be disregarded as completely unreliable, and note taken of an event that occurred in Europe in 1989–90.

The policy of the United States appears to be that all requests for information are channelled through the Central Intelligence Agency. They politely inform you that there has *not* been any attempt to collect information on unidentified flying objects since the 1950s. Any further request is referred to the National Archives and Records Administration in Washington DC.

Similarly, all requests for information in Great Britain are channelled through the British Ministry of Defence. They politely inform you that they can not answer any radar enquiries that occur beyond British boundaries because they then become the subject of national security and as such are classified information.

In reply to a detailed enquiry they confirmed that *ghost* radar returns have occurred from time to time. They state that false returns are easily detected by skilled radar operations.

They also agreed, that a radar signal – being an ultra short radio wavelength – will behave in exactly the same way as a wavelength of light. It will only reflect a signal from an object of some density or opacity.

(17)

They are, however, more forthcoming than their American counterparts on the subject of unidentified aerial phenomena. They admit to having received 147 reports of these phenomena during 1992, *some of which would seem to defy explanation.*

On the question of national security they say that the key consideration is evidence; lights or shapes in the sky – *even if radar returns are a feature of these,* and the sighting *cannot* be positively identified – *cannot be judged to exist* and therefore do not constitute a threat to national security.

They then state that the Public Records Act does not require that files should be kept, and that all files relating to this subject were routinely destroyed in 1967. They then state (to completely confuse the matter) that *some* files from the 1950s did escape the destruction process and any enquiries are referred to the Public Record Office at Richmond in Surrey.

It would appear that the rules of the Public Records Act relating to public access *enforced a period of secrecy for a period of thirty years.*

It is difficult to comprehend how a phenomenon that is deemed not to exist *can deserve such harsh treatment.*

It is also extremely dangerous for a Government Department to admit to the existence of a phenomenon that it is unable to explain, and to categorically state that it is not a national security risk.

Intentionally or unintentionally, this whole story of a phenomenon that could constitute *either* the *greatest event* or the *greatest threat* known to mankind has been a subject of ridicule for many years.

The problem of this nebulous phenomenon that has confused both national governments and the public for over 45 years is strange indeed.

If files are released, these are carefully chosen for their trivial content and are easily subjected to ridicule.

(18)

The whole phenomenon is then classified as being the prerogative of eccentrics and is subjected to derision and consequent oblivion.

Despite this ridicule the problem refuses to go away. Interest becomes more evident with the recording of factual evidence supplied by credible witnesses, making the existence of this phenomenon impossible to deny.

(19)

Section 6. The Phenomenon

Because reports have been made that attempt to bring the subject into disrepute, the time has come to lay the ghost to rest by obtaining a conclusive ruling from the European Parliament on the probability of this phenomenon – by its very concept – being extraterrestrial in its origins.

It is important that the characteristics of this phenomenon be understood.

A summary of the many descriptions given by thousands of witnesses of this object, would indicate it to be of constantly changing format.

Initial impressions would seem to be of a pinkish-white orb with many small, bright surface lights.

It would seem able to change rapidly to a diamond shape with several coloured, brighter lights situated at its extremities.

It is able to develop to a variety of other forms and has been seen to change continuously from an orb of light to platforms of square, triangular, and rectangular shapes; all are described as tumbling plethoras of light.

It is able to take the shape of a three-sided pyramid.

In its most common guise it appears as a massive triangular platform – slightly convex above and below – probably 150 feet across and relatively thick in structure. It has been described as looking like a giant steam iron when viewed from below.

It is described as having four powerful lights on its underside – one at each corner of its triangular configuration – which do not emit light, change to various colours, and yet brightly illuminate the ground below.

It has a central red light which appears to be situated underneath on a convex cupola; this pulsates and changes in intensity from dull orange to a bright red.

The object has been described as being noticeably more visible on film that has been blue-enhanced, and being dull-grey and metallic in appearance when viewed in daylight. It

(20)

72

can have circular cupola-shaped appendages on its underside, and is able to accelerate from 150–980 knots in two seconds (radar timed). It has a descent rate, also radar indicated, from 7,000 ft to 3,000 ft in one second.

In its triangular form it has been noted to display the same amount of bright lights (six to a dozen in number) on its surface as in its globular form. These small lights have the same triangular images as their parent object.

In its triangular format it has the ability to divide into two large separate triangles, each of which emits any number of the small triangular-shaped lights which proceed in various directions.

These return after a period to their respective original half triangles, which then reform to the original triangular platform.

This procedure has been witnessed many times in different instances at various geographical locations on the Earth's surface.

That then is the phenomenon. It is thus that I relate, quite objectively, the complete story of two incidents – that were the culmination of a spate of sightings – in Belgium in November 1989 and March 1990.

(21)

Section 7. Eupen

At dusk in the evening of 29 November, 1989, two Sergeant-Majors of the Belgian Gendarmerie who were on patrol on the road from Eupen to Kittenis in the Hautes Fagnes region of Belgium, noticed a phenomenon two hundred metres away on one side of the road.

It was moving slowly and was some three hundred metres above a field that bordered the road.

Both police officers noted that it appeared to be a dark triangular platform with three powerful lights shining from its underside to the ground below.

It had a central red light that pulsated from red to orange.

The object turned towards them and passed over their vehicle, illuminating the whole area and becoming more visible in its triangular format as it did so.

It appeared to be almost completely noiseless, emitting only a very soft humming sound.

It proceeded slowly towards Eupen (above the area of Van Hoek Street) and stopped motionless above the dam at Gileppe for a period of 45 minutes. It finally moved in the direction of Baelen and Spa where it disappeared.

The two police officers contacted the Belgian Air Force base at Bierset which together with Glons and Butgenbach had detected scans on their radar. These bases at Aachen and Maastricht were notified and an AWAC aircraft was vectored to the area from Gelsenkirchen.

The whole incident was to last for 2½ hours.

It was witnessed by nineteen other Gendarmes who were guests at a nearby social event.

Many witnesses from two areas of Liège, as well as Eupen, Plombières, Kittenis, Baelin, Verviers, Jalhay, St Vith, Andrimont, Lontzen, Voeren, Battice, and Herbesthal, reported this object to the Gendarmerie.

Descriptions from witnesses all tallied, and conformed to the descriptions given of this phenomenon at the beginning of this section.

(22)

All radar reports were positive readings made by skilled operatives and could not be interpreted as readings from thermal inversions, unusual electromagnetic waves or signals from other radar.

Over 55 minutes later the same two police officers witnessed another triangular platform – only this time much larger – appear from almost ground level behind a large area of trees. It described a climbing turn – all the time slowly rotating in a level plane – following the course of a nearby main road, it seemed to be maintaining a relatively slow speed of about 65 kph.

That is an accurate description of the phenomenon that appeared over the dam at Gileppe. It was reported by hundreds, followed by the Gendarmerie and confirmed by radar.

But that was only the precursor to the real event. This was concealed from the public for three months and happened at Wavre.

(23)

Section 8. Wavre (South-east Brussels)

During the night of 31-31 March, 1990, many reports were received by the police from members of the public of a phenomenon in the sky above Wavre, twelve miles south of Brussels.

This resulted in many telephone calls from the police to the radar station at Glons near Tongeren for ratification.

Glons radar confirmed the sighting of an unidentified object at an altitude of 3,000 metres.

Semmerzake radar confirmed the Glons detection and passed its confirmation to the Air Force.

The radar scans were compared with the previous Eupen radar sightings by Semmerzake and Glons and found to be identical.

Several police patrols had witnessed the same phenomenon before.

It was a massive triangular shape with the same lighting configuration as seen at Eupen four months earlier.

Colonel Wilfried De Brouwer, Chief of the operations section of the Air Force, said *That because of the frequency of requests for radar confirmation at Glons and Semmerzake – and as a number of private visual observations had been confirmed by the police – it was decided that as these parameters had been met, a patrol of F-16 aircraft should be sent to intercept an unidentified object somewhere to the south of Brussels.*

As a consequence, two F-16 aircraft of the Belgian Air Force – registration numbers 349 and 350 – flown by a Captain and a Flight-Lieutenant, both highly-qualified pilots, took off from Bevekom.

Within a few minutes – guided by the Glons radar – both pilots had detected a positive oval-shaped object on their on-board radar at a height of 3,000 m, but in the darkness saw nothing.

This oval configuration, however, caused the pilots some concern. It reacted in an intelligent and disturbing way when they attempted to 'lock-on' with their on-board radar.

(24)

Changing shape instantly, it assumed a distinct 'diamond image' on their radar screens and – increasing its speed to 1,000 km/h – took immediate and violent evasive action.

Photographs of the actual on-board radar of the F-16s recorded a descent of this object from 3,000 m to 1,200 m in 2 seconds, a descent rate of 1,800 km/h.

The same photographs show an unbelievable acceleration rate of 280 km/h to 1,800 km/h in a few seconds. According to Professor Leon Brening – a nonlinear dynamic theorist at the Free University of Brussels – this would represent an acceleration of 46 g and would be beyond the possibility of any human pilot to endure.

It was noted that in spite of these speeds and acceleration times there was a marked absence of any sonic boom.

The movements of this object were described by the pilots and radar operators as 'wildly erratic and step-like', and a zig-zag course was taken over the city of Brussels with the two F-16s in pursuit. Visual contact was not possible against the lighting of the city.

This same procedure was to be repeated several times, with this object – whenever an attempt at radar 'lock-on' was made – pursuing a violently erratic course at impossible speed and losing its pursuers.

These then, were the events that happened at Eupen and Wavre.

This object was:

1. Witnessed by many thousands at Eupen, Wavre, Liège and Brussels.
2. Reported in 2,600 statements to the police.
3. Photographed by many on camera and video.
4. Detected and confirmed by radar stations on the ground.
5. Detected, confirmed and photographed on aircraft radar screens.
6. Pursued for one hour by F-16 aircraft of the Belgian Air Force.
7. Tracked and showed intelligent evasive action.

(25)

8. Admitted by the chief of operations section of the Belgian Air Force Colonel Wilfrid De Brouwer, who confirmed the spectacular confrontation after the radar sightings were compared with those at Semmerzake and Glons and found to be strikingly similar. He said *The radar station in Glons, near Tongeren, was contacted with increasing frequency by the police for confirmation, the visual sightings made by individuals had to be confirmed by the state police and the radar stations at Glons and Semmerzake before we could decide to send up a patrol of F-16s.*

Colonel De Brouwer added *Immediately after the operation, the pilots said they had never seen anything like it. Certainly the flight pattern of the echo on their screens was in no way that of a conventional plane.* He added that the pilots were young men, and they had thought that the object was *something special.* They were convinced that it was something.

9. Admitted by Colonel A. Perrad, ACOS Air Staff Division/Operations of the Etat-Major de la Force Aérienne on 5 April, 1993, who confirmed the existence of this phenomenon on 30 March, 1990 and quoted elapsed/time details taken from the on-board radar of the pursuing aircraft. These confirmed an acceleration rate of 150 kts to 560 kts in half a second.

10. Discussed in the Belgian Parliament (Kamer Van Volksvertegenwourdigers). In reply to questions on the phenomenon that had actually appeared above the European Parliament in Brussels, the Belgian Minister of Defence, Guy Coëme, stated that *The Government did not know what they were!*

(26)

Section 9. List of Supporting Documents

a. An anomaly. A letter from the CIA dated 26 February, 1993.
Stating – that in connection with this aerial phenomenon –
there has been *no* research, studying or effort to collect
information on the part of the CIA since 1969.

b. A contradictory letter from the Ministry of Defence.
Unconfirmed radar sightings accompanied by visible lights
and shapes in the sky, cannot be classed as evidence and
consequently cannot be judged to exist. Records of any
sightings – although judged not to exist – although kept, are
subject to the Public Records Act, are subject to secrecy and
remain closed for thirty years.

Prior to 1967 all UFO files were destroyed. Some from the
fifties are available for viewing at the public records office at
Kew.

c. Confirmatory letter from the Cabinet Office stating that
records on this phenomenon have been 'preserved' since
1967 and will be released in accordance with the Public
Records Act (after 30 years).

d. A telex sent by the Ath police to the Hainault police
reporting a sighting by a resident and five police officers for
a period of one hour. A total of 75 police have been
witnesses to this phenomenon.

e. A letter from A. Perrad, Colonel, ACOS Air Staff Division,
Belgian Air Force, confirming the BAF radar sighting on 30
March, 1990, and giving elapsed time detail on acceleration
speeds taken from the pursuing aircraft's 'on-board' radar.

f. Location map showing course of phenomenon, areas of F-16
pursuit and interception, and main witness points.

g. Illustrations of phenomenon (normal and blue enhanced),
and 'on-board' radar readings.

h. An official letter, dated 26 May, 1993, from Leo Delcroix,
Belgian Minister of Defence, concerning the November and
December 1989 events at Eupen.

This letter confirms the increasing number of sightings of
these phenomena east of the province of Liège (Eupen) prior
to 21 December, 1989. It establishes observations by

(27)

79

witnesses, and detection by radar in both Belgium and Germany of the phenomenon at Eupen.

It confirms new sightings of 15 and 16 December, 1989, by witnesses and members of the Gendarmerie at Eupen.

It states that F-16 aircraft were alerted, and interceptions were attempted on both of these occasions.

The sightings of 16 December, 1989, were attributed to a laser projection at Liége. (Liége is 35 km from Eupen – and radar will not detect any form of light.)

All relevant hypotheses being excluded, the Minister at the time – Guy Coëme – *could not tell what these flying objects were.*

(28)

CENTRAL INTELLIGENCE AGENCY

26 February 1993

Dear Mr Sheffield:

In response to your recent letter to the Central Intelligence Agency, *I must inform you that there is no organized Central Intelligence Agency effort to do research in connection with the UFO phenomenon (or variations), nor has there been an organized effort to study or collect intelligence on UFOs since the 1950s.* At that time, the Air Force specifically the Air Technical Intelligence Center at Wright Patterson Air Force Base (Dayton, Ohio, USA), had the primary responsibility for the investigation of all reports of UFO sightings. The CIA's role was in connection with a scientific Advisory Panel, established to investigate and evaluate reports of UFOs. The panel was concerned only with any aspect of the UFO phenomena which might present a potential threat to the United States' national security. The panel later issued a report of its findings, the Report of the Scientific Panel on Unidentified Flying Objects – January 17, 1953, also known as the Robertson Report. The report was released by the Air Force Office of Public Information on April 9, 1958. The Air Force investigation, called Project Bluebook, was terminated in 1969. We understand that the Air Force turned its records on this subject over to the National Archives and Records Administration (NARA) where they are available for inspection and purchase. For your convenience, the NARA address is:

National Archives and Records Administration
Seventh Street and Pennsylvania Avenue, NW
Washington, DC 20408.
Sincerely
Pearl Cohen
Public Liaison Staff

From N G Pope, Secretariat (Air Staff) 2a, Room 8245

MINISTRY OF DEFENCE

24 February 1993

Dear Mr Sheffield,

Thank you for your letter dated 21 February.
In answer to your question about national security, the key consideration is evidence, without which a threat to national security cannot be judged to exist. Reports of lights or shapes in the sky cannot be classed as evidence, even if the sighting cannot be positively identified. It is not our practice to name or give details of those individuals or departments involving in looking at UFO reports.

You mentioned sightings that took place at RAF Lakenheath-Bentwaters in 1956. I am unable to comment on the point you make because, . . . I am not aware of any official access to our UFO files; *it was generally the case that before 1967 all UFO files were routinely destroyed.* After this date, files were kept, but – like all government files – *they are covered by the terms of the Public Records Act, and remain closed for 30 years after the last action.* A few files from the Fifties did escape the destruction process, and are available for viewing at the following address: Public Records Office, Ruskin Avenue, Kew, Richmond, Surrey, TGW9 4DV. The references of these surviving UFO files are as follows:

AIR 16/1199; AIR 20/7390; AIR 20/9320; AIR 20/9321; AIR 20/9322; AIR 20/9994; PREM 11/855.

I think we will have to agree to disagree about detecting the Belgian sightings on radar; from what I recall . . ., there were many visual sightings, but only one reference to radar. The definitive position on this will have to come from the Belgian government.

With regard to any questions about civil aircraft's radar returns, I suggest you write to the Civil Aviation Authority, at the following address: CAA House, 45-49 Kingsway, London, WC2B 6TE.

I hope this is helpful.

Yours sincerely

N. Pope

C

CABINET OFFICE
Historical and Records Section

23 March 1993

Dear Mr Sheffield

As I said in my letter of 8 March I have made enquiries of the Ministry of Defence about material to assist with your research into unidentified phenomena appearing over Northern Belgium in 1989/90.

I understand that the MOD has responded to several letters from you on this matter but that they have no information which would shed any light on the Belgian phenomena; suggestions have, however been made as to where further advice may be available.

As you know records relating to UFO reports have been preserved since 1967 with a view to release in accordance with the provisions of the Public Records Acts. However as no information is held on the Northern Belgian 1989/90 phenomena, these will not, *even when the files are due for release*, be of help to you in your researches.

I am sorry that I am not able to send you a more helpful reply.

Yours sincerely

Miss PM Andrews

TELEX FROM ATH POLICE TO HAINAUT POLICE

A telex sent a week ago by the Ath Police to the district of Hainaut, after a UFO sighting in the Belgian sky. In Belgium, over 75 policemen have witnessed sightings in the last four months. The Air Force is no longer alone in taking this phenomenon seriously.

```
MONS GP
FROM ATH
R 060955A APR 90
COMD DIST ATH
TO COMD GP TER PROV HAINAUT
BT
UNCLASS (.)
RE: PRESENCE OF UNIDENTIFIED FLYING OBJECT
____

REF: TELEX UNCLAS BAND/1651 OF 131650 DEC 89
____

1 060010 APRIL 1990
2 BETWEEN ATH AND GHISLENGHIEN
3 PRESENCE HIGH IN SKY OF A SHINING LUMINOUS
  SOURCE (ROTATING) OF CHANGING COLOUR
  (YELLOW/RED)
4 IDENTITY OF WITNESSES:
A MR A SIMOULIN PHILIPPE, RESIDENT IN HOUTAING,
  MADELINE STREET
B SGT GALLIET
C SGT SCHOELING
D SGT IN CHIEF CILOR
E 1ST SGT CHAIS
F CAPT BAUKENS
5 DURATION OF SIGHTING: AT LEAST 01 HOUR
6 CONTACT SOBEPS
 -BY ANSWERPHONE AROUND 00.00 HOURS
 -VIA THE ANSWERPHONE 060950 APR 1990
BT

NNNN
ATH TRIS 062008A APR 90 AR AR
```

E

FORCES ARMEES ETAT-MAJOR GENERAL

05-04-94

Sir,

Your letter dated 28th March 1993, about BAF radar sighting on March 30th 1990 got my full attention.

Out of the radar pictures, following observations were made:

-Elapsed time between 150 and 560 kts: ± $\frac{1}{2}$ second
-Elapsed time between 150 and 770 kts: ±10 seconds
-Elapsed time between 150 and 560 kts: ± 2 seconds

Yours faithfully
A. Perrad
Colonel ACOS Air Staff Division Operations

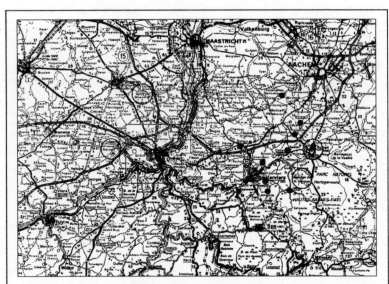

Eupen. 29/30 November 1989
Reproduced with permission from Michelin Map No. 409

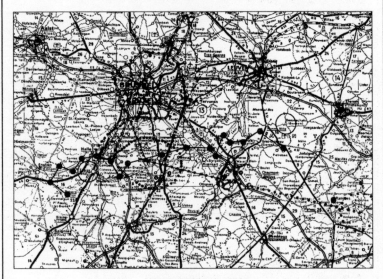

Wavre. 30 March 1990
Reproduced with permission from Michelin Map No. 409

KEY: ○ Radar/airfield and relevant locations.
      ● Main sighting points and course of phenomenon.
    ●●● Interception route and search areas of F-16 aircraft.

G

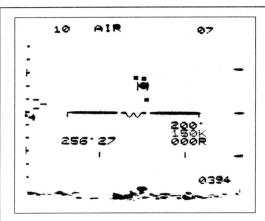

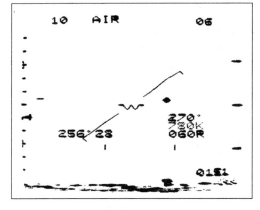

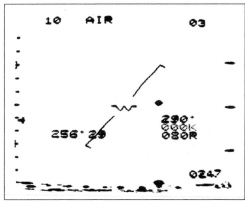

Three consecutive video photographs taken over a period of two seconds. These show an 'on-board' radar screen of a pursuing F-16 aircraft of the Belgian Air Force during one period of radar lock-on. A descent rate of 4,000 feet in ±2 seconds is indicated, together with an increase in speed from 150 knots to 780 knots in ±1 second. In one further second the speed of the target went off the scale at ±1,000 knots, the limit of indicated speed on the F-16s radar.
© Belgian Air Force/ SOBEPS

H

MINISTERIE VAN LANDSVERDEDIGING

Dear Sir,   26/05/93

I received a request from my colleague Minister G. Coëme to send you a summary of his statement to the chambre of Representatives on the 21st December 1989.

Minister Coëme, the Minister of Defense at the time being, answered to Representative Janssens about *the increasing number of UFO's above the east of the Province of Liége.*

The answer is enclosed hereby and can be summarised as follows:

1. It is not possible to establish a correlation between the observations made by witnesses on the one hand and *detection by the radars of Semmerzake (Belgium) and VEDEM (Germany) on the other hand.*

2. F-16 aeroplanes have intervened twice. The first on the 15th December 1989 *as a result of observations made by the "gendarmerie" of Eupen.*

The pilots did not observe anything and nothing was visible on the radar at the time they were operating.

The second on the 16th December 1989 as a result of observations and communications addressed to the base at Glons. It seemed that they resulted from laser-projections of a disco.

3. From military point of view, the following possibilities can be excluded:
- they were not AWACS-aeroplanes, because they are submitted to radar control when they fly over Belgian territory;
- they were not F-117 aeroplanes, as was confirmed by the General Staff of the US Air Force;
- they were not ultra light motorised aeroplanes, because these produce a different and specific sound.

4. Conclusion:

As these four hypotheses can be excluded, *the Minister could not tell what these flying objects were.*

Hoping to have answered your question with this letter, I remain,

Yours faithfully
Leo DELCROIX.
Minister of Defense.

A EUROPEAN PARLIAMENTARY QUESTION

Ref: Your letter 9/IM/RT/16. of the 26/05/93.

Dear Minister

Your reply to my letter on the events of November and December 1989 at Eupen was much appreciated.

I agree with your general comments in part 3 of your letter, and would confirm your observation that apart from the *obvious general correlation of witnesses and radar returns from Semmerzake and Vedem*, there did not appear to be any actual *pattern* to the events at Eupen.

It would seem, however, that *flying objects of some kind were in evidence above Eupen, and were detected by radar.*

Your comments that observations and communications to the radar base at Glons were attributed to laser projections at disco. I have today discussed this with a radar technical expert at Unipar Services of Tunbridge Wells in Kent. He informs me that there are *NO circumstances in which radar will detect any form of light.*

It would seem, however, that the events above Wavre and Brussels in March 1990 were somewhat different. Whilst I have obtained much information from the Belgian Air Force, concerning performance figures/radar returns and F-16 interception, and have confirmed photographs of the 'on-board' radar and the phenomenon in question, I would very much appreciate your comments – or those of your predecessor – on these particular sightings.

For your interest, the point of my requests is that I have compiled a comprehensive report on the Eupen and Wavre sightings and intend to submit these (together with very strong documentary evidence) to the European Parliament in Brussels.

I have requested that an enquiry be instigated to establish whether this phenomenon could be of possible extraterrestrial origin, and have stated that if this be so, then – in the interests of international security – it is incumbent on the European Parliament to make this fact public.

My report is complete, but I would appreciate *an urgent reply from* yourself on the attitude of the Belgian government at that time, to the events at Wavre in March 1990.

Yours sincerely
Derek Sheffield

Part 4. THE INDICTMENT

Section 10. Responsibilities of the European Parliament for International Security

Taking the evidence of this report into consideration, it is the responsibility of the European Parliament to conduct an extensive enquiry into the events that made up the Belgian incidents of 29–30 November, 1989 and the 30–31 March, 1990.

Using the 2,600 reports from members of the public purely as a guide, and only taking note of photographs and statements from specific public and professional witnesses, evidence for the enquiry should be taken from:

a. Statements of all the 75 witnesses of the Belgian gendarmerie involved over the periods of the incidents.

b. Witnesses' statements and photographs from the radar stations at Glons and Semmerzake where actual scans were confirmed and recorded.

c. Statements of the two pilots of the F-16 interceptor aircraft Nos 349 and 350 of the First Groupe de Chasse from Beauvechain (Bevekom), who pursued and attempted an interception for 1 hour in the Wavre area above Tubize 25 miles south of Brussels.

d. Studies should be made of the photographs taken of the 'on-board' radar of all the interceptor aircraft involved, with particular attention to the performance figures and times shown.

e. Studies should be made of photographs obtained (particularly where a blue enhancement shows detail not normally apparent).

If – as a result of this enquiry – this phenomenon is thought to be of probable extraterrestrial origin, it is imperative that in the interests of international security that this be recognised.

It is therefore incumbent upon the European Parliament that this declaration should be made public.

Derek Sheffield

Rolvenden 1993

(39)

CHAPTER TEN

First Apprehensions

The warning from Bruce Cathie, against involvement with governmental intelligence establishments and their recommended private agencies, was still fresh in my mind. I had some indication of this, by the lack of reply from five letters of enquiry sent to separate addresses in America. These all resulted in a single letter from the Central Intelligence Agency. Further indications of collusion were the identical policies of obstruction followed by the Central Intelligence Agency, the Ministry of Defence, and later by the Belgian Ministry of Defence. It would seem that the replies from the Ministry of Defence concerning the Belgian incidents of 1989–90 were not true.

This increased my apprehensions. I resolved to place my report with a body that did not appear to have been contaminated by such intrigue, namely the European Parliament.

Strangely enough, I simply went to my local public library and asked if they had anything that explained the workings and procedures of the European Parliament. They had. It was a publication entitled *Dod's Parliamentary Companion 1992 (160th year)*. It explained that the first course to follow, in order to obtain a ruling from the European Parliament, was through one's local Member for the European Parliament.

To start with, no one seemed to know who the local Member for the European Parliament was. After a multitude of telephone calls via town halls and council offices, who all denied any knowledge, I finally ended up with a Miss Penn of the Tunbridge Wells Town Hall Committee Section. Miss Penn advised me that my local MEP was a Mr Ben Patterson of Hawkhurst. This seemed fairly probable; Hawkhurst was relatively near, and my house is only three miles from the West Kent border. I telephoned Mr Patterson on several occasions but only managed to get an answerphone that informed me that I could either obtain Mr Patterson on a Brussels telephone number or leave a message; I left a message.

This happened on two more occasions before I actually managed to speak to a real human voice. I explained the reason for my call and was asked either to post or to deliver my report to Mr Patterson's home. As my report represented many hours of work and was irreplaceable as far as I was concerned, I chose to deliver it by hand.

One week later I received a letter from an assistant to Mr Ben Patterson. She informed me that although Mr Patterson lived 2 miles from the West Kent border, he in fact represented the East Kent constituency. My own MEP, however, was a Mr Christopher Jackson, who lived at Sevenoaks. My report had been forwarded to him.

Five weeks later the pattern was repeated, with Mr Christopher Jackson. Once again the answerphone messages, the inanimate voices, and no further contact. I made approaches to both European and constituency offices. I received very rude replies from termagant female agents, but my report seemed to have disappeared from the face of the earth.

Finally, I noted a London telephone number given at the end of one of the pre-recorded messages. It said, in effect, that a London telephone number could be contacted in the event of emergencies. As my report had been missing for five weeks I now considered the situation to be an emergency and rang the number indicated. The answer that I received from this number was, first, an enquiry as to how I had obtained their telephone number, and when I asked why there had been a five-week delay in even acknowledging receipt of my report I was told fairly testily that any recourse should be made to Christopher Jackson. As he was apparently in Brussels at the time, that was hardly appropriate. When I asked for their address in London – I intended to go personally and collect my report – I was told that that was confidential information which they were not allowed to disclose.

My report was eventually returned after having disappeared from the face of the earth for five weeks, with no comment whatsoever.

I did, however, receive a telephone call from a Susan Butler – a research assistant to Christopher Jackson. She advised me that MEPs were concerned only with commercial matters in the Common Market. She suggested that I should contact NATO (in view of my suspicions concerning the involvement of the Americans in this matter I did not deem this advisable) or even put the matter in the hands of the President in Charge, The Council of Ministers at 120 rue de la Loi, 1047 Brussels. This I immediately did – on 13 August. To date (four weeks later) I have received no reply.

My apprehensions at this point were considerable. My report had vanished without explanation for five weeks. It had been impossible to contact any MEPs. There had been no written acknowledgement of receipt of my document. My own MEP had not forwarded my report to the appropriate section of the European Parliament, nor had the respective MEPs offered any advice as to the correct procedures to follow.

I approached yet another member of the European Parliament – this time a Labour member – at the London Office for Members of the European Parliament; to date I have received no reply from that source.

I had anticipated problems of this kind. I had followed the rules. I had tried the recommendations of *Dod's Parliamentary Companion*, and made an approach through my local members of the European Parliament. These had proved to behave like typical civil servants. I did not expect anything else.

I now, however, had the bit between my teeth. I had several copies of my report printed, and followed the next recommendation to obtaining a ruling from the European Parliament. A direct appeal to the President of the European Parliament. For good measure – because it concerned the credibility of the Belgian establishment – I also sent a copy to the Belgian Prime Minister.

To date – although I followed the advice of Mr Jackson's assistant – I have heard nothing from the President in Office at the Council of Ministers. I have had a reply, however, from the Belgian Prime Minister. He stated that he had not received my report but had in fact received my reminder. He has suggested that I send a copy of my document to Egon Klepsch, President of the European Parliament. This was sent by return of post and registered.

I decided to approach Sir Leon Brittan. I knew him to be something in the Commission of the European Communities and an enthusiastic European. Sir Leon was to be another iron in the fire. I wrote to him asking for advice in obtaining a ruling from the European Parliament.

My estimation was correct. I received a reply from David Coyne of the office of Sir Leon Brittan within five days of having written my letter. I could not believe my good fortune. David Coyne requested details of the ruling I was seeking; these I sent by return of post.

I felt that things were beginning to happen.

It had also transpired that the European Parliament did *not* deal only with purely commercial matters. Evidently there are many different committees – probably 12 in all – that deal with all manner of things that could concern a European Parliament. This was contrary to the information given to me by Christopher Jackson's research assistant, something that added to my apprehensions.

I had, of course, exerted pressure in other ways.

At the time that I sent copies of my report to the Kent Members for the European Parliament, I issued a general press release to the effect that this submission had been made. It seemed to make interesting reading. In effect a concise summary of my 40-page report was as follows.

PRESS RELEASE

An application for a ruling by the European Parliament, has been made by Derek Sheffield, the Rolvenden author, in a letter to Mr G. B. Patterson, the Member for the European Parliament for West Kent.

The application takes the form of a legal document and is divided into four parts: the Postulation. The Witnesses. The Testimony. The Indictment.

It contains calculated postulations by Professors Lovell and Sagan, and scientists, Morrison and Coccini, that there can be no doubt that planets exist by the million within our own Galaxy in which there are highly-advanced extraterrestrial civilisations at the present time. These extraterrestrial civilisations would have technologies so in advance of ours as to be beyond our understanding.

It deals in depth with the development of intelligence and the evolving of life within the cosmos.

Derek Sheffield provides, under the title 'The Witnesses', an impressive list of the world's top astronomers, scientists, academics, leaders of the world's armed services, top politicians and political leaders, six presidents of the United States of America, and many astronauts and test pilots, who all believe in the existence of extraterrestrial phenomena in the heavens above the Earth.

Because of the state of apparent confusion that exists in both the American CIA and the British Ministry of Defence, and the difficulties – for whatever reasons – in obtaining honest information from either the American or the British scenes, the time has come for the ghost to be laid by the study of a series of events that occurred in Europe in November 1989 and March 1990.

Derek Sheffield then quotes testimony in the form of a detailed study – backed by a comprehensive list of documents – of the appearance above Eupen and Wavre in Belgium in 1989–90 of a phenomenon that was seen by many thousands of witnesses.

Over 2,600 of these made statements to the police. Seventy-five members of the Belgian Gendarmerie were among witnesses who submitted statements.

It was filmed by the media, photographed by the public and tracked by three radar stations.

When these sightings were confirmed by police and the radar stations involved, the Belgian Air Force sent up two F-16 interceptor aircraft which were vectored to the target by two of these radar stations.

The two pursuing aircraft picked up the target on their 'on-board' radar but when they attempted to 'lock-on', the object took violent evasive action attaining acceleration speeds of 150 kts to 780 kts in $\pm\frac{1}{2}$ second, and a rate of descent from 7,000 ft to 3,000 ft in 1 second.

These figures have been confirmed by the Belgian Air Force.

This interception continued for over one hour above Brussels (the home of the European Parliament) and Wavre, South of the Capital.

During this time the object showed by its evasive action, a remarkable degree of intelligence.

Derek Sheffield shows illustrations of the phenomenon – in the first instance as four strange lights – and secondly (when enhanced by blue light), in its triangular format.

Special attention should be paid to the light patterns shown when various light enhancements are made.

These illustrations have been confirmed as genuine by the Belgian Royal Military Academy.

Also shown are illustrations of the actual 'on-board' radar screens taken from the pursuing F-16 Interceptors, and confirmed by the Belgian Air Force.

The Belgian Minister of Defence – in reply to a question on this phenomenon – stated that 'he did not know what it was'.

'The Indictment' states that as this event could be either the greatest event or the greatest danger to mankind, and as the credibility of the Belgian Air Force, Police and Ministry of Defence are in question, then it is the responsibility of the European Parliament to conduct an extensive enquiry into the events that made up the Belgian incidents of the 29th–30th of November 1989 and the 30th–31st March 1990.

If, as a result of this enquiry this phenomenon is thought to be of probable extraterrestrial origin, it is imperative that in the interests of International security that this be recognised.

It is therefore incumbent upon the European Parliament that this declaration be made public.

Derek Sheffield
Rolvenden, 1993

CHAPTER ELEVEN

The Spider's Web

This press release had strange results in more ways than one. Not very long ago, General Manuel Noriega (an ex-CIA agent) allegedly caused the Americans some problems in Panama. President George Bush stated in a television interview that there was a local fracas between warring factions of the Panamanian national army. He said, replying to a suggestion that there was American involvement, 'If this is some American operation, I can tell you this is not true.'

The story that was issued was that there had been a small skirmish that resulted in 250 casualties. What in fact had happened was that 25,000 American troops, supported by many attack helicopters, had attacked at night and had completely devastated a large area of Panama City. Houses were torched and the estimated dead were put at 4,000. Bodies were buried in 15 mass graves and many atrocities were committed by American troops.

Rear-Admiral Eugene Carroll of the Center for Defense Information said that there had been complete collaboration between the American media and the military authorities to block all news of this event. He said that a visit to the scene of destruction by a visiting contingent of six journalists was completely stage-managed by the military authorities to avoid sensitive areas.

There was no report in the media of the United Nations condemnation of the attack, or of the invasion of Panama.

No journalists were allowed in the devastated areas and eight press agencies seemed unable to get past the military:

The Associated Press
The National Broadcasting Corporation TV
Time magazine
The American Broadcasting Corporation
Reuters
The *Houston Post*
The *Dallas Morning News*
The *Houston Chronicle*.

The door was slammed and nothing got out.

The reason for recounting this incident is to illustrate to the reader how easily a degree of censorship can be imposed on an innocent society.

I issued my press release to 14 different press agencies. A well-known reporter said that it was a very relevant news item, particularly as it concerned an event that had not been publicized in the UK.

This press release was sent to:

Independent Television
Meridian Television
BBC Television
The Associated Press
The Press Association
Reuters
BELGA (Belgium)
DPA (Germany)
AFO (France)
ANP (Holland)
The *Daily Telegraph*
The *Daily Express*
The *Daily Mail*
The *Daily Mirror*.

All the above declined to comment.

Copies of my press release were sent to two local newspapers and BBC Radio Kent. I had formed an association with them because of their reviews of my previous book, *A Question of Reason*. Both newspapers carried the story and I was invited to another live broadcast at the Canterbury studios of BBC Radio Kent.

This time the broadcast was different. I was on the offensive. I was going to talk about this incredible event that the media had kept very quiet about. I was determined to get the details over to the public.

The first statement by the interviewer was an attempt at ridicule. I had anticipated this and quickly corrected him. I moved to the much more serious business of the Belgian radar detections. I managed to broadcast all the relevant details of the Belgian sightings in a 10-minute period. As is usual with this subject, any television or radio coverage is given out in the early hours. In this case it was at 8 am and 9 am and then nothing more – one correspondent even enquired if the radio station had been served with a 'D' notice – but the response was incredible. Within the next few weeks I became the recipient of letters and telephone calls from all over the world. I became acquainted with some very interesting people.

One of these was an attractive American lady who went by the very English name of Linda Moulton-Howe.

Another was an equally attractive English lady known as Maria Ward.

And the third was Michael Soper, Chairman of Contact International (UK). All – in their respective ways – provided me with aspects of this story that I would not have thought possible.

Within a few days of my BBC Radio Kent broadcast, I received a telephone call inviting me to meet Linda Moulton-Howe.

By this time I was beginning to have apprehensions concerning any strange occurrences that did not fit my normal routine. Liaisons with attractive young ladies were certainly not my usual routine.

To look at things objectively, odd things were happening that had not happened before. People who ought to have co-operated did not do so, letters and documents that should have been delivered did not arrive, false information was given to me by the Ministry of Defence, information given by MEP assistants was incorrect, Belgian police departments referred any questions to the Belgian Air Force like a hot potato (despite the fact that 75 officers of the Belgian police were involved), and my telephone began to behave in a most mysterious manner.

I viewed this invitation with some caution.

The venue was a large roadhouse near the M2 motorway named The Black Prince. This was chosen because of ease of access for both parties. The meeting was arranged for Friday, 6 August at 3 pm.

Linda Moulton-Howe arrived on schedule, accompanied by two tall men dressed in dark suits. It was like some scene from a spy story. My worries were, however, groundless, because their presence at the meeting was quickly explained.

Probably because of my unease, my first reaction – after initial introductions – was to ask Linda Moulton-Howe and her two companions exactly who they were, and what their business was. It was explained that Linda Moulton-Howe was – amongst other things – an author; one of the reasons for her presence was that her two companions were in the process of setting up a book marketing concern, and were negotiating distribution arrangements with her.

Before Linda explained the purpose of our meeting, I said quite bluntly that I did not believe in any of the more outrageous aspects of some of the lunatic groups that had formed in connection with this phenomenon.

I said that my approach was – because the American and British scenes were corrupt to the point of deception – to ignore any reference (both past and present) to these areas, and to concentrate, in a completely factual and truthful way, on a series of events that had occurred on our own doorstep, the Belgian incidents of 1989 and 1990.

The opening remark went down like a lead balloon.

Linda Moulton-Howe, an obviously very intelligent young lady, then gave me details of her background. She is a graduate of Stanford University with a Master's degree in communication. She has devoted her film and television career to documentary and studio productions concerning science, medicine and the environment. Linda has received local, national and international awards, including three Emmies and a national Emmy nomination for her documentaries. These films have included *Fire in the Water*, about hydrogen as an alternative energy source to fossil fuels; *A Radioactive Water*, which investigated uranium contamination of public drinking water in Denver; *A Strange Harvest*, which explored the worldwide animal mutilation mystery that has haunted the United States and other countries since the 1960s – and continues to date.

In 1989, she wrote and published a hard-cover book entitled *An Alien Harvest*. She was also Director of International Programming for *Earthbeat*, an environmental series broadcast on Turner's WIBS Superstation, Atlanta, Georgia.

Her television productions in 1990 included the creation of the CNN Reel News series; a two-hour special, *Earth Mysteries: Alien Life Forms*, in association with WATL-Fox, Atlanta; and a documentary, *The Pressure of Fact*.

In 1991, she was contracted with Paramount Studios as Supervising Producer and Original Concept Creator for a one-hour special based on her *Earth Mysteries* programme. That hour, *UFO Report: Sightings*, was broadcast on 18 October 1991 and 25 January 1992, and led to the *Sightings* series on the Fox network.

In 1992, Linda Moulton-Howe was voted winner of the international MUFON Award, honouring her contributions to advancing understanding of complex alien life-form phenomena. She has been interviewed on the *Montel Williams* TV show and other national and international media. Linda continues to write, produce and speak at national and international conferences and symposiums, including NASA Goddard Space Flight Center. She helped to co-ordinate scientific investigations of the crop circle mystery in England in 1992, and has distributed *Crop Circle Communiqué* in association with Circlevision, England. She is currently writing a new book, *Glimpses of Other Realities*, and producing a documentary, *Strange Harvests – 1993*.

I was suitably impressed – humbled in fact. But I am no longer young and am wise to the ways of the world. I also have very firm ideas of my own. One of these is that I refuse to be drawn in to some of the strange assumptions made by fellow believers regardless of how pretty and how intelligent they are.

This is not to say that their hypotheses are not correct – they probably are. It is just that when confronted with an enigma that consists of lies and deception, then I would rather conduct my own enquiry; at least I know that it is truthful and honest in every way.

If – when I have pursued my quest to the conclusion that I already suspect it to be – I find that the observations of Linda Moulton-Howe are relevant, then I will gladly accommodate them and accept them willingly. But at this time, as far as I am concerned, it must be a case of a clear, step-by-step, factual investigation. Nothing must be added that – in the eyes of the British public – could be interpreted as unacceptable in any way.

I think Linda Moulton-Howe had been interested in my broadcast because I had expressed a new approach. She said several things that had intrigued me. The first was that she would be surprised if I got anywhere in requesting any European government for assistance in obtaining an inquiry. She said that security in Great Britain was tighter than in Libya; at least, she said, in America they had the Freedom of Information Act, and were able to have access to information that was just not possible in this country.

Linda said, very convincingly, that she had researched the subject for many years and had discovered facts that were almost unbelievable. When I pressed her on this point she made a statement that put things into the realms of horror.

She said that she had conducted an investigation into cattle mutilation in Canada and America. She said that there had been instances where dead cattle had been found mutilated at the locations of the appearance of this phenomenon. Evidently investigations had been carried out pathologically on these animal cadavers with the most extraordinary results.

It would seem that parts of these carcasses had been removed; namely lips, eyes, nipples, reproductive organs and parts of stomachs. These parts had been removed clinically and with great precision.

There were, however, sinister aspects of a different kind.

It had not been possible to determine how the incisions had been made. Pathologically, it was possible to determine that these incisions were not made by conventional surgical instruments. Cutting by laser was ruled out; laser incisions leave carbon deposits at the edge of any cut. The only other method of incising, it was deduced, was by the use of some form of sonic instrument.

All the cadavers were also completely bloodless, there being no evidence of any blood in the surrounding area of the dead animals.

I remarked, at this point, that the fact that one cow had been attacked by an imbecile with a knife did not really prove a thing. Was it not an over-reaction on her part? Her answer stopped me dead in my tracks.

'I'm not talking about one dead cow,' she said, 'I'm talking about *ten thousand!'*

Linda then associated this obscenity with hypnotic regressions at which she had been present. Apparently, unimpeachable citizens – who had claimed to have been abducted – recounted operations in which it can only be assumed that semen was surgically removed from their bodies.

Linda Moulton-Howe is, above all else, a very intelligent woman of integrity. Of course she is in the business of making money, but she is well known and is dependent upon her reputation for her livelihood. It would not be in her interests to over-sensationalize any aspect of this subject. Despite my own opinions, I find it difficult to comprehend that she would have stated these views had she not considered them very carefully before expressing them.

She said that she *knew* that all information on this phenomenon was coming from – and being directed by – America.

Her conclusions are the nightmare scenario: that contact has already been made by the United States, that there is intense collaboration with this phenomenon, that this has resulted in the exchange of animal tissue and human semen in return for highly advanced technology.

Linda qualified her point by pointing out the extraordinary advance of American technology in the last twenty years compared with that of any other nation on Earth.

Because my philosophy is to have an open mind on any subject, I accepted all that Linda Moulton-Howe had said – but with reservations.

My original purpose, however, must still remain: to prove beyond any doubt that these phenomena exist, and, if they do, what their reasons are for being here.

During our conversation, one of Linda's companions mentioned 'the present wave of sightings'. This intrigued me. On enquiring what they were, I was told that Linda was on her way to investigate one of these sightings that had been witnessed on the north Kent coast. There had also been another at Harcliffe, near Bristol. According to newspaper reports, dozens of families had left their beds to watch coloured lights hover in the sky for five hours. Residents in Harcliffe, Bristol, saw eight different lights change from blue to red until 5.30 am. A witness said that they were definitely not stars, aircraft or helicopters. Bristol Airport Control and the Civil Aviation Authority were said to be baffled.

It was now, however, that I found that I was becoming involved in a weird aspect of this phenomenon that I did not want to be associated with. I was being sidetracked into the general UFO aura; I was becoming involved with a train of events that could give my research lack of credibility.

Because it was a local event I was interested in the north Kent sightings. Linda Moulton-Howe's companion advised me to contact a Maria Ward, who apparently knew of these.

This was to be my next insight into another aspect that caused me some concern. I telephoned Maria Ward and made an appointment.

Maria Ward was different again; she would be best described as attractive with an air of mysticism. She knew of the north Kent sightings, but felt that I would be better informed by interviewing a local resident; she gave me the appropriate telephone number. Maria then said that sightings in this area were numerous; she mentioned, in passing, its close proximity to Manston Airport. At this point, I began to see all talk of 'a wave of sightings' in its proper perspective. I relegated it to the realms of the imagination. People will always see what they want to see, and an active airfield will always produce its crop of lights in the sky. Maria Ward was also intelligent. She informed me that she was a member of MENSA – an organization of the highly intelligent – and she had taken some odd photographs which she claimed were UFO photographs. These were identical to star photographs taken with an unsteady hand and did not particularly convince me. Maria's interest was mainly in the psychic aspect of the phenomenon, which was not mine. Once again, the views of Maria Ward – like those of Linda Moulton-Howe – are probably correct, but remain to be proven.

I have recently read a report of a United Nations committee dated January 1993. It stated that five academics had debated for six hours (at a symposium held on 2 October 1992), on Extraterrestrial Intelligence and Human Nature. It would seem from this summary that the members present, despite holding differing views, had reached a common conclusion. They decided that too much emphasis had been placed on proving the existence of extraterrestrials, and not enough on why they are here, what we can learn, and how we should deal with them. Some speakers wanted scientists to go one step further and accept extraterrestrial existence based on eyewitness accounts rather than on replicable laboratory-controlled evidence.

Other academics tried to establish that the most effective language is not the spoken one but telepathy (which they claim is already used by alien intelligences). They also say that we should accept abduction which is a means used to conduct human experiments for our own benefit.

It was decided to attempt to revive United Nations GA Decision 33/426 which called for a central UN body to deal with exchange of information between countries with advanced extraterrestrial programmes.

The committee also stressed the need to test the credibility of telepathic messages and automatic writings dictated by invisible entities, especially by cosmic colleagues who claim they serve a cosmic plan.

These were the observations and resolutions discussed by a committee of the United Nations. They certainly make the beliefs of Maria Ward and Linda Moulton-Howe infinitely more credible. I believe, however, that they are putting the cart before the horse.

All the time people are asked to believe in apparently supernatural forces without any physical evidence, they will reject them out of hand as figments of the imagination. Provide them with real proof and the picture is completely different. They will accept any new postulations as being credible.

The plot deepens. Evidently, concern is now at a very high level indeed.

A fitting end to this chapter must be that I was advised by a friend that there would be a talk on BBC radio by an American, Bob Oechsler, at 10 pm the following evening. The subject was to be the UFO situation. The date, by coincidence, was exactly two months *after* the meeting that I had with Linda Moulton-Howe.

Nothing much in that, you might say. There was when you knew the context of the interview.

Bob Oechsler appeared to be a highly qualified space technician, previously employed on many projects by NASA. His qualifications appeared to be almost as impressive as those of Linda Moulton-Howe, but more in the field of pure space technology.

What brought me down to earth with a jolt was the feeling of *déjà-vu* that I had, as I listened to his broadcast. I had been here before. It was as if I was listening to a gramophone record that I had heard at an earlier time. Then I realized that

I had. I could even tell what was coming next. It was almost word for word – in the correct sequence – the conversation that I had had with Linda Moulton-Howe *two months previously*.

Coincidences of that kind just do not happen. Could they possibly be associates?

During the Bob Oechsler interview, the interviewer asked how it was possible for him to disclose such highly classified information. Mr Oechsler's reply was that he had not the slightest idea. He did, however, think it was possible that the fact that he was allowed to release this information was all part of a plan, and quite intentional. This phrase brought to mind Linda Moulton-Howe's statement that this whole phenomenon was being controlled by the Americans, who were releasing details as and when they thought suitable.

While both Linda Moulton-Howe and Bob Oechsler are no doubt entirely genuine, I must keep firmly in mind that the phenomenon we are dealing with *is intelligent in the extreme*. They are possibly correct in all that they say, but this could be intentional disinformation, or even part of a conditioning programme for the acceptance of this phenomenon. It could be that if one became involved with their theories, then one would be classed as involved in the realms of the weird. It must be remembered that ridicule is a very effective weapon of this intelligence. I must stick to my first principle: prove the existence of this phenomenon and all else will fall into place.

I have recently had a further example of this practice. I have made the acquaintance of Michael Soper. Michael is National Chairman of Contact International (UK), an organization with a titled President and an impressive council of academic members. It was recommended to me by the Ministry of Defence as probably being able to give me some assistance in researching the Belgian sightings. I followed this line of enquiry despite my apprehensions in dealing with anyone recommended by the Ministry of Defence – one has, after all, to start somewhere. We found our subject to be of mutual interest. This resulted, after many conversations, in my being invited as a guest speaker to a conference held by his organization in Oxford. This was enlightening. I suppose that I came away from the meeting feeling that although the opinions expressed were many and varied, the sum total would be that we all believed in the existence of this phenomenon, but its form and purpose were the subject of great variance. I also met my first abductee.

During a break for refreshment in the latter part of the conference I noticed a quiet man standing apart from the mass of people. He was probably 28 years of age, well groomed, of above average height, and physically athletic in stature. He was dressed quite casually and seemed to be keeping himself to himself.

I made my way over and asked him if he was enjoying the meeting. He replied that he was, but with reservations. He said that most of the subjects discussed had been above his head but that he had particularly related to my attitude to the subject and had greatly enjoyed my talk.

He seemed to be extremely tense and acted as if he wanted to speak to me further. Several times he started to talk in an abrupt way but then stopped. He said that he wanted to discuss something with me but that he had never spoken of it to any other person and did not know how to begin. I said that I had got time, and suggested that the beginning was a good place to start.

He was obviously terribly embarrassed. He stammered a story in which he told me that a particular hobby of his was mountaineering. He said that this was a lonely sport and there were many occasions when he was in isolated locations. One such occasion had been in Wales, when, high on the side of a mountain, an orb had appeared. He did not quote its size, but I imagine from his description for it to have been 30–50 ft across. Its upper surface was silver, and it was dull grey and black underneath. He said that it remained stationary in the sky, and then moved slowly towards him until it was some 200 feet directly above him. He remembers being aghast and rooted to the spot and then being aware that he was on another part of the mountain and that the time was some hours later. He was obviously very distressed at this point and seemed to take a few moments to compose himself. He said that this had not been the first occasion of involvement with this phenomenon; he had been taken from a cornfield on the outskirts of Oxford at the age of 7. He stammered that odd bits of memory kept coming back. He said that semen had been taken from him.

At this point he speculated that he had said enough. He apologized for his outburst but said that he had to talk to someone. Would I mind if he telephoned me at a later date? I replied that I would have no objection at all. I said that it must have been a nightmare for him and that he must have had fears for his sanity. I told him that in view of the statements that I had heard over the last few weeks, it could be that he was one of over five thousand to have experienced the same fate.

I gave him my telephone number; he looked uneasy and said that he would have to think about it. Depending on how he felt about the matter, he *might* give me a ring at some time in the future. I said that if it would give him some reassurance he would be very welcome to do so.

Linda Moulton-Howe, Bob Oechsler and a complete stranger – though very credible – had all stated that abusing of the human species was taking place *by the forcible extraction of semen*. This can only mean either that these people are telling the truth, or that a weird spreading of disinformation is taking place with some ulterior motive in mind.

Whatever it is, *there is decidedly something most peculiar going on.*

CHAPTER TWELVE

Contact International

B ruce Cathie cautioned me in his letter to be wary of UFO groups recommended by defence establishments. In spite of his expressed caution, when a group called Contact International were recommended by the Ministry of Defence as a source of information on the Belgian detections, I had no particular hesitation in seeking their help.

It was Contact International that asked me to speak at their conference in Oxford. My first apprehension concerning this group came when I was asked not to be too critical in any reference to the Ministry of Defence. It was said that a good working relationship was had with this department and they had no wish to jeopardize this. I had greater apprehensions when a video tape was made of the proceedings. It was explained that a video film would be made of the conference; this would evidently be for sale at a later date. When I

DEREK SHEFFIELD – BELGIAN CASES:

Derek Sheffield is to be congratulated on his efforts to bring Ufology into the political arena after the events of 1990 (which in a way is concurrent with the aims of John Holman – which I will return to later). I have read of the Belgian events, and learnt more from Derek. Although I agree that the whole situation was of concern to the Belgian Military at the time, conversely it was hardly considered a real threat to national security. Surely any real perceived threat would have warranted more than flights of an Air Patrol nature? If it had been aircraft coming in from Eastern Europe, there would have been rather more defensive aircraft scrambled including Belgian USAFE aircraft. Derek made much of the aversion of our own Ministry of Defence to admit that they were notified through NATO channels of the radar contacts, but I wonder if other European Air Commands have been any more forthcoming? Although the Belgian Air Force have declared the objects as unidentified, something seems amiss in the reaction, or possibly the interpretation by Ufologists. The same might be said of the well-known Puerto Rico events – which I will again return to.

BRIAN P. JAMES

---

requested a copy of this film, it was explained that the film had to be edited and this could take several months. It all seemed most odd. Despite my five-hour journey to and from Oxford, no note of appreciation has ever been sent. No further reference to a video film has been made in over two years.

I have received a copy of volume 19, number 3, of *Awareness*, the journal of Contact International, in which there is a write-up of my contribution to the Oxford Conference by Brian P. James, which reads as shown opposite.

It is odd that the comments expressed by Mr James are similar, to an interesting degree, to the opinions expressed by the Ministry of Defence and the Minister of State for the Armed Forces:

- The statement that this was of concern to the Belgian military only.
- The doubts that these detections constituted a threat.
- Apparent support for the MOD's attitude to radar disclosures.

Taking all these factors into account, I have reason to doubt the motives of Contact International. It could be that their actions are purely circumstantial. I hope that they are. I suspect, however, that they are being used in a deception by an intelligence that is beyond their wildest dreams.

A correspondence was entered into with Mr James which is reproduced as follows.

A Letter to Contact International

22nd March 1994

Dear Mr James

Thank you for your congratulatory comments on my efforts to bring Ufology into the political arena.

I would correct your comment. Ufology is tainted with a radical view that I have no wish to be connected with. My purpose is to firstly prove the existence of a phenomenon above Belgium in 1989/90, and that the MOD *did* have knowledge of these phenomenon.

This I have done. I have confirmation from the Belgian Government that: 'from a military point of view, all hypotheses could be excluded, there were flying objects above Belgium on the dates mentioned, and the Belgian Government did not know what they were'.

I have been informed by the Belgian Air Force that strict parameters were met before action could be taken. Witnesses observations have to be confirmed by the police. Police observations have to be confirmed by Belgian radar. When these conditions have been met, the Belgian Air Force will, after consultation with the radar stations involved, attempt an interception. All these parameters were met. Interceptions were ordered.

To your comment that a real threat to national security would have warranted more than *flights of an air patrol nature*, I would add that the Belgian Air Force considered this intrusion to be of the utmost gravity. Their interceptions were not of an air patrol nature. They resent any implication to the contrary. For your interest, the event of any intrusion into our own air space, very rarely results in any more than two RAF interceptor aircraft being alerted.

Concerning your comment that I made much of the aversion of the MOD to admit that they were notified through NATO channels of these radar contacts. I would suggest that because of the blank by the UK media, you probably were not well informed. The German and French military were very much involved. *Their* media coverage illustrated the point.

On the question of the MOD. We have an interesting situation. I have a letter from Mr Pope stating that the MOD had *no* knowledge of the Belgian detections. We have a letter from the Minister admitting that the MOD *did* have knowledge of these detections.

I also have proof that NADGE advised UK radar of these detections and that the MOD *were* advised of these.

Action is pending to ratify these contradictions.

Once proof of these detections are admitted by the MOD (they now have no alternative but to admit to this) the next logical step will be to ascertain the reasons for their denials.

Bearing in mind the associations of Contact International with the MOD, I would be interested to see whether you include this in your next issue.

Yours sincerely, Derek Sheffield

REPLY FROM CONTACT INTERNATIONAL

30 March 1994

Dear Derek

Many thanks for your letter regarding my comments in the last issue of CONTACT's *Awareness*, which has been forwarded to me. I have only recently joined CONTACT, and only in the past few weeks taken on an active role as an investigator, so my attendance of the Conference last October was as an individual, and it was in this context that I assumed that you were a UFO researcher as such, so please accept my apologies for any incorrect inference I have made on that matter.

My notes on the Conference have sadly been altered in places, whether it is editorial amendment, typing errors or poor proof reading, or a combination of all three I'm not sure, but it has led to several of my comments in 'Awareness' having a rather different context to my original notes, not a situation I am pleased about as I'm sure you can imagine, and I will be taking this up with the editor.

Really my only knowledge of the Belgian events at the time came from Tim Good's coverage in the annual *UFO Report*, and the much quoted letter by Colonel De Brouwer – so it was the combination of those on which I was basing my comments – and your address to the Conference increased my knowledge, and interest. I am very keen to know where I can obtain more data on what happened at the time, and subsequent investigations into the events. I was very interested to hear of the necessary chain of command in Belgium for dealing with this sort of event, leading to an attempted interception.

Unfortunately the line you picked up on in my article, 'flights of an air patrol nature' was not how I had worded it, I specifically referred to a Combat Air Patrol and interception. While I have never been in the Air Force, or indeed any of the services, I am a keen enthusiast of military aviation, so I am aware of the point you make about it being common practice for an interception of an intruder to be by only two aircraft that had been on standby, but I would suggest that the situation that existed between both NATO and the Warsaw Pact forces did mean that most 'interceptions' of intruders, by both sides, were not really of true 'unidentified' aircraft, since both sides were well aware

113

of the almost daily cat and mouse probing, so when scrambled, an RAF intercept unit would be 99% sure that they were going to encounter a Tu-20 or other Soviet aircraft, and exchange various gestures before both parties completed their little charade. I am sure that you have access to more data on the Belgian events that would confirm that once the interceptors had found a true 'unidentified' intruder, then a new sequence of actions would have been initiated, as indeed I would expect them to have been in any other NATO country, but based on the admittedly little data on the events that I have read, that didn't seem to happen. As far as I know there were only two F-16s involved at any one time, which brings me back to my original comment of intercepting a 'known' intruder, and then watching this intruder. I am not sure that at any time the Belgian AF attempted to use the weapons on the F-16s against these intruders in Belgian airspace, and I have to wonder why, unless they already knew the possible consequences. At a time when the Cold War still existed to some extent, surely if there was any possibility that these unidentified craft were actually Soviet aircraft or weapons systems, then action would have been taken, after all, it's only in the past few months that NATO and what remains of the Soviet forces have agreed not to target our nuclear arsenals at each other. It was very interesting to hear that the Belgians regard the matter with great concern, and resent implications otherwise, but to me something isn't adding up.

I appreciate that you will have vast amounts of information that may well correct my possible misinterpretation – and I would be grateful if you can point out my erroneous thoughts – but based on the data that I have seen, I still feel there is a doubt as to the degree of threat perceived by the Belgian AF in these events. I realise that I may be coming across as a sort of debunker of these events, far from it, I accept that something very unusual did occur, my doubt is to the perception of what was occurring at the time against the political and military background that existed.

I am grateful for you updating me on the coverage given in particularly France and Germany on the matter, these are significant aspects which have not been given enough publicity, even in the UFO literature which I have seen, and clearly show part of a much greater picture of events. *I agree that the behaviour of our own MOD and its involvement is curious, and you have confirmed one of my own personal suspicions, namely that as a member of NATO, our MOD and RAF would have been informed, along with France and Germany, and also presumably Holland and possibly Denmark.* Have the USAFE authorities ever admitted to being involved at the time, as they would surely have had F-15 interceptors on standby?

It is true that CONTACT has recently used associations within the MOD to enable them to view at the Public Record Office, specific documents of RAF interceptions, from what I have seen they date back to the mid-1950s, but one document that I have seen a copy of does suggest an exchange of data on sightings when an object flew back towards Europe. I was not involved in this visit, and I am not sure if others are planned in the future, but I doubt if I will be invited to participate.

I have no direct involvement in the production of *Awareness*, but I will pass a copy of your letter to the editor – Geoff Ambler – so that he can include it next time in reply to my article.

Thanking you once again for your interest.

Your colleague,

Brian P. James

A LETTER TO BRIAN P. JAMES

10th April 1994

Dear Brian

Thank you for your letter of the 30th March. Your comments are appreciated. You will understand – bearing in mind my application to the European Parliament – that it would be unwise for me to become involved with any UFO groups. A very effective weapon of the establishment is ridicule. Unfortunately UFO groups leave themselves open to this charge.

Your observations concerning the curious involvement of the MOD is noted. To this I would add that I have been informed by a senior defence staff member that Mr Pope is a very junior civil servant . . .

I am in a strange situation concerning information from the Belgian Air Force. I was advised by an airline pilot who heard a radio broadcast that I had made, in which I stated that the MOD refuted that there had ever been radar detections that had been confirmed by airline pilots; he advised me that this was quite wrong, and to contact the Belgian Air Force.

Initially I made two contacts. They supplied me with information that was beyond belief. Basically that there had been many radar detections over a four-month period involving four Belgian radar stations and one German. Officially, interceptions were attempted by F-16 fighters on 20th November 1989, 15th December 1989, 16th December 1989, and 30th March 1990. I have strong reasons to believe that there were many others.

I have been sent details of radar detections on these incidents, as well as twelve pages of typescript of the conversations by the Belgian pilots with each other and their radar control centres. These contain the performance figures on the night of 31/31st March 1990, of courses followed, and details of avoidance by the phenomena when radar lock-on was attempted (for your interest, in one lock-on of 22.5 secs, there were 5 changes of direction, 14 changes of speed, and 14 changes in altitude).

The task set for these aircraft was VID (verify and identify) and on two occasions control asked that the armament be checked as safe.

I have an admission by the Belgian Minister of Defence that there were flying objects over Belgium. He stated that all known hypotheses had been taken into account and that he did not know what these flying objects were. The Belgians have informed me that the main detection was by Glons (CRC) radar, which is part of the NADGE radar defence system which covers the whole of Europe. I have been advised by my defence staff contact that it is inconceivable that the MOD did not know of the Belgian radar detections, 'because that is how the system works!'

I note your comment that something does not 'add up' in the Belgian affair. It could be, that after chasing shadows for four months, that later incidents assumed a lack of realism for the Belgian Air Force. It would seem that their final conclusions were that the phenomena indicated a very strong electromagnetic force indeed.

For your interest, a comparison of statements by Belgian witnesses with those of 40 witnesses in north Kent in September indicates that the Kent and Belgian phenomena are the same. It has a constantly changing format.

Yours sincerely
Derek Sheffield

A FURTHER LETTER TO BRIAN P. JAMES

30th July 1995

Dear Brian

Just a note to let you know that things are now on the move. It would seem that one of the largest publishers in the country is very interested in publishing my book on the Belgian events; it is to be entitled *UFO: A Deadly Concealment*. I am in the process of putting it all together – no small task! It consists of a very detailed account of the actual events of both the sightings at Eupen in November 1989 and Wavre in March 1990, and a statement by the Belgian Air Force giving details of the conversations between the F-16 pilots and their radar stations as they were being vectored to their targets (you will be able to form your own opinion as to whether these were 'flights of an air patrol nature' or not!)

The book was originally simply a file on my appeal to the European Parliament requesting an investigation into the Belgian phenomenon. The nature of things, however, has changed. It would seem that I have uncovered a can of worms. The contradictory statements between the Ministry of Defence and the Minister of Defence, the observation by the Minister that we were *not* automatically advised by Belgian radar (NADGE) and a statement by De Brouwer that UK radar (NADGE) at Neatshead in Norfolk *were* advised automatically, all form part of a story that can only lead to a charge of a massive deception of some kind.

To this end, I would like to mention my experience concerning Contact International, and wonder whether you would have any objection to my reproducing either your complete letter of the 3rd March 1994, or the parts of it relevant to my case?

Thank you for your past interest,

Yours sincerely

Derek Sheffield

CHAPTER THIRTEEN

A Parliamentary Breakthrough

When I returned to the Oxford conference after the abduction discussion, John Holman was on the rostrum. I had not noticed him in the audience at the time that I was speaking. I was interested to note that he was talking about the Belgian phenomenon. A summary of his speech would be that we *know* that this phenomenon exists; what positive course of action can we now take? I was greatly interested in the point of view that he expressed but sadly I was running out of time and, with a 4½-hour train journey in prospect, had to leave before the conclusion of his speech.

During the return journey I reflected on his point of view.

I was absolutely sure – because I had irrefutable evidence – that unidentified aerial objects of some kind had been detected above Belgium.

I was equally sure that the British Ministry of Defence (either by ignorance or design) were obstructing the release of information on these phenomena.

I *knew* that the NATO Air Defence Ground Environment had detected this phenomenon.

Because the UK is part of this defence system we should have been advised of this detection.

The Ministry of Defence say that they were not.

Either the Ministry of Defence are being economical with the truth, or they have instructions to obstruct the release of information, or NADGE (NATO) are withholding details of this phenomenon from them. This must mean that either the MOD or the CIA, or both, *know what it is*. I have written to John Holman since my return and explained to him that I had missed part of his speech, but on the basis of what I had heard

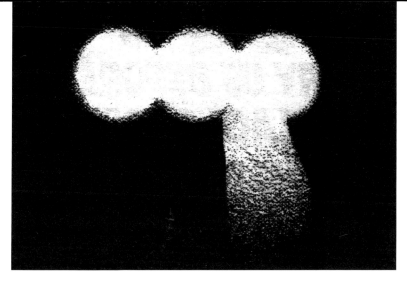

1 *One form of the 'North Kent phenomenon' witnessed by many people in the Canterbury area of southern England, 17–20 September 1993.*

Kent:	Three bright, greenish-white lights in a flat triangular shape.
Eupen:	A triangular platform with three powerful lights at its points.
Kent:	An oval, ellipsoid-shaped light.
Eupen:	An orb of light.
Kent:	A silvery oval object with flashing lights around the rim.
Eupen:	A white orb with coloured lights situated at its extremities.
Kent:	A large object with bright, white lights zig-zagging through the sky at an incredible speed.
Eupen:	This object pursued a wildly erratic and step-like zig-zag course.
Kent:	A bright silvery stationary object that was turning over itself.
Eupen:	A continual changing format; a tumbling plethora of light.
Kent:	A very bright light – out of which four identical shapes emerged – they were moving all around it; the four shapes all seemed to merge into the main one and it disappeared.
Eupen:	It has the ability to divide into two separate triangles, each of which emit a number of small replicas of itself which proceed in various directions. These return after a period to their respective half triangles, which then reform to the original triangular platform.
Kent:	A large, round thing with sparkling lights on it, over towards Ramsgate. It seemed to have lights *in* it as well as round it.
Eupen:	A large, pinkish-white orb with many small lights both on its surface as well as *in* it.

2 *Comparison of witness statements of the Kent, UK and Eupen, Belgium sightings.*

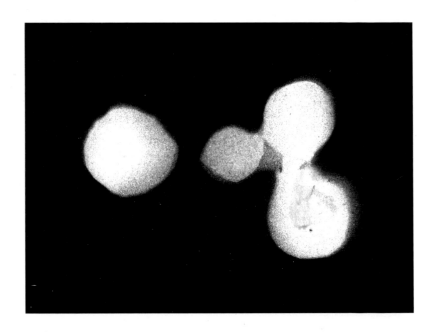

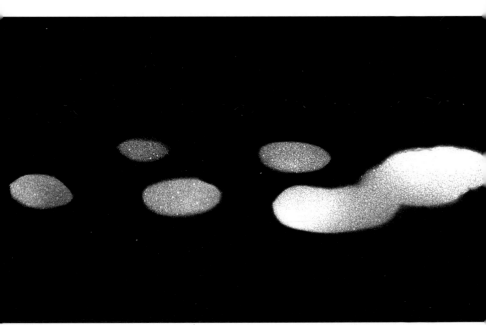

3 and 4 *Artist's impressions, based on photographs, as comparison of the object seen over Central America in 1990 (top) and in 1991 (bottom).*

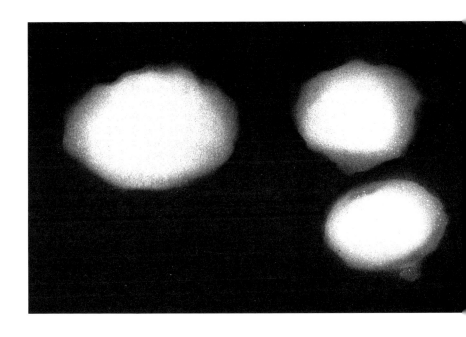

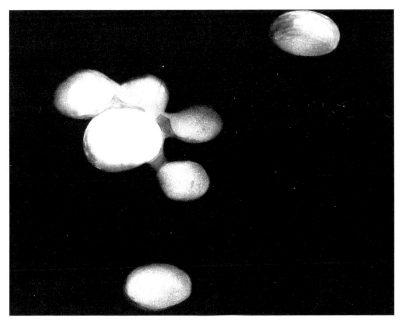

5 and 6 *Artist's impressions, based on photographs, as comparison of the objects seen over Belgium 1990 (top) and Southern Russia (bottom).*

Minister Coëme, the Minister of Defense at the time being, answered to Representative Janssens about the increasing number of UFO's above the east of the Province of Liège.

The answer is enclosed hereby and can be summarised as follows :

1. It is not possible to establish a correlation between the observations made by witnesses on the one hand and detection by the radars of Semmerzake (Belgium) and VEDEM (Germany) on the other hand.

2. F-16 aeroplanes have intervened twice. The first on the 15th December 1989 as a result of observations made by the "gendarmerie" of Eupen.

The pilotes did not observe anything and nothing was visible on the radar at the time they were operating.

The second on the 16th December 1989 as a result of observations and communications adressed to the base of Glons. It seemed that they resulted from laser-projections of a disco.

3. From military point of view, the following possibilities can be excluded :

- they were not AWACS-aeroplanes, because they are submitted to radar control when they fly over belgian territory ;
- they were not F-117 aeroplanes, as was confirmed by the General Staff of the US Air Force ;
- they were not teleguided military machines, because they were not used during these particular weeks ;
- they were not ultra light motorised aeroplanes, because these produce a different and specific sound.

4. Conclusion :

As these four hypotheses can be excluded, the Minister could not tell what these flying objects were.

Hoping to have answered your question with this letter, I remain,

Yours faithfully,

Leo DELCROIX.
Minister of Defense.

7 *Letter from Belgian Defence Minister Guy Coëme (1990) to the author; endorsed by later Defence Minister Leo Delcroix (1993).*

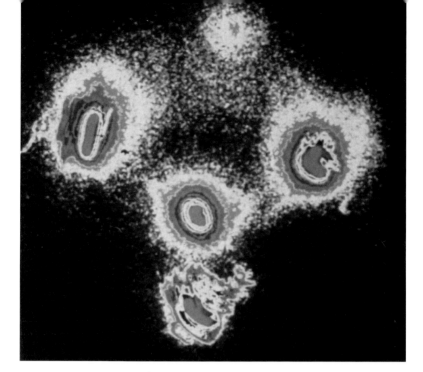

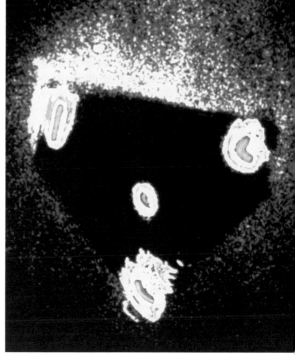

8 and 9 *The only close-up – estimated range 100–150 m – of the Belgian phenomenon 30–31 March 1990. Taken on Kodak 200 ASA film, using a Praktika BX20 with Cokin 1A skylight filter on zoom setting 100–150 mm, the exposure (above) was 2 seconds at f4. There is no evidence of camera shake; any distortion appears to be due to the object's movement. Evidence of its triangular shape is revealed by blue enhancement (right) of the same photograph.*
(Reproduced with permission; © E. Mossay –SOFAM- SOBEPS.)

4. Moreover in your letter to Dr Clark, U.K. Shadow Secretary of State of Defence, you stated that the Belgian Minister of Defence "confirmed" that the UFO-sighting (30th March 90) has been classified as HOSTILE and that the "UFO" was on a heading towards U.K..

This is completely "wrong" because the "UFO" was not only flying on an EASTERLY heading, but aswell at any moment it neighter fullfilled the NATO identification-criteria to be treated as a HOSTILE. And even if it would have been, all surrounding radarstations (including NEATESHEAD, U.K.) would automatically have been alerted of this fact.

W. DE BROUWER
Maj-Gen
Deputy Chief of Airstaff
Plans, Operations and Personnel

10 (top) F-16 interceptors, the same type of Mach 2 aircraft type used by the Belgian Air Force in the incident of 30–31 March 1990.
(Courtesy Air Pictorial.)

11 (Extract) letter to the author from Major-General W. De Brouwer, Deputy Chief of Airstaff Plans, Operations and Personnel, Belgian Air Force.

Dear Mr Sheffield,

Thank you for your letter, and the copy of your dossier for the European Parliament. I have now had time to read the report, but not to study it carefully. I shall send it back to you this week by Recorded Delivery. You are not the first of my UFO correspondents to believe that his mail is tampered with, but I find it very difficult to credit.

Let me say at once that I find the account of the two Belgian sightings entirely convincing. What is unusual is that the Belgian MOD, police, Air Force and Politicians have been so forthcoming. This will be useful to your cause. There was a piece in the Financial Times on 2.12.93, by the way, stating that the EU was to set up an observatory for the study of UFOs. They may, perhaps, have got wind of your initiative.

I must make my position clear. If NADGE had this object via the Belgian and German radar stations I consider it inconceivable that UK NADGE would not have been aware of it. I also consider it inconceivable that the Operations Division of SHAPE at Mons was not aware of it. I disregard your letter from Pope, because he is a very junior civil servant, programmed to write that sort of letter. No admission will be made by the MOD until they are absolutely forced to it by one means or another. I may feel inclined to table a Written Question, or write directly to Mr Rifkind, rather depending on how you get on. You are right in saying that the question in the forth paragraph of your letter is the one that matters.

I do not feel inclined to nit-pick my way through various bits of your report, but I am rather uneasy (simply for verisimilitude) at the claims on p. 30 that the F.16 pilots saw the shape of the object, and its change of shape, on their aircraft radar scopes. I was not aware that this could be seen.

As you want the report back, would you kindly let me have a copy of Section 6 and Section 8 for my file, in due course?

I hope you will let me know later how you got on with Brussels.

Yours sincerely,

[signature]

You will know that our sole reason for examining reports of UFO sightings is to establish whether or not there is evidence of any threat to the United Kingdom. The Belgium authorities have indicated that they did not notify us of these sightings at the time because there was no evidence of any threat, and because they occurred over the central part of Belgium. I should add that notification of NADGE radar detections is at the discretion of the operators, and does not occur automatically.

12 *Letter to the author from UK Admiral of the Fleet, The Lord Hill-Norton GCB; sent in 1994 (top).*

13 *(Extract) letter to Admiral of the Fleet, The Lord Hill-Norton GCB sent in 1994 by Malcolm Rifkind, then UK Secretary of State for Defence (bottom).*

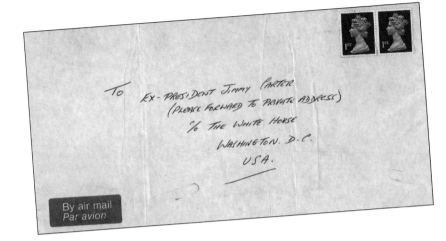

To EX-PRESIDENT JIMMY CARTER
(PLEASE FORWARD TO PRIVATE ADDRESS)
% THE WHITE HOUSE
WASHINGTON. D.C.
USA.

By air mail
Par avion

Thank you for your letter of 1 October.

I have examined the envelope you sent in which you sent to Jimmy Carter, but regret that I have been unable to determine why it was returned to you. It appears that you are quite correct in your assumption that the letter did not leave the country, because otherwise there would be some kind of markings on the envelope. The letter would have been opened by our Return Letter Section in order for them to find the return address. However, obviously it should never have been sent to them in the first place. I am sorry for the error, but unfortunately I do not know who was responsible for it.

I have been in contact with the office of Colonel Bouzette at the Belgium Embassy in London. The telephone number of the office I contacted is 071-235-4012. I spoke to a gentleman there, but I regret I was very remiss and did not take a note of his name. However, the gentleman found a copy of the letter to you in a file, but was not prepared to send a copy of this letter to you on my authority. He did say that he would be prepared to consider sending a copy if he was contacted directly by yourself.

I hope this information is of use to you, and if I can be of any further help please do not hesitate to contact me.

14 *(top) The 'Carter envelope' returned to the author by the Royal Mail without explanation.*

15 and 16 *(Extracts) letters to the author from the Royal Mail in respect of the 'Carter envelope' (above) and proof of the non-delivery of the letter from the Belgian Government (below).*

it would seem that we were probably on the same wavelength.

I explained my research into the Belgian phenomenon and my degree of involvement with the Belgian Defence Ministry and armed forces. I explained my document requesting that an inquiry be established by the European Parliament into these phenomena.

I received a letter on 30 October 1993 from John Holman. In it he stated that his sentiments are as mine and he wished me success in bringing about European Parliamentary debate on the Belgian phenomenon. He requested that he be kept updated on any response to my efforts and offered me any assistance should I ever need it.

John Holman's strategy is to exploit *any* situation that would bring this subject to the attention of the public. While I think this is admirable – he mentions American public demonstrations at Post Offices – and says that while this represents the sharp end of any campaign and is not everyone's particular choice of method, it did produce results. My own opinion is that to bring the truth of this phenomenon into the open, such is the degree of censorship, it must be exposed at the topmost level. Only then will governments and the media take notice. That is why my approach is on three levels: an approach to the European Parliament; to obtain a serious question in the House of Commons; to take the matter to the United Nations.

The European Parliament approach was on the move. It was time to start on a question in the House of Commons and a reminder to the United Nations.

There is a strange establishment in an isolated area of the Yorkshire Dales. It is at a remote and lonely place called Menwith Hill. It occupies 560 acres of moorland and has an impenetrable barbed perimeter fence that marks its boundary; it stretches for 5½ miles.

The buildings that occupy this vast site are many and strange indeed; they are many-faceted spheres of immense size that enclose electronic listening devices. The employees at this establishment are expressly forbidden to form friendships or have any association with British nationals who live in the surrounding area.

This establishment is classified as absolutely top secret. So top secret that any enquiries made by British Members of Parliament are unanswered and totally classified.

It is here that covert electronic surveillance is carried out in all spheres of Western Europe. This means that *every* form of electronic communication – mobile, private, business and continental telephone calls, computer and satellite communication, radio and television communication – is subject to intense covert surveillance.

This establishment is run by the National Security Agency of America. It employs only Americans. It is a CIA operation and is directly involved with the Ministry of Defence establishment at GCHQ at Cheltenham.

That is the degree of involvement of the Central Intelligence Agency with the Ministry of Defence. This degree of co-operation with the Ministry of Defence by the American Central Intelligence Agency, and the consequent obstructive attitude of the Ministry of Defence, would indicate a joint operation involving both intelligence agencies.

In short, it would appear that the American Central Intelligence Agency is controlling surveillance operations in Western Europe via the National Security Agency of America at Menwith Hill and GCHQ at Cheltenham. They are consequently also covertly controlling – through the North Atlantic Treaty Organization – all defence and security systems within this same area. It would appear on the evidence, therefore, that it is NATO who are controlling the release of all information on this phenomenon, and NATO who know the form of this entity.

These are the precise sentiments expressed by Linda Moulton-Howe and Bob Oechsler.

With the power of its total electronic surveillance, its increasingly obvious media censorship and control, one ponders as to the form and purpose of this entity and the degree of its penetration of our society.

Bearing in mind the enormity of this situation, how does one even approach the task of factually exposing this phenomenon? How can an entity of this intelligence – which is even now demonstrating its intellectual contempt by openly displaying itself in our skies with no fear of exposure – ever be outwitted and exposed? An insurmountable task, like playing chess with a thought reader. The course to pursue would seem impossible, but is it?

CHAPTER FOURTEEN

Strange Contacts

On 28 January 1994, I received a telephone call from a Mr Neil Fleming. This is the person who telephoned me to arrange a meeting with Linda Moulton-Howe. I originally met Mr Fleming and a colleague, together with Linda Moulton-Howe, at 3 pm on Friday, 6 August 1993, at the Black Prince roadhouse near the M2 at Bexley in Kent. When asked to explain the reason for Miss Moulton-Howe's visit to this country, Mr Fleming and Miss Moulton-Howe said that, apart from negotiating terms for her publications with an agency that he was proposing to set up, the prime reason for her visit *was to investigate a wave of UFO sightings that had occurred in the Bristol Channel, and at an area of the north Kent coast.*

They were interested in the action that I was taking on the Belgian sightings, and in my request to the European Parliament for an inquiry to be set up to investigate these incidents.

The purpose of Mr Fleming's telephone call was supposedly to enquire on how the situation was developing. He suggested that we arrange a meeting to discuss this further.

I explained that with a book launch in progress it would be difficult at the present time. He said that perhaps we could discuss this in the near future.

I said that I had found one particular fact concerning our previous meeting difficult to comprehend, namely, that the wave of sightings on the north Kent coast did not occur until two months *after* our meeting at the Black Prince. Mr Fleming did not answer and rang off. I have not heard from him since.

I must now evaluate a situation that is causing me some concern.

Original contact was made by Neil Fleming, who arranged

a meeting with Linda Moulton-Howe. Is there an association of sorts – because of the context of my discussion with Linda Moulton-Howe, and the identical radio broadcast by Bob Oechsler – between Linda Moulton-Howe and Bob Oechsler?

Because I was referred to Maria Ward, as someone who could give me details on the north Kent sightings, by Neil Fleming, is there an association of sorts between Neil Fleming and Maria Ward?

Is there an association of sorts between Linda Moulton-Howe, John Schuessler (space scientist, Houston, Texas), and Stanton Friedman (nuclear physicist), in the Parapsychology Society of the United Nations?

Because Maria Ward has apparently been invited to speak at the Parapsychology Society of the United Nations, is there an association of sorts between Maria Ward and Linda Moulton-Howe in the United Nations?

Maria Ward has recently had centre-page publicity in the *People* newspaper of 20 February 1994 concerning an alleged rape charge involving aliens.

Linda Moulton-Howe has written a book strongly suggesting that aliens cause cattle mutilations.

Bob Oechsler also quotes cattle mutilations and recounts the stories of supposedly dead aliens at Roswell.

Bearing in mind the 20-year lack of activity on this subject by the United Nations, could this not all be part of a disinformation exercise intended to create ridicule? Is Neil Fleming the common denominator? He has twice telephoned me to enquire on the progress of my application to the European Parliament. Whatever is going on?

CHAPTER FIFTEEN

Missing Mail

I now felt that things were beginning to move. The office of Sir Leon Brittan now had a detailed letter from me – sent on 11 September 1993 – giving all the information that they had asked for; it will be interesting to see what their reply will be.

I have also received a reply from Eric Vanderheiden, written on behalf of the Belgian Prime Minister. Eric Vanderheiden is Counsellor for Foreign Affairs. It acknowledged my reminder of 17 August but said that the Belgian Prime Minister had *not* received my report that had been sent to him on 29 July. It said, however (as I hoped it would), that regarding my European Parliamentary question, he would suggest that I send a copy of this report to:

Mr Egon Klepsch, President of the European Parliament
Belliardstrasse 97–117,
1047 Brussels, Belgium.

I sent this by registered mail the next day: Friday, 10 September 1993.

Four weeks later, having received no acknowledgement of this document I sent a reminder to Egon Klepsch, again by registered mail.

The situation is that either the following documents have not been delivered by the Post Office or, for some unknown reason, have not been passed to their respective addresses within the Belgian establishment or the European Parliament:

Document Ref: RR 0070 6316 9GB
The Council of Ministers,
120 rue de la Loi, 1047 Brussels, Belgium.

Document Ref: RR 0005 8108 4GB.
To Jean-Luc Dehaene, Belgian Prime Minister,
Belliardstraat 113,
1047 Brussels, Belgium.

Document Ref: RR 0005 8110 7GTB.
To Egon Klepsch,
President of the European Parliament,
Belliardstraat 97–117,
1047 Brussels, Belgium.

My only comment is that these missing documents, when added to the unexplained return of a letter sent to President Carter which did not leave this country, the official letter sent to me by the Belgian government of September 1993 which I did not receive (and which the Belgian government now refuse to send me) and at least 34 other letters which have disappeared without trace, indicate that something very strange is happening to my mail.

On 27 September 1993, I sent three letters which were translated into French (this being the language spoken in the Brabant region of Belgium) to each of the following persons. They concern the events of the night of 30–31 March 1990.

Monsieur A. Renkin, Gendarmerie MDL,
Ramillies,
Brabant,
Belgique.

Monsieur Renkin was the police officer who telephoned the Glons radar CRC (Control Reporting Centre) at 23.00 hours. He reported that he could see, from his home at Ramillies, three unusual lights, much brighter than stars, that were stationary in the sky. They were continuously changing colour from red to green and yellow.

Captain Pinson, Gendarmerie Jodoigne,
Jodoigne (Geldenaken),
Brabant,
Belgique.

Captain Pinson was the police officer of a gendarmerie patrol (probably from Wavre) who confirmed the sighting by officer Renkin. Captain Pinson gave a graphic description of this phenomenon and its movements, and of three more lights that formed a triangle and joined the first. Glons radar CRC confirmed the phenomenon on its radar.

> A. Perrad, Colonel, Forces Armées Etat-Major Général
> Etat-Major de la Force Aérienne, ACIS Air Staff
>   Division-Operations,
> Quartier Reine Elizabeth,
> rue d'Evere,
> 1140 Bruxelles,
> Belgique

Colonel Perrad was the Belgian Air Force commander who confirmed to me the existence of these flying objects. He supplied me with performance data taken from both the Belgian Air Force pilots involved in their pursuit, and confirmed by figures taken by the video cameras of the aircraft on-board radar screens.

The letter sent to these three correspondents was as follows:

In view of the fact that the opinion expressed by the Belgian Government of the sightings in November 1989 and March 1990 was: *That ALL possible hypotheses could be excluded. The Minister could not tell what these flying objects were.*

In your own opinion – because these objects were not known to the Belgian authorities – could they possibly have been of extra-terrestrial origin?

Your early reply would be appreciated.

                    Yours sincerely
                    Derek Sheffield

A REPLY FROM COLONEL PERRAD

Dear Mr Sheffield
   I acknowledge receipt of your letter dated 27th September 1993.

With reference to the observed phenomena of November 1989 and March 1990.

I feel that at the present time there are neither satisfactory explanations nor understandable data. Given these reasons, *one can only come to their own conclusions*. . . .

I hope that at some time in the future, more light will be thrown on this subject. At the present time I have no comment, only great doubts. Until there are any new developments, this matter will have to remain as dormant status in my pending file.

Yours sincerely

A. PERRAD, Colonel BAF

Chief of Section: Operations

The following is a letter of appreciation to Colonel Perrad, together with a request for radar details, and advising him of my forthcoming book.

13th October 1993

Dear Colonel Perrad

Just a letter of appreciation for your most helpful correspondence in the past.

Your letter of the 1st October was particularly enlightening. It left a lot unsaid, as you say 'one can only come to their own conclusions. . . .'

I am endeavouring to raise the question of the Belgian sightings with the European Parliament by requesting an Inquiry at committee level.

My only reason for this is to establish the true story of the phenomena above Brussels in 1989/90.

I have obtained a multitude of conclusive information from the Belgian Air Force, including on-board radar film taken of the radar screens of the pursuing F-16 aircraft, and typescript of the conversations between the two pilots and the Belgian radar stations involved.

As – at some time in the future – the credibility of the Belgian Air Force could be discussed, could I count on your support should this matter ever reach committee level?

I also have one last question. As this was a top alert, and the detections were made by Glons CRC (part of NATO Air Defence Ground Environment), would this information have been passed to UK radar?

A simple yes or no would suffice.

For your interest, we have had a series of sightings at Canterbury - very similar to the events at Eupen - within the last two weeks. Reports would indicate it to be an identical object.

I will send you a copy of my book when it is published. *I am sure that you will find it interesting reading.*

Yours sincerely
Derek Sheffield

A REMINDER TO COLONEL PERRAD

27th December 1993

Dear Colonel Perrad

A short note of reminder; could you please answer my request of the 13th October for your support should my application to the European Parliament reach Committee level?

And would the Glons CRC (NADGE) detections have been passed to UK radar? A simple yes or no would suffice.

Yours sincerely
Derek Sheffield

To date there has been no reply from Colonel Perrad.

On the advice of a copyright expert, I abstracted a two-page section from a Time-Life publication which I purchased from Amsterdam, and included this – stating quite clearly that it was a section from that publication – in my report to the European Parliament.

This purports to show an actual photograph of the lighting configuration of this phenomenon, and – when the photograph is enhanced under blue light – a distinctly triangular outline. It also shows, quite clearly, an extremely odd pattern at the centres of each of the four lights.

Also shown are video photographs of the on-board radar screens of the pursuing interceptor aircraft.

Although the picture credits in this publication state that they were supplied by courtesy of the Belgian Air Force and SOBEPS, all requests to these sources for permissions to reproduce the F-16 on-board radar screens have failed to bring forth any response.

Colonel Perrad stated that actual on-board radar photographs from the pursuing fighters were not for release, yet these were already being displayed in the Time-Life publication.

SOBEPS referred me to Patrick Ferryn (obviously an agent for the actual owner of the photograph). Despite five letters, two reminders and five telephone calls to the Brussels home of Patrick Ferryn, no reply has been forthcoming.

From the moment I informed Tim Vankerom of SOBEPS (and Mr Patrick Ferryn) of the purpose of my report, there has been either a complete clampdown on the subject, or a total censorship of any mail deliveries.

It stated in the Time-Life article that the photographs shown had been ratified by the Belgian Royal Military Academy. According to the Time-Life publication, this is the top photographic analytical establishment in Belgium. The Academy apparently fully endorsed the authenticity of these photographs.

Because I felt some foreboding concerning the silence of SOBEPS and Patrick Ferryn, I contacted the Belgian Embassy in London and obtained the address of the Military Academy in Brussels. It is:

The Belgian Royal Military Academy,
avenue de la Renaissance 30,
B-1040 Brussels,
Belgium.

To date I have sent three letters to this address asking them to confirm the authenticity of this photograph. I have also sent a reminder stressing the urgency of a reply. I have emphasized that I am in correspondence with the Belgian Prime Minister concerning this photograph, which forms part of my report.

After a delay of four months, a reply was finally received from SOBEPS.

THE LONG-AWAITED REPLY FROM SOBEPS

20 November 1994

Dear Sir,

Re: Your letters dated 10.8.93, 8.10.93 and 24.10.93
to Professor Marc Acheroy of the Brussels Royal Military
College.

Professor Marc Acheroy of the Brussels Royal Military
College has passed to us your three letters on the
results of the study of the Petit Rechain photo. He has
asked us to reply on his behalf, and this is also our
own reply.

We are currently in the final stage of publishing a
second book relating to the study and the
characteristics of the Belgian wave, and we are sure
that you will understand that we aim to be the first to
publish the results of the study carried out at our
request at the Royal Military College.

In addition, the Petit Rechain photo is copyright, and
you are not allowed to publish it without paying
royalties.

Professor Marc Acheroy shares our point of view. The
results of the study will therefore be first published in
our book, which is due to be published in the first half
of 1994.

If after this publication you wish to publish the
study yourself, you would be obliged to seek
authorisation from us.

In the meantime, we remain

Yours faithfully.
Lucien CLEREBAUT
General Secretary
SOBEPS

MY SUBSEQUENT CORRESPONDENCE TO SOBEPS

24 July 1994

Dear Lucien CLEREBAUT,

I have just completed a manuscript on the Belgian
phenomena of 1989/90. This deals with the implications
of the radar detections involved.

Your letter of 20th November 1993 advises me that your
book on the study of the results of the Petit Rechain

photograph will be published in the first half of 1994 and that you will be prepared – after the release of your own publication – for me to use this photograph to illustrate my own book.

Professor M. ACHEROY informs me that SOBEPS is responsible for the use and distribution of this · photograph on which I understand that a royalty would be payable.

I would request this authorization and information of the royalty charges.

Yours sincerely
Derek Sheffield

It does seem odd that five letters to the United States of America, a letter to President Carter, three copies of my report (to the Belgian Prime Minister, the President of the Council of Ministers, the President of the European Parliament), three reminders (to the Belgian Prime Minister, President of the Council of Ministers, President of the European Parliament), letters to three European Members of Parliament, three letters to the Société Belge d'Etude des Phénomènes Spatiaux, two letters to Patrick Ferryn, four letters to the Belgian Royal Military Academy, and fourteen press releases to all press agencies in the United Kingdom and Western Europe should all – apart from that to the Belgian Prime Minister – have disappeared without trace.

It would seem to make no difference if I send my mail by registered post.

One wonders at the enormity of what is really going on.

On 20 September 1993, the following letter was sent to Lynn Bachelor of the Customer Service Centre, Royal Mail, Tonbridge, Kent:

Dear Lynn Bachelor,

Thank you for your letter TON/10007946 of the 17th September 1993. I am an author. I am involved in research concerning an application for an inquiry to be instigated by the European Parliament.

The missing document that you mention is a 40-page report which is a case for presentation to the European Parliament. You are aware that this is the item that is missing.

I have sent an identical copy - by the same registered mail - to the President in Office, The Council of Ministers, 120 rue de la Loi, Brussels, Belgium. This has also failed to arrive.

I would advise that these reports have taken me over a year to research and compile. Could you advise me of any method - apart from personal delivery - by which I can be guaranteed actual delivery?

Apart from these two items, I recently had cause to write to ex-president Jimmy Carter (to be forwarded to personal address) c/o The White House, Washington D.C., United States of America. This letter was returned to my home address: unfranked, opened along the bottom of the envelope, with no comment whatsoever. It would appear that this letter never left the country. Could you please offer me some explanation.

I have now sent another report at the request of the Belgian Prime Minister - also registered by international mail - to Egon Klepsch, President of the European Parliament, Belliardstraat 97-117, 1047 Brussels, Belgium. This was posted on 8/9/1993. I trust that with luck this will arrive. For your interest, this saga will form part of a chapter in my current book.

                    Yours sincerely
                    Derek Sheffield

On Friday, 1 October 1993, I received the following letter from Miss Bachelor:

Dear Mr Sheffield
    Thank you for your letter of the 20th September.
    I am sorry that a further package to Belgium appears to have gone astray. I have now passed the details of both of these registered items to our International Customer Care Unit. They will make detailed enquiries into this matter and I will advise you again once I receive a reply from them. However, I must advise you that international enquiries can sometimes take up to four months.

    I was concerned to learn that the letter you sent to Jimmy Carter was returned to you unfranked and opened. I have made enquiries into this matter but regret that I have been unable to determine why the letter was returned or who actually returned it. If you still have the envelope and would like to send it to me I will make further enquiries.

I am sorry that I cannot send a more helpful reply, however, I will contact you again once I receive some further information.

Yours sincerely
Miss L. Bachelor
Customer Care

I trust my reader will note that it could take *four months* for an international enquiry to be made.

There is also no mention of an answer to my question as to what method of postal delivery would guarantee delivery to my correspondent.

A FURTHER LETTER FROM LYNN BACHELOR

9 November 1993

Dear Mr Sheffield

Thank you for your letter of 1 October.

I have examined the envelope which you sent to Jimmy Carter, but regret that I have been unable to determine why it was returned to you. It appears that you are quite correct in your assumption that the letter did not leave the country, because otherwise there would be some kind of markings on the envelope. The letter would have been opened by our Return Letter Section in order for them to find the return address. However, obviously it should never have been sent to them in the first place. I am sorry for the error, but unfortunately I do not know who was responsible for it.

The Registered service is really the safest way of sending mail to Belgium, but I am sorry that you have experienced problems with this service. The only other service I could suggest would be Datapost. This is a courier service however; anything up to 500 g would cost you £25.00. Datapost would guarantee delivery of an item to Belgium within two days.

I will chase up your enquiries for you, and as soon as I receive a reply from our International Office I will contact you again.

I have returned your envelope to you, and I enclose a booklet of stamps as a refund of your wasted postage on the letter.

Yours sincerely
Miss L. Bachelor
Customer Care

The whole point of writing to ex-president Jimmy Carter was to obtain verification, from a former President of the United States, of a personal incident involving a sighting of an unidentified phenomenon. My reason was that in the order of things, one cannot get a person of greater standing than a President of the United States of America.

While my letter to Jimmy Carter was intercepted and returned to me, I have been able to research this sighting by an alternative route.

At the time of this incident – 7.15 pm Eastern Standard Time in the evening of 18 October 1969 – Jimmy Carter (who had a background in the United States Navy and was a graduate in nuclear physics) was Governor of Georgia, and waiting with 10 other members of the Lions Club at Leary, Georgia, for a meeting due to begin at 7.30 pm.

It was shortly after dark on a moonless night, with many stars in evidence. A very bright object attracted the attention of all members present. It was situated some 30 degrees above the horizon and (while the distance was difficult to estimate), could have been anything between 300 yds and 1000 yds away. In the 10–12 minutes of observation, it appeared to come close and then moved away. It repeated this manoeuvre, and on moving away became smaller and disappeared. There were no aircraft in the vicinity. Its size varied; at its smallest it could be described as brighter than, but larger than, a planet. At its largest it was estimated to be fractionally smaller than the Moon.

Governor Carter, who at this time was campaigning for the Presidency of the United States, reported this incident and stated that it was his intention to pursue the matter.

NASA was reputed to have denied Governor Carter's request to review UFO data. Governor Carter has declined to make any further comment. He has not carried out his promise to pursue the matter and to disclose any information known to the public.

A LETTER TO THE CUSTOMER SERVICE CENTRE: GPO TONBRIDGE

30th August 1994

Dear Miss Bachelor

You may remember that several times, during the latter part of 1993, I had complained to you that my mail to various addresses in Belgium seemed to be going astray. It seemed that the chance of any of my letters actually reaching their destinations was remote; indeed, in order to get one very important document to the Belgian Government I had to resort to having five copies made. One of these – the most important one – actually reached its destination.

I now have a situation where it appears that the Belgian Government sent me an extremely important letter which I did not receive.

I have been sent a letter by Dr David Clark, MP, Shadow Secretary of State for Defence, with an enclosure from Colonel J. Bouzette, Defence Attaché at the Belgian Embassy in London.

This enclosure states that an official answer was sent to me by the Belgian Government in September 1993.

At no time did I receive this communication.

I enclose a photocopy of the letter from Colonel Bouzette.

I am involved in an inquiry with the European Parliament; this document is of prime importance. I would appreciate an inquiry by your department as to why I did not receive it.

Yours sincerely
Derek Sheffield

AN UNCONVINCING REPLY FROM ROYAL MAIL CUSTOMER CARE

8 September 1994

Dear Mr Sheffield

Thank you for your recent enquiry, from which I was most concerned to learn of a letter sent to you from the Belgian Embassy that has not been delivered.

I have made extensive enquiries into this matter but unfortunately, in view of the time that has elapsed since posting and the fact that it is not possible for us to maintain a record of individual items sent by the ordinary service, I have been unable to trace the missing item or find out the reason why it was not delivered.

A letter which for any reason cannot be delivered is whenever possible returned to the sender, but a record is not kept of the disposal of such items.

I would like to assure you that we do treat any report of missing mail very seriously, all enquiries possible have been made into this matter. I have also passed the details of this enquiry to our Investigations Department and they will contact you directly should they have any further information.

I hope that you will accept my sincere apologies for the concern and inconvenience you have been caused by this matter.

Yours sincerely
Mrs S. Sexton
Customer Care

THE CUSTOMER CARE SECTION OF THE ROYAL MAIL, HAVING MANY OF THEIR FACTS WRONG, WERE SENT THE FOLLOWING LETTER.

12th September 1994

Dear Mrs Sexton

Thank you for your letter of the 8th September.

I would correct you on a most important point: as the photocopy sent to you indicates, the missing letter was not sent to me by the Belgian Embassy in London, *It was sent to me by the Belgian Government from Brussels*.

This fact has come to light because Colonel Bouzette of the Belgian Embassy has referred to it in his correspondence to Dr David Clark, the Labour Shadow Minister of Defence.

As the responsibility for the delivery of this letter was entrusted to the GPO, I would suggest that your investigators contact Colonel Bouzette, Defence Attaché at the Belgian Embassy in London (who obviously has a copy of this letter), and either obtain a copy to forward to me, or obtain from him the address of the Belgian governmental office which were alleged to have sent this, and ask them for a copy which must be forwarded to me.

To date, it would now appear that almost 40 letters – to the Belgian Police/MOD/Air Force and other Belgian

agencies, the European Parliament, various American
agencies, NATO, the United Nations, and all press
agencies in the UK and Europe – all dealing with a
matter of international security, have now either been
unanswered or have disappeared without trace. As this is
now to be discussed under Petition 990/93 by the
European Parliament, it will be seen that it is a matter
of some importance. This letter from the Belgian
Government is yet another to add to the list.

Prompt action by your investigators would be
appreciated.

Yours sincerely
Derek Sheffield

A FURTHER LETTER TO MRS SEXTON

12th September 1994

Dear Mrs Sexton

I wrote to you four weeks ago concerning a letter from
the Belgian Government which for some obscure reason was
not delivered to me.

Would you please acknowledge that you received this
letter (dated 12th September), and please explain why I
have not yet received a reply.

It does not take four weeks to telephone Colonel
Bouzette at the Belgian Embassy to obtain a copy of the
missing letter (of which he apparently has a copy), or
to find out from him the Belgian government department
from which this letter originated.

I did stress in my letter that this matter was of
extreme urgency. I find this whole situation quite
unbelievable and would advise that unless some prompt
results are forthcoming, I will have no alternative but
to take the matter to a much higher authority.

I will expect your reply by return of post.

Yours sincerely
Derek Sheffield

MRS SEXTON'S REPLY

25th October 1994

Dear Mr Sheffield

Further to your recent enquiry about a letter sent to
you from the Belgian Government.

I have been in contact with the office of Colonel

137

Bouzette at the Belgian Embassy in London. The telephone
number of the office I contacted is 071-235-4012. I spoke
to a gentleman there, but I regret I was very remiss and
did not take a note of his name. However, the gentleman
found a copy of the letter to you in a file, but was not
prepared to send a copy of this letter to you on my
authority. He did say that he would be prepared to
consider sending a copy if he was contacted directly by
yourself.

I hope this information is of use to you, and if I can
be of any further help please do not hesitate to contact
me.

Yours sincerely
Mrs Sue Sexton
Customer Care

LETTER TO MICHAEL HERON, CHAIRMAN OF THE POST OFFICE

17th October 1994

Dear Mr Heron

I am concerned at a most peculiar anomaly concerning
the delivery of my mail. I have very strong evidence –
of which the Post Office is aware – of two letters in
particular that have been intercepted and not delivered.

It would seem that a letter written to President
Carter requesting information on an incident that
occurred prior to his election to the presidency was
unfranked, never left this country, was opened and
returned to me with no comment whatsoever. The Post
Office was not able to offer any explanation: they *did
not offer to re-accept this letter for future delivery*.
Luckily I was able (via another source) to obtain the
details required.

It has now come to my notice that a letter written
officially to me by the Belgian government in January
1993 has never been delivered. Colonel Bouzette,
Military Attaché at the Belgian Embassy, evidently has a
copy of this letter (a section of which he has quoted to
David Clark, Shadow Secretary of State for Defence).

I have been informed by Mrs S. Sexton of Customer
Service Centre at Tonbridge that this has been placed in
the hands of the Investigations Department for their
action. This was five weeks ago; it does not take five

weeks to telephone Colonel Bouzette to request a copy of this letter to be forwarded to me, or find out from him the Belgian government department that was the source of this letter and obtain a copy of it from them.

These anomalies apparently began at the time that I was researching a defence matter for the compilation of a report for submission to the European Parliament. It would seem that any correspondence on this subject was subject to disappearance, indeed even the Registered service did not seem able to guarantee delivery (anticipating problems I actually had five copies of my report compiled and posted – luckily the most important one got through!). The only guarantee that the Post Office could give on delivery was the courier service, and at £25 per item the cost was prohibitive. It would seem that 38 letters have gone astray.

As the European Parliament have now accepted my document as Petition 990/93, to be discussed by the Committee on Energy, Research and Technology, I would appreciate a serious inquiry and some guarantee on mail delivery in the future.

Yours sincerely
Derek Sheffield

RESPONSE TO MY LETTER TO MICHAEL HERON

24th November 1994

Dear Mr Sheffield

Thank you for your letter of 17 October which has been forwarded to me from the office of Mr Michael Heron, Chairman of the Post Office.

I was sorry to learn of your concern over the service you receive. I can, however, assure you that Mrs Sexton took all possible action to investigate the matters raised in your letter. Unfortunately, as she points out in her letter, the time elapsed between posting and your enquiry does mean that there is little positive action that can be taken and our avenues of enquiry are somewhat limited.

I hope you have now received Mrs Sexton's letter confirming that she has contacted the Belgian Embassy. Unfortunately, they were unable to send a duplicate letter on the request of a third party but I hope the telephone number provided was of use to you.

As you are aware, full details of this matter have been passed to our internal Investigation Department. This will be held on their files but they are currently unable to pursue an active inquiry.

I have noted your comments about the Registered Service but have to advise you that the service has now changed. For your future information you may wish to make a note of the services available.

Recorded Delivery – the items travel with the ordinary mail but a signature is obtained on delivery.

Inland –	1st or 2nd class postage plus 55p
Overseas –	Airmail Postage plus £2.50
Registered –	added security in the UK (and guaranteed delivery) and abroad with a signature on delivery. Compensation available for the intrinsic value of any contents.
Inland –	1st class postage plus £3 for £500 cover
Overseas –	Airmail Postage plus £3 for £500 cover (additional cover is available for extra fees)

Special delivery – guaranteed delivery and a signature on delivery

Inland only –	1st class mail plus £2.70
Swiftair –	express airmail
Overseas only –	Airmail postage plus £2.70

You will also be interested to know that items sent using the above services are bar-coded and their whereabouts can be checked by contacting a local call rate telephone number (0645 272100).

I hope this information is of use to you. Please do not hesitate to contact me again if I can be of any further help.

Yours sincerely
Sue Knight-Smith
Customer Care Manager

MY REPLY TO SUE KNIGHT-SMITH'S LETTER

2nd December 1994

Dear Sue Knight-Smith,

Thank you for your letter FCU/0015814 of 24th November 1994.

As you are probably aware, I have spoken with the office of Colonel Bouzette of the Belgian Embassy on the number given to me by the Customer Service Centre at Tonbridge. The Belgian Embassy have denied that the Post Office have ever been in contact with them. I would like your comments on this please.

I have been advised by the Military Attaché at the Belgian Embassy that an approach must be made to the Belgian Minister of Defence for a copy of this letter to be sent to me.

The address given is:

Mr L. Delcroix, Minister of Defence,
Lambermontstraat 8, 1000 Brussels,
Belgium.

As it is the responsibility of the Post Office (who have accepted this letter but not delivered it!) to carry out the business of mail delivery, I do not understand why your Investigations Department are not able to pursue this further; surely an approach by the Investigations Department to the above minister would be a matter of the utmost simplicity.

Your comments on both of these matters would be appreciated.

Yours sincerely
Derek Sheffield

MY LETTER TO COLONEL BOUZETTE AT THE BELGIAN EMBASSY

27th October 1994

Dear Sir,

I spoke with your office last week, concerning a letter which you apparently have, that was sent to me by the Belgian Government in January 1993, and which was not delivered.

I have taken this matter up with the Post Office who say that they have spoken with your office who have refused to send a copy of this letter on to me.

On taking this matter up with your office, I was informed that they had not been contacted by the Post Office. The Post Office have said that this is untrue.

I have today received a letter from the Post Office; I attach a copy for your observations.

As per the contents of this letter: I understand that

you would be prepared to send a copy of this letter if contacted directly by me; please consider this as a direct request to you for a copy of that letter.

I await your reply with interest,

Yours sincerely

Derek Sheffield

THE RESPONSE FROM THE BELGIAN EMBASSY

3 November 1994

Dear Mister Sheffield,

In reply to your letter dated 27 October 1994 concerning a letter supposedly sent by the Minister of Defence – Belgium I can give you the following information.

To obtain a copy of his letter I suggest you write to the Minister himself at the following address:

Mr L. DELCROIX;
Minister of Defence
Lambermontstraat 8
1000 BRUSSELS
BELGIUM

Yours sincerely

J. BOUZETTE

Colonel, Defence Attaché

LETTER TO LEO DELCROIX, BELGIAN MINISTER OF DEFENCE

12th November 1994

Dear Minister,

Please find copies of attached letters from myself to the Belgian Prime Minister, and from Colonel Bouzette, Defence Attaché at the Belgian Embassy in London. These are self explanatory.

I would ask for a copy of the letter sent to me in January 1993, together with affirmation of your co-operation if required, in an inquiry (listed as Petition No. 990/93 of the Committee on Energy, Research and Technology) into the – declared hostile – unconfirmed radar detections by NADGE radars above Belgium in 1989/90.

Yours faithfully

Derek Sheffield

The Minister has not replied to this letter.

CHAPTER SIXTEEN

A Crack in the Armour

Because of the free flow of information from the Belgian Air Force and the confirmatory evidence from the Belgian Minister of Defence, it would seem that the penetration of our society, in the form of surveillance and censorship by this phenomenon, is not, as yet, complete.

Undoubtedly, within a short period, this will be total, but at present there are still cracks to be found and it is these that must be exploited before the door is slammed shut.

To penetrate this censorship has been to probe all avenues. Where I have been blocked, I have pursued alternative courses.

To date I seem to be making some progress. Having been blocked by the normal channels in my appeal to the European Parliament, I tried a direct appeal to the President of the European Parliament; was this somehow lost in the post? A reminder failed to bring any response. An appeal to the Belgian Prime Minister, however, resulted in a suggestion that I send a fresh copy of my report to Egon Klepsch, President of the European Parliament. This caused an immediate reply to the effect that my second report had been received, but there was no avenue by which this could be pursued. I replied that there were 12 committees to cover all aspects of the Parliament and that I would have thought that the committee covering petitions would have been applicable.

On 27 October 1993, I received a letter from Mr Robert Ramsay of the office of the Director-General, Directorate General for Research, of the European Parliament in Luxembourg. It says:

'Thank you for your letter of the 12th October. As you have requested, I am passing your letter and earlier document to the Petitions Committee.'

It seemed that the first hurdle was over. It was now up to the committee to consider my report.

On 20 October 1993, I sent the following letter to Robert Ramsay of the Office of President Egon Klepsch of the European Parliament with copies to the Belgian Prime Minister, the Belgian Minister of Defence, the Belgian Ministry of Defence, the Belgian Air Force and the Belgian Gendarmerie.

29th October 1993

Dear Mr Ramsay

Thank you for your letter of the 25th instant advising me that you are forwarding my earlier document to the Petitions Committee of the European Parliament for their consideration.

I would ask that you advise the committee of the inconclusive statement of the Belgian Minister of Defence: *From a military point of view, all relevant hypotheses could be excluded. The Minister could not tell what these flying objects were.*

This statement, when taken with the appearance of an identical phenomenon to those of Belgium in 1989/90 – and witnessed by many – above Canterbury in Kent on the 20th September 1993, provides a strong case for an inquiry to ascertain the nature of this phenomenon, and its relevance to the security of the European member states.

I would state that as the credibility of the Belgian Minister and Ministry of Defence, the Belgian Air Force, and the Belgian gendarmerie is involved, I would expect their full cooperation in this petition.

I am giving them details of this letter and am requesting their confirmation should the Petitions Committee wish to pursue this matter further.

Thank you for your kind assistance.

Yours sincerely,
Derek Sheffield

CONFIRMATION OF ADMISSION OF THE PETITION

11 April 1994

Subject: Petition 990/93

Dear Mr Sheffield,

I would like to inform you that the Committee on Petitions considered your petition at its meeting of 24 and 25 February 1994 and, having decided that the issues which you raise therein fall within the sphere of activities of the European Communities, declared it admissible, pursuant to Rule 156 of the Rules of Procedure of the European Parliament.

The committee considered it appropriate that your observations be brought to the attention of the committee with responsibilities in this area, and decided therefore to forward your petition to the Committee on Energy, Research and Technology of the European Parliament, for further action.

I would like to thank you for the interest you have shown in the work of the European Parliament, and to inform you, on behalf of the Committee on Petitions, that its consideration of your petition has thus been concluded.

Yours sincerely,
Ana Miranda de Lage
Vice-Chairman of the
Committee on Petitions

MY REPLY TO ANA MIRANDA DE LAGE

14 April 1994

Dear Ana Miranda de Lage,

Thank you for your letter informing me that the Committee on Petitions have considered my petition, and decided that the issues that I raise fall within the sphere of activities of the European Communities. The Committee has consequently declared it admissible, subject to Rule 156 of the Rules of Procedure of the European Parliament.

I understand that the Committee considered it appropriate that my observations be brought to the attention of the Committee with responsibilities in this area, and have forwarded my petition to the Committee on Energy, Research and Technology of the European Parliament, for further action.

It is to this end that I would make a request. I have spent countless months of research on this matter. It is imperative that it is completely understood, and that the Committee are aware of other ramifications. Would it be possible for me to be involved - purely in a consultative capacity - in any discussions on my report?

Thank you for the courtesy of your comments and your prompt reply.

Yours sincerely
Derek Sheffield

The European Parliament's reply

9 June 1994

Subject: Petition 990/93
Dear Sir,

Thank you for your letter of 14 April 1994.

I would like to inform you that your letter has been forwarded to the Committee on Energy, Research and Technology, to which your petition was forwarded for further action.

Yours sincerely
Rosy Bindi
Chairman, Committee on Petitions

A letter to Rosy Bindi

26 September 1994

Dear Rosy Bindi,

You may remember that I wrote to the Committee on Energy, Research and Technology on 14th April 1994, asking - because of various ramifications - if I could be present, either in an advisory capacity or purely as an interested spectator, when this matter is discussed by the Committee.

I know that since I have been engaged on this project, my mail has been subject to interception. Many letters have not reached their destinations (a letter to President Carter was unfranked, never left this country, was opened along the bottom of the envelope, and returned with no explanation whatever, and an official letter on this subject from the Belgian Government sent in January 1993 has never been received by me). The Post Office does not appear to want to investigate these discrepancies, and does not offer to accept these letters for further delivery.

In view of this fact, and the three months' delay in an answer from the Committee, I would request that in any future correspondence, an acknowledgement of receipt should be asked for. At least this should eliminate the enigma of my disappearing mail and guarantee a postal delivery of some kind.

Yours sincerely,
Derek Sheffield

A REPLY FROM MR E. NEWMAN

15 December 1994

Subject: Petition 990/93
Dear Mr Sheffield,

Thank you for your letter of 26 September 1994.

As in the case of your previous correspondence, the above-mentioned letter has been forwarded to the Committee on Energy, Research and Technology, to which your petition was forwarded for further action.

Yours sincerely,
E. Newman
Chairman, Committee on Petitions

A LETTER ACCOMPANYING AN APPENDIX TO MY PETITION

26 January 1995

Reference: Appendix to Petition 990/93
Dear Mr Newman,

Thank you for your letter 037648 of the 15th December 1994.

Please find enclosed an appendix to be added to Petition no. 990/93. I trust that you will forward this to the Committee on Energy, Research and Technology, for their due consideration.

Would you please confirm receipt of this document.

Yours sincerely,
Derek Sheffield

AN APPENDIX TO THE REPORT ON
UNIDENTIFIED AERIAL PHENOMENA FOR
RATIFICATION BY THE EUROPEAN PARLIAMENT

PETITION NO. 990/93

THE COMMITTEE ON ENERGY, RESEARCH
AND TECHNOLOGY

(A1)

An Appendix
to the Report on Unidentified Aerial Phenomena
for Ratification by the European Parliament
PETITION NO. 990/93
The Committee on Energy, Research and Technology

My particular interest in the incidents above Belgium in 1989/90 has been in the unidentified radar detections involved, and the implications that these may have.

There is no doubt that detections were made by radar stations in Belgium; at Bertem (near Leuven), Semmerzeke, Glons, St Hubert, and at Vedem in Germany. These are radar stations that are part of the NATO Air Defence Ground Environment radar complex that covers the whole of Europe: the United Kingdom is part of this complex.

There is no doubt as to the credibility of radar detection; radar will only detect the reflection of its own wavelength from an object of opacity and substance.

There are certain circumstances when ghost reflections are observed; these are easily recognised by skilled operators.

The detections made by Belgian radar were confirmed as positive detections by highly-skilled operators of the Belgian Air Force.

In the first incident at Eupen in December 1989, apart from a general correlation between witnesses and radar detections, there did not appear to be an accurate co-ordination between the two.

The second incident, which terminated at Tubize, was different. There was a complete correlation between witnesses, police, and radar. Aircraft were vectored by radar stations. Aircraft on-board radar confirmed the same detections. Video recordings were made of these by on-board video cameras.

When radar lock-on was attempted, extreme intelligence was shown by violent evasive action taken by these objects.

(A2)

In a Press Release to the media on 11 July, 1990, General-Major De Brouwer of the Belgian Air Force, stated that strict parameters were met governing the rules of interception. Because these detections were not identified they were declared hostile. Only when an unidentified radar detection is declared hostile, can interceptions be ordered by the Belgian Air Force. Consequently, interceptions were made by the Belgian Air Force.

In a letter dated 22nd December, 1994, General-Major De Brouwer stated that all surrounding radar stations (including Neatshead, UK) would *automatically* have been alerted to this fact.

In a reply dated 11th June, 1994, from the Secretary of State for Defence, Malcolm Rifkind, to Admiral of the Fleet, the Lord Hill-Norton, GCB (a former Chief of Defence Staff and Chairman of the NATO Military Committee) the Secretary of State for Defence states: I should add that notification of NADGE radar detections is at the discretion of the operators and *does not occur automatically.*

The Secretary of State for Defence stated in the same letter (11th June, 1994) that the Ministry of Defence were *not informed* at the time of these detections, because the Belgians did not consider these (classified hostile) detections a threat.

The British Ministry of Defence have stated (although apparently having *not* been informed?) that their Air Defence experts did not consider these unidentified detections a threat.

Bearing in mind these substantiated facts, does it not seem odd that these radar detections, which would automatically have been passed by NATO radar to Neatshead UK, and which are disclaimed by the British Minister and Ministry of Defence, are now denied by the Belgian Air Force?

In my research on this subject, a distinct pattern – which you will confirm should you decide to take the matter further – has become apparent.

All approaches for information to the United States are diverted to the Central Intelligence Agency. These, in turn, are referred to selected private groups.

(A3)

All approaches for information in the United Kingdom, are diverted to the Ministry of Defence. These, in turn, are referred to selected private groups.

While initially, information from the Belgian Air Force was given in great detail, it would now appear that enquiries are diverted to the Belgian Ministry of Defence. These are now referred to a private group.

This private group has not taken up the obvious radar anomaly.

Repeated requests have been made over the last 18 months; to the Belgian Minister and Ministry of Defence, the Belgian Police, and the Belgian Air Force, for their assistance in this matter.

I have asked for their co-operation in my Petition to the European Parliament.

To date, there has been no reply to this request for assistance.

This Appendix is to notify you of this fact.

(A4)

A REMINDER TO MR E. NEWMAN

21 February, 1995
Reference: Appendix to Petition 990/93

Dear Mr Newman,

I wrote to you on the 26th January, enclosing an appendix to be added to my petition 990/93. I asked for this to be forwarded to the Committee on Energy, Research and Technology, for their due consideration.

In view of the fact that odd things seem to be happening to my mail, I particularly asked for confirmation of receipt of this document.

To date, I have not received this confirmation.

Would you please reply at your earliest possible convenience.

Yours sincerely
Derek Sheffield

A REMINDER TO ANA MIRANDA DE LAGE

5 March 1995
Subject: Petition 990/93

Dear Ana Miranda de Lage,

I wrote to Mr Newman, Chairman, Committee on Petitions, Secretariat General, L-2929, Luxembourg, on the 26th January 1995, enclosing an appendix to be added to my Petition 990/93. I requested that this be forwarded to the Committee on Energy, Research and Technology, for their due consideration.

You are aware of the problem that seems to exist with my mail and my request that confirmations be made of receipt of correspondence from me. (I have another instance of a letter from the Belgian government that has never arrived, and which they now refuse to send to me.)

I particularly asked Mr Newman to acknowledge receipt of this document which was sent by International Mail Ref.: RR 0071 3056 6GB. This requires a signature of receipt.

I have written to Mr Newman again on 21st February 1995, asking once again for acknowledgement of receipt of this document.

To date, I have received no reply to either of these letters.

Could you please drop me a short note acknowledging receipt of my appendix of the 30th January. If you have not received this document, I will take the matter up with the International Mail section of the General Post Office.

Thank you for your assistance.

Yours sincerely,

Derek Sheffield

A FURTHER REMINDER TO MR E. NEWMAN

26 April 1994

Reference: Appendix to Petition 990/93
Reminders of the 21st February 1995
and 5th March 1995 to Ana Miranda de Lage

Dear Mr Newman,

I wrote to you on the 26th January enclosing an appendix to be added to Petition no. 990/93.

I specifically asked for confirmation of receipt of this document. I wrote on the 21st February, once again asking for your confirmation of receipt.

Having still not received your confirmation, I wrote on the 5th March to Ana Miranda de Lage asking if she could assist me in this matter.

To date I have not received replies to any of these letters.

Once again I enclose a copy of my appendix to be forwarded to the Committee on Petitions to be added to my Petition 990/93, and once again I would ask for your confirmation of receipt.

Yours sincerely

Derek Sheffield

A REPLY FROM THE ROYAL MAIL REGARDING THE MISSING APPENDIX

23 March 1995

Dear Mr Sheffield,

Thank you for your enquiry of 22nd March concerning the letter you sent to Mr Newman of the Committee on Petitions, Secretariat General, European Parliament, L-2929 Luxembourg.

Your enquiry has now been passed to our International Customer Care Section in London who will make enquiries on our behalf with the foreign authorities. I will write to you again as soon as I receive any information from them. However, I would like to mention that overseas enquiries can sometimes take up to four months to be finalised.

I am sorry that I cannot send a more helpful reply at this stage.

Yours sincerely
Sue Sexton
Customer Care Officer

THE FOLLOWING REPLY WAS SENT, WHICH QUESTIONS THEIR UNSATISFACTORY RESPONSE

10th April 1995

Dear Ms Sexton,

Thank you for your reply concerning my letter sent to Mr Newman, Chairman, Committee on Petitions, Secretariat General, European Parliament, L-2929 Luxembourg, on the 22nd March 1995.

I used this particular service because a signature of receipt is required on delivery. It must therefore follow, that if this letter was delivered, then an actual signature of receipt was obtained. It should not take four months for this signature to be passed to me.

Bearing in mind that there have now been many instances of my letters not being received by the European Parliament, I have specifically asked them to acknowledge receipt of any letters that I send them.

They have not acknowledged receipt of either the document in question, or two reminders sent to two different sources.

It would seem that, as there has been no signature of receipt from Mr Newman, and no acknowledgement of receipt from the Parliament, my letters have not actually been received.

I would like your comments on the above, and your assurance that my mail is not being intercepted and tampered with.

Yours sincerely
Derek Sheffield

AN ASSURANCE FROM THE ROYAL MAIL

2 May 1995

Dear Mr Sheffield,

I am replying to your recent correspondence regarding International Recorded item RR 0071 3056 6GB which you sent to the European Parliament, Luxembourg.

I can confirm that this item was dispatched from the UK on 31 January and after making enquiries through our International Department, with the Luxembourg Postal Authorities I can also confirm that this item was delivered to the European Parliament on 1 February. The letter would have been delivered to a general post room together with many other recorded and registered items and signed for by a member of staff.

I am afraid I cannot say why your petition has not been acknowledged by Mr Newman but I can assure you that your mail is not being tampered with. It would be impossible to target out your mail amongst the many millions of items travelling through the mail system each day.

I hope the above information is of use to you.

Yours sincerely
Mrs S. Sexton
Customer Care

THE FIFTH ATTEMPT FOR CONFIRMATION OF RECEIPT

10th May 1995

Reference: Appendix to Petition 990/93.
Reminders of 21st February 1995 to Mr Newman; on 5th March 1995 to Ana Miranda de Lage, and again on 26th April 1995 to Mr Newman.

Dear Sirs,

I wrote to you on the 26th January enclosing an appendix to be added to Petition no. 990/93.

I specifically asked for confirmation of receipt of this document. I wrote on 21st February, once again asking for confirmation of receipt.

Having still not received confirmation, I wrote on the 5th March to Ana Miranda de Lage asking for assistance in this matter.

I wrote again on the 26th April 1995. Confirmation of delivery to the general post room of the European

Parliament has been given to me by the Post Office. To date I have not received replies to any of these letters.

Once again I enclose a copy of my appendix to be added to my Petition 990/93, and for the fifth time I would ask for your confirmation of receipt.

Yours faithfully
Derek Sheffield

A LETTER TO THE RECIPIENT OF THE APPENDIX

22nd May 1995

Dear Mr Figus,

I have recently sent to the European Parliament two copies of an appendix to be added to my Petition no. 990/93, now with the Committee on Energy, Research and Technology.

I have particularly asked for acknowledgement of receipt of these documents.

The first was sent to Mr Newman, Chairman, the Committee on Energy, Research and Technology. It was sent as an International Recorded item, no. RR 0071 3056 6GB, to the European Parliament, Secretariat General, L-2929 Luxembourg. The United Kingdom Royal Mail have informed me that it was delivered and signed for, by your post room.

A reminder asking for acknowledgement of receipt, was sent to Ana Miranda de Lage, Assistant to the Chairman of the Committee on Energy, Research and Technology.

A second copy was sent to the Committee on Energy, Research and Technology by a private mail service. I was advised by them that it was signed for by yourself.

Could you please advise me whether these documents have been passed on by you to the respective addressees as requested.

Yours sincerely,
Derek Sheffield

To date, no reply is forthcoming from Mr Figus.

However, Mr Newman did eventually reply confirming receipt of the Appendix. This letter crossed in the post with my communication to Mr Figus.

A CRACK IN THE ARMOUR

22 May 1995
Subject: Petition no. 990/93

Dear Mr Sheffield,

I would like to confirm that I have received your recent correspondence.

When petitions are referred to other committees for further action, it is up to the committee concerned to decide whether or not to give any follow-up. You may, of course, if you wish, contact the Chairman of the relevant committee directly.

Yours sincerely
E. Newman

CHAPTER SEVENTEEN

The Belgian
Ministry of Defence

My letter of 16 March 1994, to the Belgian Prime Minister, with a copy to General-Major Schellemans of the Belgian Ministry of Defence, appears to have brought a quick response.

I was informed on 15 July 1993 by General-Major Schellemans that my enquiries on the events of 30–31 March 1990, had been sent to the appropriate service to answer. After four letters of reminder and a delay of six months, it would seem that no replies would be forthcoming. A lame excuse was given, that owing to military reorganization and a reduction in military personnel, all replies should now be directed to Professor A. Meessen at the Université Catholique de Louvain, Leuven, Belgium. Professor Meessen is a member of SOBEPS, the civil organization that worked with the Belgian Air Force in the investigation of the phenomena in the period November 1989–March 1990.

I have apprehensions as to this organization. Their investigations came to no conclusion. Their only help was in referring me to Patrick Ferryn, who said that I would get nowhere with my request to the European Parliament for an inquiry and stressed the monetary side of the use of the Petit Rechain photographs. They did not follow up the obvious radar anomaly: the positive detections by five radar stations, and the denial by the British Ministry of Defence of any knowledge of these events. The British media ban on this subject should also have formed part of their enquiries. Bearing in mind the hostile classification by the Belgian Air Force, Professor Meessen's answer as to whether this intrusion constituted a national threat is awaited with interest.

CORRESPONDENCE WITH THE BELGIAN MINISTER OF DEFENCE, LEO DELCROIX

4th June 1993

Ref: Your letter 9/IM/RT/16 of the 26/05/93.

Dear Minister,

Your reply to my letter on the events of November 1989 at Eupen was much appreciated.

I agree with your general comments in part 3 of your letter, and would confirm your observation that apart from the obvious *general* correlation of witnesses and radar returns from Semmerzake and Vedem, there did not appear to be any actual *pattern* to the events at Eupen.

It would seem, however, that flying objects of some kind were in evidence above Eupen, and were detected by radar.

You comment that observations and communications to the radar base at Glons were attributed to laser projections at a disco. I have today discussed this with a radar technical expert at Unipar Services of Tunbridge Wells in Kent; he informs me that there are *no* circumstances in which radar will detect any form of light.

It would seem, however, that the events above Wavre and Brussels in March 1990 were somewhat different. Whilst I have obtained much information from the Belgian Air Force concerning performance figures/radar returns and F-16 interception, and have confirmed photographs of the on-board radar and the phenomenon in question, I would very much appreciate your comments – or those of your predecessor – on these particular sightings.

For your interest, the point of my requests is that I have compiled a comprehensive report on the Eupen and Wavre sightings and intend to submit this (together with very strong documentary evidence) to the European Parliament in Brussels.

I have requested that an inquiry be instigated to establish whether this phenomenon could be of possible extraterrestrial origin, and have stated that if this be so, then – in the interests of international security – it is incumbent on the European Parliament to make this fact public.

My report is complete, but I would appreciate *an urgent reply* from yourself on the attitude of the Belgian government at that time to the events at Wavre in March 1990.

Thank you for your kind assistance,

Yours sincerely, Derek Sheffield

Having received no reply to my letter to Leo Delcroix I pursued the matter with a letter stressing the importance of the comments of the Belgian Ministry of Defence:

4th July 1993

Dear Minister,

I corresponded with you on the subject of unidentified aerial phenomenon at Eupen in November 1989 and again at Wavre/Brussels in March 1990.

You kindly replied on 26th May concerning the November 1989 incidents at Eupen but omitted the more important events at Wavre/Brussels in March 1990.

I have written to you on 4th June, requesting 'very urgently' a reply on the Wavre/Brussels incidents, but to date have had no reply.

The credibility of the Belgian Air Force, police, and Ministry of Defence is involved. I have no wish to state in my request to the European Parliament that I have been unable to obtain any comment from your department.

My report is complete - I have enough factual and documentary evidence to provide a sound case for an inquiry to be set up. Press releases have been made out to all the European press agencies to this effect. I feel that more credibility would be given to this incident by a statement from you or your predecessor rather than having to include in my report a deafening silence from your department.

I would once again stress the importance of this situation and ask for the matter to be given your urgent attention.

Yours sincerely,
Derek Sheffield

Eleven days later I received a reply from General-Major J.E. Schellemans of the office of the Belgian Minister of Defence:

15 July 1993

Dear Sir,

The Minister of Defence, Leo DELCROIX, thanks you for your letter dated 04.07.93, and has read it with attention.

Your demand has been forwarded to the appropriate service for investigation and answer.

Yours sincerely,
J. SCHELLEMANS
General-Major

No reply was forthcoming from any service (with the results of an investigation) over the next three months. Having received confirmation that my report had been forwarded to the Petitions Committee of the European Parliament I wrote again to the Belgian Ministry of Defence.

29 October 1993
Your Ref: 7/ME/00510

Dear General-Major Schellemans,

Thank you for your letter of the 15th July 1993.

I have been informed that my application for a ruling from the European Parliament has now been forwarded to the Petitions Committee for their consideration.

I enclose my reply to Mr Robert Ramsay of the Office of the Director-General for your information.

Bearing in mind the observations concerning the Belgian Minister and Ministry of Defence, I would request an answer to your letter of the 15th July concerning the events of the 30/31st March 1990 in which you state that my request has been forwarded to the appropriate service for investigation and answer.

I would also ask for your confirmation that full co-operation will be given to me in the event of the Petitions Committee pursuing this matter further.

Thank you for your assistance,

Yours sincerely,
Derek Sheffield

Two further reminders were necessary on 27 December 1993 and 29 January 1994, which elicited the following reply.

3 February 1994

Dear Mister Sheffield,

I received your letter dated 29th January 1994, in which you remind me your former letters dated 20 October 1993 and 27 December 1993.

Your question was sent directly to the General Staff of the Airforce with the request to formulate an answer as soon as possible. Therefore I can only reply in the same way as I did in my latest letter, i.e. the General Staff will supply you with an answer.

Yours sincerely,
J. SCHELLEMANS
General-Major

Six weeks later, no reply being forthcoming from the Belgian Air Force, I wrote two letters: one to General-Major Schellemans and one to the Belgian Prime Minister:

16th March 1994

Dear General-Major Schellemans,

I am concerned at the lack of response, to my enquiry of five months ago, from the General Staff of the Belgian Air Force.

This delay is unreasonable and unacceptable.

I can see no reason for a five-month delay on a subject that received so much coverage in the Belgian press.

I urgently need the details requested in my letter of 29th October 1993, to prepare my submission for the European Parliament.

I have written to the Belgian Prime Minister, asking for his backing to my request for an immediate reply from the Belgian Air Force.

Yours sincerely
Derek Sheffield

MY LETTER TO THE BELGIAN PRIME MINISTER

16th March 1994

Dear Prime Minister,

I am writing to ask for your backing to my request for a reply to a letter sent to the General Staff of the Belgian Air Force.

I am concerned at the lack of response to an enquiry sent five months ago.

This delay is unreasonable and unacceptable.

There can be no possible reason for a five-month delay on a subject that received so much coverage in the Belgian press.

The details are urgently needed to prepare a final submission to the European Parliament.

I have written to General-Major Schellemans of the Belgian MOD on numerous occasions. He seems unable to obtain an answer.

Yours faithfully,
Derek Sheffield

These two letters elicited a prompt reply from General-Major Schellemans which is reproduced below:

24 March 1994

Dear Mister Sheffield,
Your letter dated 16th March 1994 received my full attention.

Seen the number of questions concerning the observations made on UFO, the Minister of Defence decided that all available elements should be provided to the 'SOBEPS' and to Professor MEESSEN, who is still working on the subject. In the context of the military reorganization, the reduction of personnel and all the military activities outside Belgium, the General Staff is not in a position to answer this subject any more.

May I suggest to contact Professor A. MEESSEN. His address is:
Université Catholique de Louvain
Département de Physique
chemin du Cyclotron 2
B-1348 LOUVAIN-LA-NEUVE
BELGIUM

Yours sincerely,
J. SCHELLEMANS
General-Major

After this disappointing response from the Belgian Ministry of Defence, I wrote again to General-Major Schellemans requesting a straight answer to a simple question:

30th March 1994

Dear General Major Schellemans,
Thank you for your prompt reply 3/pg/30016 of 24th March 1994.

I have now obtained all the information that I require from the Belgian Air Force.

Thank you for the address of Professor MEESSEN.

Whilst Professor MEESSEN is probably able to answer any questions concerning the *observation* of the phenomenon of the 30/31st March 1990, the information that I require directly concerns the Belgian Minister of Defence at that time, Minister G. Coëme.

The question is a simple one. It only requires a negative or affirmative answer:

Bearing in mind that the necessary prerequisites were met before the F-16 aircraft achieved their interceptions did Minister of Defence Guy Coëme consider that this intrusion of Belgian airspace constituted a threat to national security?

Should you not be able to give me an answer to this, I would ask that you forward this letter to Minister G. Coëme with great urgency.

Yours sincerely,
Derek Sheffield

General-Major Schellemans replied as follows:

12 April 1994
Dear Mister Sheffield,
In answer to your letter dated 30th March 1994, I can assure you that until now, the UFO phenomenon has never been considered as a threat to national security.

Yours sincerely,
J. SCHELLEMANS
General-Major

Bearing in mind all the evidence available, his reply caused me some concern. I sent the following letter to General-Major Schellemans asking for clarification of the reasons for the nature of his reply, and giving a brief résumé of the evidence:

17 April 1994

Dear General-Major Schellemans,

Thank you for your prompt reply to my letter of the 30th March 1994. The general context of your letter causes me some concern.

I am sure that you do not need me to remind you that positive detections were made by skilled radar operatives at Bertem, Semmerzake, Glons, St Hubert, and Vedem (German) radar stations. These detections proved beyond any doubt that flying objects of opacity/substance were present in Belgian air space. All necessary confirmations were made (witnesses, police, radar). Belgian Air Force interceptors were alerted many times to visually identify (VID) these flying objects. Checks were made on armament in flight, and instructions given many times to take the maximum number of pictures. Many interceptions were made achieving radar lock-on, and establishing performance details of these phenomena. Because of the European radar defence system, many NADGE radars were alerted. All this was confirmed on 21st December 1989 by Minister G. Coëme, the Minister of Defence at that time, and corroborated by Leo Delcroix, the present Minister of Defence, on 26th May 1993.

In a letter 9/IM/RT/16 of the 26th May 1994 Leo Delcroix stated 'All hypotheses can be excluded, the Minister could not tell what these flying objects were.'

Bearing in mind all the above facts, by what premise do you assume that these unidentified intrusions into Belgian airspace did *not* constitute a threat to Belgian national security?

> Yours sincerely
> Derek Sheffield

At the time of writing, General-Major Schellemans has declined to answer this letter.

Prior to receiving General-Major Schellemans' reply, I had written to Professor Meessen at the Université Catholique de Louvain, Département de Physique, asking the same question posed to the Belgian Ministry of Defence regarding the perceived threat to national security.

7th April 1994

Dear Professor Meessen,

I am in the process of compiling a document for the Petitions Committee of the European Parliament. This concerns the phenomenon of 30/31st March 1990 and its interception by aircraft of the Belgian Air Force.

General-Major Schellemans of the Ministère de la Défense Nationale has advised me to contact you for information on this subject.

The information I require is very simple. It requires only a negative or affirmative reply:

Bearing in mind that the necessary prerequisites were met before the F-16 aircraft achieved their inter-ceptions; was it deemed that this intrusion of Belgian air space constituted a threat to national security?

As there has been a delay of over six months from the Belgian Ministry of Defence in answering this question I

would request an answer at your earliest possible
convenience.

                    Yours sincerely,
                    Derek Sheffield

At the time of writing, Professor Meessen has declined to
reply to this letter.

It would seem that General-Major Schellemans is being
obstructive. After five letters requesting details of the radar
detections and sightings of 30–31 March 1990, the only reply
that I had received was a letter from the General-Major
stating that my requests had been passed to the Belgian Air
Force for an answer.

After five months of delaying tactics by Schellemans, a
direct appeal was made to the Belgian Prime Minister for
assistance.

This resulted in an immediate reply on 24 March from
General-Major Schellemans: the delaying tactics continued;
he advised me that because of reductions in personnel in the
Belgian Air Force, they could not answer any further
questions on this matter. He stated that I should direct any
further enquiries to Professor Meessen of the Université
Catholique de Louvain.

A letter from Dr David Clark, MP, the Shadow Secretary of
State for Defence on 22 August 1994, contained an enclosure
from Colonel J. Bouzette, Defence Attaché at the Belgian
Embassy. This enclosure stated that 'an official answer was
forwarded to Mr Sheffield by the Belgian Government in
September 1993'. Not only was *no* letter ever received by me
from the Belgian Government in September 1993, but this is
in complete contradiction to the statement by General-Major
Schellemans in his letter of 24 March 1994.

Whatever is going on?

It would appear that either my mail is being intercepted,
or General-Major Schellemans – and by implication the
Belgian Ministry of Defence – is, *for some odd reason*,
attempting to obstruct an inquiry into this subject. By his
track record to date, I would suspect the latter.

THE BELGIAN MINISTRY OF DEFENCE

On 12 November 1994, I again wrote to the Belgian Prime
Minister requesting a personal reply from his office in an
attempt to get an answer to my queries:

12th November 1994

Dear Prime Minister,

I have submitted a 40-page document to the European
Parliament concerning unidentified radar detections above
Belgium in 1989/90.

This document concludes that the statement made by the
Belgian Minister of Defence, M. Coëme, to the Belgian
Parliament on the 21st December 1989 was inconclusive
and, as these detections were not identified by NADGE
radars and had consequently been declared hostile, were
a case for an extensive inquiry to be held by the
European Parliament.

The Parliament have agreed to discuss this matter, and
the Petitions Committee have forwarded my document to
the Committee on Energy, Research and Technology as
Petition 990/93 for further action.

I have requested assistance from the Belgian
Government and Ministry of Defence in this enquiry;
could I please be given an answer? General-Major
Schellemans has been obstructive in the extreme; he has
employed delaying tactics by not answering letters for
many months, has stated that requests had been passed to
the Belgian Air Force, and after five months has said
that because of military re-organization, all matters in
relation to this subject would be passed to Professor
Meessen of Louvain University. Professor Meessen does
not reply.

My last letter - asking for a specific answer - to
General-Major Schellemans, was written on 17th April
1994 - 7 months ago! To date there has been no reply.

I now understand from Doctor David Clark (Shadow
Minister of Defence) that a letter from the Belgian
Government was sent to me in January 1993. At no time
was this ever received by me.

The Belgian Embassy in London have quoted sections
from this letter to Dr Clark, and I have been informed
that they have this on file, but despite a request from
the Post Office and a letter two weeks ago from me, they
refuse to send me a copy! The situation is made more
complicated by the office of the Military Attaché denying

that the Post Office have been in contact with them, and
the Post Office saying that the Belgian Embassy are not
telling the truth!

Whatever is going on?

I find this whole situation very strange and most
suspect. What began as a simple matter of proving the
existence of a phenomenon above Belgium in 1989/90 has
now - by overwhelming circumstantial evidence - assumed
implications of a clandestine nature.

When the Committee on Energy, Research and Technology
of the European Parliament discuss this problem, I have
asked for permission to acquaint them of these
anomalies.

Your personal answer is requested, and not that of
General-Major Schellemans.

Yours faithfully,

Derek Sheffield

The preceding letter to the Belgian Prime Minister resulted
in the following reply from General-Major W. De Brouwer,
Deputy Chief of Airstaff, Plans, Operations and Personnel of
the Belgian Armed Forces, specifically the Belgian Air Force –
the same W. De Brouwer (then a colonel) who, at the time of
the sightings at Eupen and Wavre in 1989–90, had handled
the release of information to the media by means of a press
conference, etc., during which time information on the events
that took place over Belgium seemed freely available. During
the three and a half years between the actual sightings of the
unidentified objects and the following letter this policy
would appear to have changed.

General-Major W. De Brouwer's letter is reproduced in its
entirety, *exactly* as written:

22 December 1994

Ref: Your letter dated 12 November 1994.

Dear Sir,

Thank you for your letter in reference.

Allow me first to state that during the last two years
the Belgian Authorities have been extremely patient in
regard to your never ending request to get information
on the Belgian UFO sightings. Although the Air Force
does not have an office especially dealing with this

matters and although your letters are often quite offending, yet we always answered your letters until now, e.g.:

*May 1993:   a summary of the statements made by the Minister of Defence, Guy Coëme.
*April 1993:   distinct figures on F-16 radardata.
*September 1993: details of the Press Conference given by Col DE BROUWER on 11 Jul 1990.
*September 1994: an answer to your "Alleged intrusion into Belgian Airspace" via our Embassy in London.
*December 1994: this letter.

Notwithstanding all our help, following facts, which we fully disapprove, were noticed:

1. In your letter of 4th June 1993 you informed us that a radar technical expert at UNIPAR SERVICES OF TUNBRIDGE WELLS (KENT) denied the possibility that a radar can detect any form of light. Apparently you "twisted" the words of the Minister of Defence (May 1993) by stating to this technician that the radar of CRC GLONS "detected" laser projections of a disco, which was definitely not mentioned as such in the letter of the Minister of Defence to you.

   By the way: some sensors, called LIDAR (LIght Detection And Ranging), do detect emissions of light because these sensors are using another part of the electromagnetic spectrum than the proper "RADAR" systems.

2. In your Press Release (Jun 1993) you "adapted" the F-16 radardata to your needs and stated that these figures were confirmed by the Belgian Air Force;

3. This Press Release contains as well "mis-information" to the public because the UFO phenomenon in BELGIUM was NOT filmed by the media and only ONE person was able to take TWO pictures of it. The Royal Military Academy and the University of Leuven investigated these photographs later on but NEVER stated that these were genuine.

   They only stated that the above mentioned photographs were not "counterfeited" in a technical way known to them because these Institutes were not able to "reproduce" those pictures with the means and the knowledge they presently have. Therefore they especially stressed that proving the pictures are not technically "falsified", does not mean that they are genuine.

4. Moreover in your letter to Dr Clark, U.K. Shadow Secretary of State of Defence, you stated that the Belgian Minister of Defence "confirmed" that the UFO-sighting (30th March 90) has been classified as HOSTILE and that the "UFO" was on a heading towards U.K.

   This is completely "wrong" because the "UFO" was not only flying on an EASTERLY heading, but as well at any moment it neighter fullfilled the NATO identification-criteria to be treated as a HOSTILE. And even if it would have been, all surrounding radarstations (including NEATSHEAD, U.K.) would automatically have been alerted of this fact.

Furthermore the Belgian Authorities do not like to be put under pressure. As a few examples we quote:

1. Your letter to our Minister of Defence (4th July 93):
   "The credibility of the Belgian Air Force, Police and Ministry of Defence is involved, and I have no wish to state in my request to the European Parliament that I have been unable to obtain any comment from your department."

   And in the next paragraph of that same letter:
   "My report is complete – I have enough factual and documentary evidence to provide a sound case for an enquiry to be set up, and press releases have been made out to all the European press agencies and media to this effect – I feel that more credibility would be given to this incident by a statement from you (Minister DELCROIX) or your predecessor (Minister COEME) rather than having to include in my report an ominous deafening silence from your department."

   Apparently you forgot that in the meantime you received already two letters from us, one of them signed by Minister of Defence DELCROIX where he gave you a summary of the events and the conclusions thereof!

2. Your letter to General-Major Schellemans (16th August 93):
   " . . . and (I) would request an immediate reply to assist me with these details."

3. Your letter to P. VAN DOORSLAER, the Belgian Superintendent of Police, (29th October 1993):

"I would state that as the credibility of the Belgian Prime Minister and Ministry of Defence, the Belgian Air Force, and the Belgian Gendarmerie is involved, I would expect their full co-operation in this petition."

4. Your letter to our Prime Minister (12th November 1994):

"Your personal answer is requested, and not that of General-Major Schellemans."

Especially in the light of what you mentioned just above:

"What began as a simple matter of proving the existence of a phenomenon above Belgium in 1989/90, has now – by overwhelming circumstantial evidence (???) – assumed implications of a clandestine nature."

For all the above mentioned reasons, the Belgian Authorities do not wish to reopen the debate.

Concerning your request to get a copy of the letter mentioned by Doctor David Clark because *"At no time was this ever received by me"*, we must state that this is impossible. As our correspondence only started in May 1993, no letter could have been sent to you in Januari 1993.

Nevertheless, if you still require further information on UFO sightings in Belgium, we kindly suggest you to contact the:

"Société Belge d'Etude de Phénomènes Spatiaux (SOBEPS)
Avenue Paul Janson, 74
B-1070 Brussels,

an organisation which not only published already two books on this issue but which as well is very pleased with the helpfullness of the Belgian Air Force and Police in this delicate matter.

Yours sincerely
W. DE BROUWER
General-Major
Deputy Chief of Airstaff
Plans, Operations and Personnel

I was somewhat disappointed to receive this letter from the Belgian authorities, as I considered that prior to this, apart from their recent prevarication, my relationship with them had been quite good. It struck me as curious that the Belgian Air Force should be aware of a letter I had sent to the Belgian Superintendent of Police on 29 October 1993. Presumably this letter had been forwarded either to the Belgian Air Force or some central agency that holds a file of all my correspondence to all agencies in Belgium with whom I have been in contact. This seems a little 'over the top' considering that the subject matter is not considered to be of a threat to national security. Incidentally, I never received a reply to the letter in question, but at least I now know that it was delivered.

General-Major De Brouwer's letter mentions a reply sent to me in September 1993, from the Belgian authorities. I should mention that in my communications to the Belgians I had quoted the date of this letter as being January 1993. I was incorrect, taking the date from correspondence with the Royal Mail. It was remiss of me not to have checked and double-checked my facts, as I mention in my reply to General-Major De Brouwer:

```
                                    30th December 1994
Ref: Your letter dated 22nd December 1994
Dear General-Major De Brouwer,
   Thank you for your letter of the 22nd inst:
   Apart from your latest letter, I have only ever
received two letters from the Belgian authorities; those
of April and May 1993. I do not understand how this
constitutes 'being patient by the Belgian authorities'.
If you feel that my letters have been 'quite offensive',
I would plead frustration. The Belgian Air Force have
previously been free with their information. Since the
acceptance of my request for an inquiry by the European
Parliament, there has obviously now been a clampdown on
anything concerning this subject. If you consider
constantly requesting assistance from the Belgian Air
Force as 'offensive', and asking for the backing of the
Belgian authorities as 'putting pressure on them', then
that is your opinion.
   If the European Parliament decide to take this matter
further, they will not accept your 'offensive/putting
pressure' ploys; you will have to truthfully answer to
them on all these points.
```

THE BELGIAN MINISTRY OF DEFENCE

I was misinformed by the Post Office, who obtained
their information from the Belgian Embassy. Although the
actual date in question was September 1993, the date is
irrelevant. What is relevant is that the Belgian Embassy
quoted this letter to Dr Clark, the Shadow Secretary of
State for Defence, and alleged that it had been sent to
me. I have never received this letter. The Belgian
Embassy have refused to send it to me. I find this most
odd!

Taking your letter in context, my main interest has
been in the radar implications involved. I stand by my
observation that *radar*, is the detection, by reflected
radio frequency, of objects of opacity and substance.

In the letter from Leo Delcroix, Minister of Defence,
of the 26th May 1993, he states that F-16 aircraft
intervened on the 15th and 16th December 1989. And 'as a
result of observations and communications addressed to
the base at Glons. It seemed that they resulted from
laser projections of a disco.'

Glons is a *radar* station that is part of the NADGE
complex. Radar will *not* detect the wavelength of light.
In your own words, 'the Belgian Air Force is only
empowered to attempt interceptions providing certain
parameters are met. Witnesses' statements have to be
confirmed by the Belgian Police; these in turn have to be
confirmed by radar. If radar can not identify their
detections, they are classified as *hostile*. All these
parameters were met. The Belgian Air Force attempted
interceptions.' These are your words and not mine.
Because the Belgian Air Force attempted interceptions,
Glons radar *must* have made detections that were not
identified.

*The Minister's statement is a direct suggestion that
Glons radar detected laser projections from a disco.*

You state that in my press release (June 1993) I
adapted F-16 radar data to my needs and that these
figures had not been confirmed by the Belgian Air Force.
General-Major De Brouwer, all the information that I
have is on record, and came from the Belgian Air Force!

Concerning your observation that my press release
'misinformed the public' by stating that this phenomenon
was filmed by the media. Apart from the fact that I have
a video and photographs sent from Belgium of this
object, I find it difficult to believe that something that
was *witnessed by 13,500 people (2,500 of whom provided*

*statements), witnessed by 75 members of the Belgian
Police, detected by 5 radar stations, intercepted on
many occasions by the Belgian Air Force, and discussed
by the Belgian Parliament, WAS NOT FILMED BY MANY WITH
CAMERAS AND VIDEO CAMERAS - AND BY THE MEDIA!* Indeed, by
the amount of occasions that your pilots were instructed
to take as many photographs as possible, the Belgian Air
Force were very remiss *not* to have obtained photographs
of this object. The fact that 'on-board' radar videos
were taken, but none by the public or the Belgian Air
Force, is surely stretching imagination to its limits
and a subject for investigation.

I find the definition by Leuven University that '*proving
the pictures are not technically falsified, does not mean
that they are genuine*', to be double-talk in the
extreme. It would seem that the course being pursued by
the Belgian authorities is in line with those of the
American and United Kingdom defence establishments. All
enquiries are referred to civilian groups that are
controlled by the security/defence establishments of
their respective countries. . . .

You have confirmed the NATO identification-criteria for
a *hostile* classification. Once again I would quote the
parameters for interceptions by the Belgian Air Force:

1. Witnesses' observations have to be confirmed by the
Belgian police.

2. Belgian radar must confirm the observations of the
Belgian police.

3. If the Belgian radar are not able to identify their
detections, they are *classified as hostile*.

4. The Belgian Air Force can only attempt
interceptions if a radar detection has not been
identified and has been classified as *hostile*.

5. All these parameters were met. The highly skilled
NADGE radar operators at Glons and other radar stations
could not identify their detections, they were classified
as *hostile* and interceptions were ordered.

6. You are being selective with your answer: all
sixteen previous movements, from 7 km south of
Beauvechain (Bevkom) to a point near to Enghien, *were
all due west* towards the United Kingdom. *The last 3 km
only, to Rebecq, were on a south-easterly heading.*

7. As you have already stated: your aircraft would not
have been in the air if the NATO identification-criteria
had not been fullfilled.

8. Your statement that: – 'all surrounding radar stations (including NEATSHEAD, UK) would automatically have been alerted to this fact' is interesting. The British Secretary of State for Defence has stated in a letter to Admiral of the Fleet Lord Hill-Norton that notification of NADGE radar detections does not occur automatically!

Whatever is going on?

Your entire 3rd page is taken up with observations concerning my requests for the backing of the Belgian Air Force, police and Ministry of Defence in my application for an inquiry into the events in Belgium in 1989/90.

It would now seem that, in spite of continual appeals to these three agencies, no co-operation is to be forthcoming.

This in itself is strange. It is odd that such a series of incidents well documented by the Belgian Police, given such publicity by the media, authenticated by yourself on television, and given credibility by the Belgian Parliament, should now be disclaimed by all these agencies.

As was admitted by the Belgian Minister of Defence, flying objects of some kind were apparent above Belgium in 1989/90. It is not known what they were.

What makes this whole matter a subject of concern is not that there were objects present, but the recent attitude of the various Belgian agencies in disclaiming this.

It is this attitude that makes the whole issue highly suspect.

In closing, I would once again repeat my requests for:

1. The letter (Sept 1993) as quoted by the Belgian Embassy to Dr Clark.

2. Details of the March 1990 sightings over Wavre.

3. Confirmation that there will be no co-operation from the Belgian agencies involved, in an enquiry by the European Parliament.

Yours sincerely,
Derek Sheffield

There has been no reply from General-Major De Brouwer to this letter.

CHAPTER EIGHTEEN

The Canterbury Wave

It would seem now that a reappraisal of some kind is called for. It is now a proven fact that flying objects of some kind appeared many times in the skies above Belgium between November 1989 and March 1990.

The very fact of their appearance, their performance, their ability to disappear and appear at will, to detect and confuse radars of any pursuing aircraft, would indicate an entity with an intelligence far greater than anything that exists on Earth.

It would appear that as apparently no one knows what they are, *no* defence ministries, British, American or Belgian, would be able to state whether they constituted a threat or not. What is perplexing, therefore, are the claims by these defence ministries that these entities are *not* hostile. If it is not known what they are, how can they possibly be construed as not being hostile? The only possible deduction from this, therefore, is that these ministries know what these entities are, and their covert attitudes *must* indicate a degree of involvement.

This being so, one must now consider all options. These must include the beliefs of Linda Moulton-Howe, and the strange wave of sightings in Kent, north of Canterbury, that began on 20 September 1993, six weeks *after* Linda Moulton-Howe arrived in Kent to investigate them.

Carol Davies is a senior reporter for a provincial newspaper. She is highly thought of by her editor, is a responsible and serious person, and would do nothing to jeopardize her professional integrity. The 8 October 1993 copy of her weekly newspaper was almost entirely devoted to a series of events that had happened over a two-week period, 17–30 September 1993, over an area of Kent to the north of Canterbury, a series of events that were almost identical to the occurrences above

Eupen in eastern Belgium three years before. It was an editorial decision – because the 14-year career of Carol Davies had earned the respect of her editor – to carry her report in its entirety.

Because of the similarity to the Eupen sightings, I had a meeting with Carol. It lasted for two hours.

Carol's experience began in the evening, at approximately 8 pm on Monday, 20 September, 1993. She and a companion, Adrian Williams, a watercolour artist, were travelling by car on the London-bound A2 road towards Canterbury. Both she and her companion became aware of a close configuration of lights above and to one side of their car.

Carol's recollection was of an oval, ellipsoid shape that was bright bluish-white in colour. She said that it was difficult to make a detailed study and to drive her car at the same time. Her companion was able to make a better observation and described the phenomenon as being three orbs of light connected together in a horizontal plane. It was while he was observing this configuration of lights (much larger than any aircraft illumination) that the object, which appeared to be quite stationary in the sky, performed a startling manoeuvre. A cone of light appeared from the underside of the rear of this phenomenon, projecting downwards. Carol described this as 'light-plasma'. She said that it appeared to have a spiralling density and was a moving, contained area of light. Fractionally after this cone of light appeared, the object vanished at a speed too quick for the eye to register.

It then reappeared, probably a mile away. Carol and her companion followed it, and the same sequence of events happened again; it remained stationary in the sky, emitted the cone of light-plasma, and disappeared at a speed beyond the ability of the eye to follow.

Carol and her companion scanned the sky for a further appearance but could see nothing, but when they turned for home it was again noticed by Adrian Williams, only this time behind the car.

The duration of these sightings over the various locations involved was of the order of 20 minutes. It was fortunate that

Adrian Williams, being a watercolour artist, was able to form an exact judgement on colour. He sketched an impressive charcoal impression of what he saw, the accuracy of which was verified by Carol Davies.

This is the series of events that was reported by her newspaper. The response by members of the public was considerable. Carol was impressed by the integrity of the witnesses that she interviewed; they were a general cross-section of the community. All were convinced of what they had seen. Their descriptions matched *exactly* all the descriptions given by the many witnesses of the phenomenon at Eupen in Belgium in November 1989, and again at Wavre (Brussels) in March 1990.

Carol Davies said that only *some* of the statements given to her were published; there were a total of over 40 from all witnesses.

Witnesses' descriptions spoke of:

Kent: Three bright, greenish-white lights in a flat triangular shape.

Eupen: A triangular platform with three powerful lights at its points.

Kent: An oval, ellipsoid-shaped light.
Eupen: An orb of light.

Kent: A silvery oval object with flashing lights around the rim.
Eupen: A white orb with coloured lights situated at its extremities.

Kent: A large object with bright, white lights zig-zagging through the sky at an incredible speed.
Eupen: This object pursued a wildly erratic and step-like zig-zag course.

Kent: A bright silvery stationary object that was turning over itself.
Eupen: A continual changing format; a tumbling 'plethora' of light.

Kent: A very bright light, out of which four identical
            shapes emerged – they were moving all around it;
            the four shapes all seemed to merge into the main
            one and it disappeared.

Eupen: It has the ability to divide into two separate
            triangles, each of which emits a number of small
            replicas of itself which proceed in various
            directions. These return after a period to their
            respective half-triangles, which then re-form to the
            original triangular platform.

Kent: A large, round thing with sparkling lights on it, over
            towards Ramsgate. It seemed to have lights *in* it as
            well as around it.

Eupen: A large, pinkish-white orb with many small lights
            both on its surface and *in* it.

This, then, is an account of the events in the Kent area, north
of Canterbury on 20 September 1993. It is also a list of
statements from witnesses, providing a direct comparison
with Eupen and Wavre in 1989–90, and Canterbury in Kent in
September 1993 – *conclusive proof that the phenomenon in both
places is the same.*

I have written to Robert Ramsay of the Directorate General
for Research of the European Community. I have asked him
to indicate to the Petitions Committee that it must be
emphasized that my request has the backing of the Belgian
Minister and Ministry of Defence, the Belgian Air Force and
the Belgian gendarmerie. I have also stated that because the
Belgian phenomena of 1989–90 and the Kent phenomenon of
1993 are exactly the same, the two events must be correlated
and included together in the same application to the
Committee.

I have telephoned Carol Davies at her newspaper and
asked her three questions. I said that I would respect her
answers and would not compromise her in any way. I would
understand completely should she not wish to involve
herself in my investigation.

I first said that it looked as if my request to the European Parliament was now on the move. I said that I had received no practical help from my local Member of the European Parliament.

Only on direct appeal to the Belgian Prime Minister was I asked to send a copy of my petition direct to Egon Klepsch, President of the European Parliament. President Klepsch had my application forwarded to the Petitions Committee for their consideration. It would be up to them to consider if my request was suitable for submission to the appropriate committee of the European Parliament.

I informed Carol that I had asked Robert Ramsay to advise the Petitions Committee that my request for an inquiry should include the support of the Belgian establishment and armed forces. I said that – because the Canterbury and Belgian phenomena were one and the same – I would request her assistance should matters in the European Parliament progress further. I asked Carol Davies if she would keep on file details of the statements made to her by the 40 witnesses involved.

I also asked her if I could use the charcoal drawing made by her companion on the night of the incident.

I asked if I could rely on her as a personal witness, should the matter ever reach the inquiry stage in the European Parliament.

Carol Davies replied in the affirmative in a very positive manner.

CHAPTER NINETEEN

The Lamberhurst Sighting

I have included this chapter to illustrate an experience of a witness whom I know to be completely normal and absolutely trustworthy in every way. I have carried out extensive local enquiries and have been unable to fault her statement.

Mrs Brigit Ferguson lives in a period property that faces the main London–Hastings road at Lamberhurst in Kent. Her property is situated on a hill that leads to Pembury and Tonbridge. To the rear she has an elevated cottage garden that overlooks a lush unkempt meadow that forms part of the valley of the river Teise. This meadow is fallow and appears to be unused. At the far end of this meadow the land rises to meet the boundary of a local abattoir. To the left is a row of cottages, the rear gardens of which form the end of this section of the meadow boundary.

At this corner of the meadow there is a clump of assorted trees that form a mushroom-shaped copse approximately 30 feet across.

Enquiries at the company that own the abattoir resulted in the statement that although there were occasions when deliveries were made late at night, the only illumination used was normal industrial lighting.

Enquiries made at nearby cottages (one of which was barely 50 feet from the site of the phenomenon I am about to describe) revealed nothing untoward on the night in question.

A small, derelict forge nearby is used only to shoe the occasional horse. There was nothing in the area that could give rise to the luminescent, green orb seen by the witness. A comment made by the occupant of the cottage nearest to the phenomenon was to emphatically endorse the integrity of Mrs Ferguson.

Mrs Brigit Ferguson is an extremely intelligent and articulate person. She is sensible, completely normal, and not prone to flights of the imagination. She has an inquisitive and enquiring mind.

Because Mrs Ferguson found herself in a situation that she was not able to understand, she approached her local newspaper to enquire whether there had been any reports of a phenomenon that she had witnessed to the west of Lamberhurst in Kent. She wanted an explanation for this phenomenon. Her experience was reported in the newspaper and linked to my report to the European Parliament. I telephoned her and arranged a meeting. Phenomena were seen on the night of 31 May 1994. A different phenomenon was witnessed three nights later on 3 June 1994. Confirmation was obtained from a friend that a similar sighting took place over Camber on the Kentish coast on 30 May 1994.

Mrs Ferguson explained that often, on retiring, she takes in the view from her bedroom window. This overlooks – to the west – the small meadow that is part of the Teise valley, and a collection of buildings, the major one of which is an asbestos building used as an abattoir. Mrs Ferguson said the time was 10.30 pm, it was an overcast night and there were no visible stars. She described the phenomenon as being in a north-westerly position. As far as she was able to ascertain at night, it appeared to be only about 500 yards away. It took the form of a crucifix-type cross with the longer arm shorter than normal. Because of its brightness and configuration it attracted Mrs Ferguson's attention; she said that 'it moved without moving'. (By this, she meant that it disappeared from one position and instantly reappeared at another.) It moved several times but generally stayed in the same area. The duration of this sighting was approximately 25 minutes. In this period it changed its appearance from a cross to an arrow. This was an arrow with a configuration similar to the Radiation Danger symbol (three arms of the same length that converge at a point). While this was happening, another object, this time of an elongated box-like shape, appeared to the north-west. This was similar in size, and three-quarters the length of a container vehicle. It appeared to be covered in translucent film. It had many coloured lights on all edges of its construction; because of its transparency, all these lights were visible *through* the body of the object. This then moved smoothly towards the west, and, passing by the cross, turned down, where it disappeared behind the abattoir.

Mrs Ferguson expected an explosion of some kind but there was none.

On 3 June at 10.30 pm the cross appeared again, but on the part of the meadow where it begins to rise towards the collection of farm buildings. Only 200 yards from the bottom of Mrs Ferguson's garden an orb of green light appeared. It was completely covering a copse of trees, semi-circular in form, and translucent, as if covered with a semi-opaque film. It was probably 30 feet in diameter and similar to half a giant bubble. Mrs Ferguson said the striking thing about it was its colour. It was the most beautiful shade of translucent apple-green that she had ever seen. During this sighting, Mrs Ferguson took photographs with an Instamatic-type camera. She simply pointed the camera and snapped. There were three exposures, two of which showed nothing. The third – in which she used a flash – seemed to show the reflection of her double-glazed bedroom window and a light of some sort to one side of the exposure. This appeared to be an anomaly in the film exposure. I said that as I suspected these objects to be a phenomenon of light, it would take either luck or a good camera to obtain a worthwhile result. The observation of this orb, for such a long period, seemed pointless, so Mrs Ferguson simply retired to her bed.

I have been back to the scene of the green orb. It is situated on the edge of the meadow next to the back fence of an empty cottage. The copse is a mixture of elder, hawthorn, and a conifer. The elder was in bloom, which made it easily visible in the twilight of a summer's night. Mrs Ferguson's description of the general shape of this copse as 'mushroom-like' is very accurate. She said that the green orb completely covered this copse. Mrs Ferguson also said that at the time of the appearance of the orb, another light became apparent.

This was situated some 10 or 15 feet to the right of the orb, and had the appearance of a bright, sparkling ball of light, very much smaller than the green orb. This light seemed to be of moderate intensity but to continuously emit bright flashes of light from its surface to no particular pattern.

The management of the abattoir stated that they were clearing some scrub from the ground at the rear of their property. They said that they were burning this scrub and that could account for the white, spluttering light seen by Mrs Ferguson. This is a plausible explanation except for the fact that from Mrs Ferguson's garden, the site of the green orb around the copse and the close proximity of its sparkling white light are probably 100 yards from the site of any scrub bonfire. These relative positions are easily distinguishable in the half-light of a summer's night.

I have quoted Mrs Ferguson's experience to illustrate an example of a sighting of a phenomenon that is becoming increasingly commonplace. Hers is only one of an estimated 80,000 that have appeared on the surface of the Earth over the last twenty years.

After two interviews on BBC local radio, I began to receive letters and telephone calls from many sources. Several of these letters were from airline pilots debunking the statement by the Ministry of Defence that no radar detections had been made that could not be accounted for.

Several letters were from religious eccentrics.

The most amazing of all were letters containing photographs and illustrations from all parts of the world.

After the Belgian photographs, the incident and illustration by Carol Davies, the descriptions and illustrations of the same phenomenon seen by 40 witnesses above north Kent, and the Lamberhurst incident, it seemed obvious that something very strange was going on.

It was the next discovery that – when added to the graphically illustrated evidence obtained in these incidents – gave strong indications that we are *not* dealing with a purely localized affair.

It was as I was studying several of the actual photographs sent to me that the realization came that – with a certain amount of rearranging – they were all variations of the same object.

Although I cannot vouch for the authenticity of these photographs, because of the diversity of their sources, and their obvious similarity I decided – purely for comparison – to alter four of them by enlarging or reducing the images so as to make them appear the same size, and arranging their juxtaposition so that their image is the same in each photograph. It is highly likely that these four different photographs are of the same phenomenon.

They were taken at different times, at different places, at the four corners of the Earth.

What governmental design is it, I wonder, that allows this entity the freedom to roam unchallenged over the entire surface of our planet?

CHAPTER TWENTY

Letters to the Ministry of Defence and NATO

Following my broadcasts on BBC radio, the many and various communications I received as a direct result (some of which contradicted statements made by the Ministry of Defence in an earlier exchange of letters) prompted me to enter into the following correspondence with Mr N. G. Pope of the Ministry of Defence in Whitehall:

27th September 1993

Dear Mr Pope,

You may remember that earlier in the year we had some correspondence concerning unidentified radar returns.

Your observations refer: 'There are certainly no instances where solid objects have been detected but not identified' (Ref: D/Sec(AS)12/3) and on the subject of anomalous propagation of radar 'it is easy for skilled operators to distinguish between these sort of returns, and the track made by a solid object such as an aircraft.' (Ref: D/Sec(AS)12/3).

I was recently invited by BBC radio to discuss an application that I have made to the European Parliament for an inquiry into the Belgian incidents of 1989/90.

A direct result of this broadcast was several letters and telephone calls from airline pilots, who had indeed been alerted by radar stations of objects that had been detected on converging courses, and who had witnessed, together with other crew members, the detected object/objects passing where indicated. A telephone conversation with a radar operator also confirmed similar incidents.

A conversation with a radar technologist also confirmed that *radar will act in much the same way as a wavelength of light. It will only detect another radar signal or its own reflection from an object of reflectability, in the latter case an object of some substance or opacity.*

Note: This must be the case, or there would be no point in radar detection.

I have had considerable correspondence with the Belgian Air Force, the Belgian Minister/Ministry of Defence, and the Belgian Prime Minister. Because the credibility of the Belgian armed forces and Ministry of Defence is in question, my report has been forwarded to:

Egon Klepsch, President of the European Parliament, Belliardstraat 97–117, 1047 Brussels, Belgium.

I have also been informed that detections were made by Belgian radar at Semmerzake (array type, military), Belgian radar at Glons (multi-purpose impulsion type), and other NADGE radars at Bertem and St Hubert (Belgium), and Vedem (Germany). All observations were made by skilled operatives. You are aware, of course, that these radar stations are part of the 80-station NADGE radar complex that covers the whole of Europe. I presume that you are also aware that all the detections of these radar stations are co-ordinated.

We are part of the North Atlantic Treaty Organisation Air Defence Ground Environment and of the same radar complex.

The Ministry of Defence must therefore have been aware of the many radar detections by these five radar stations, and of the 13 contacts made by the F-16 interceptor aircraft which were vectored to their targets by the three main radar stations involved.

In view of: (1) the statement by the radar technologist involved stating that radar will only positively detect a reflected radar wavelength from an object of opacity and substance.

(2) The statement concerning – on two occasions – prior warning by radar to a civil airliner, of an object that was witnessed by three aircrew members.

(3) I would be interested in your observations as to whether you agree with statement (1), whether you will confirm that the MOD have never had an unidentified radar return as advised in statement (2), and how you would qualify your comments in your letter D/Sec(AS)12/3 of the 24/2/93 that – concerning the Belgian incidents and the detections by three NATO radar stations that – *there was only ONE reference to radar.*

Your comments would be appreciated

Yours sincerely,
Derek Sheffield

Mr Pope's reply was prompt and contradicts information I had received regarding the notification of radar detections across the NADGE network.

29th September 1993

Dear Mr Sheffield,

Thank you for your letter dated 27 September.

I agree that radar will only positively detect a radar wavelength or an object of opacity and substance, although it is important to remember that a radar blip does not necessarily correspond to the location of an object; as I explained in my letter dated 18 February, the phenomenon of Anomalous Propagation can give an indication that an object of some sort is in the air, when in fact there is no such object; the radar will be picking up a natural feature such as a coastline.

I am not aware of instances where radar operators have detected an object, judged it to be solid, and not been able to identify it; if there have been such cases then they probably relate to weather balloons. The point I was trying to make in my 18th February letter was that we have never detected a structured craft flying in UK airspace, that has remained unidentified.

Although, as you point out, there is a chain of radar stations stretching across NATO, it is not the case that they all automatically exchange data, so it is not correct to say that the Ministry of Defence must have been aware of radar detections that occurred during the 1989/90 UFO sightings in Belgium. When I said, in my letter dated 24th February, that I remembered only one reference to radar sightings, I made it quite clear that this was a personal recollection of comments made in Timothy Good's book *Alien Liaison*.

I really must stress again that while the sightings that you are researching are doubtless very interesting, they occurred outside UK airspace, and as such lie outside our remit.

I wish you the best of luck with your continuing attempts to get to the bottom of this mystery.

Yours sincerely
Derek Sheffield

Mr Pope's letter confirmed the facts on radar detections and concurred with the Belgian Ministry of Defence position. As

Mr Pope and, by inference, the UK Ministry of Defence purported to have little knowledge of the Belgian incident I decided to impart the facts, as I knew them, in my reply to him, a copy of which was sent to the Secretary of State for Defence.

2nd October 1993

Dear Mr Pope,

Thank you for your very welcome letter of confirmation that radar will only positively detect a radar wavelength or an object of opacity and substance.

This is also the opinion of the Belgian Air Force and the Belgian Minister of Defence.

As you apparently have no knowledge of the Belgian incidents, I trust that you will not think me patronising if I give you details of one of these.

On the night of the 30/31st March 1990 at 23h.00 (local time) in the vicinity of Wavre (south-east of Brussels), many witnesses reported a configuration of lights in the sky.

As a result of these reports and their confirmation by members of the Belgian gendarmerie, the Belgian radar stations at Semmerzake and Glons were alerted. They confirmed a strong signal where indicated by witnesses. This was also confirmed by the German radar station at Vedem.

These confirmations by the three main radar stations were considered to be a threat to Belgian national security.

The Belgian Air Force were alerted to scramble two F-16 aircraft to intercept these targets.

These two aircraft were vectored to their targets by the two radar stations involved.

13 interceptions were made. Radar lock-on was achieved on each occasion, times varying from 0.1 sec to 45.0 sec.

Video film is available of on-board radar confirming these interceptions. Acceleration figures were recorded of this object from 150 knots to 1,000 knots in ± $^{1}/_{2}$ sec, and a rate of descent from 10,000 ft to 4,000 ft in 2 secs. Pursuit and interception continued for over 1 hour.

2,600 witnesses provided statements. 75 of these were Belgian police officers.

The Belgian Minister of Defence, Guy Coëme, admitted the existence of these flying objects; he stated in the Belgian Parliament that *all* hypotheses could be excluded – he did not know what these flying objects were. This was confirmed on the 26th May by Leo Delcroix, the present Belgian Minister of Defence.

At one period of interception, both F-16 aircraft were in pursuit of one of these unidentified objects, which was on a westerly heading, towards UK airspace at speeds of +1,000 knots per hour.

This incident was regarded by the Belgian authorities as a major alert. Actual time to infringe UK airspace would have been less than six minutes.

I note your observation that because the Belgian detections were outside UK airspace they were beyond your area of remit.

Whilst I acknowledge that this was so, I do not see how it is possible to ensure UK security by such rigid parameters.

When an unknown object of some substance – treated as a threat by the armed forces of a fellow NATO member state – is only six minutes from our national boundary and is being pursued at speeds in excess of 1,000 knots per hour by two interceptor aircraft, then it is not practicable or possible, in the interests of security, to impose statutory limits involving national boundaries.

I have discussed your observations with a NATO colleague, and find it difficult to accept that – as you say in your letter – even though we are part of NATO Air Defence Ground Environment and are covered to some extent by AWAC aircraft, there are occasions when we are not advised by the NATO 80 radar station complex of possible intrusions into our airspace.

It would seem, however, that because this incident was regarded by the Belgian military as a major alert, we should have been notified by Glons CRC (NADGE) of their radar detection. There would seem little point of a radar defence system that did not do this.

It would seem incredible that the Ministry of Defence were not aware of this imminent infringement of our national security, particularly when an event of such magnitude was being enacted only six minutes away.

Your comments would be appreciated.

Yours sincerely,
Derek Sheffield

Mr Pope replied to my letter on his own behalf and on behalf of the Secretary of State for Defence – an interesting letter:

13th October 1993

Dear Mr Sheffield,

Thank you for your letter dated 2nd October, copied to the Secretary of State for Defence. Please treat this reply as the response to both letters.

I was interested in the information that you provided, but I have yet to see any official documents relating to these UFO sightings. We have no record that the Belgians (or anybody else) passed us any information relating these sightings, and can only assume that the appropriate military authorities did not believe that there was any threat to the UK.

I can assure you that the Air Defence of the UK is taken very seriously; you may recall from the days of the cold war that Soviet aircraft used to test our defences on a regular basis, by attempting to penetrate the UK Air Defence Region. You may also recall the very effective way in which the RAF detected and intercepted these aircraft.

Yours sincerely,

N. Pope

A curious letter: it is what it does *not* say that makes it interesting.

One must wonder at this letter.

Why did the Ministry of Defence not know of the Belgian sightings when they were so widely reported in the continental press?

Why have they not seen any official documents relating to these incidents? I have obtained an abundance of these without any problems from the Belgian Defence Minister, the Belgian Ministry of Defence and the Belgian Air Force.

I find the fact that the Ministry of Defence have not been passed any information relating to these detections as extremely odd. Glons CRC (NADGE) radar was on a major alert involving F-16 interceptor aircraft. *We are part of NADGE* (NATO Air Defence Ground Environment). This object was six minutes from our air space and closing at more than 1,000 knots. Not only would I have thought that notification of some kind would have been mandatory, but I wonder if the Ministry of Defence have now questioned this omission?

Although NADGE detection was involved in a full alert only six minutes away, by what premise was it that NATO considered that there was *no* threat to the UK?

It would seem that NADGE considered the detection serious enough to involve military pursuit aircraft in Belgium, but not serious enough to inform either the RAF or the Ministry of Defence in the United Kingdom

One wonders whether the NATO Air Defence Ground Environment is more involved in this situation than they would care to admit.

A FURTHER LETTER TO THE MINISTRY OF DEFENCE

23 October 1993

Dear Mr Pope,

Thank you for your reply of the 13th October on behalf of yourself and the Secretary of State for Defence.

I would like to comment on the first paragraph of your letter.

I wonder why the Ministry of Defence did not know of the unidentified Belgian radar detections, when they were so widely reported in the Continental press?

I also wonder why the Ministry of Defence have not seen any official documents relating to these incidents? I have obtained an abundance of these from the Belgian Defence Minister, the Belgian Ministry of Defence and the Belgian Air Force.

I find the fact that the Ministry of Defence have not been passed any information relating to these detections extremely odd. Glons CRC (NADGE) radar was on a major alert involving F-16 interceptor aircraft. *We are part of NADGE* (NATO Air Defence Ground Environment). This object was six minutes from our air space and closing at 1,000+kts. Not only would I have thought that notification of some kind was obligatory, but I wonder why the Ministry do not now query this omission? Although a NADGE detection was involved in a full alert only six minutes away, by what premise did NATO consider that there was *no* threat to the UK?

It would seem that NADGE considered the detection serious enough to involve military pursuit aircraft in Belgium, but not serious enough to inform either the RAF or the Ministry of Defence in the United Kingdom.

Your statement that: 'I can only assume that the appropriate military authorities did not believe that there was any threat to the UK' causes me some apprehension. Do you not *know* whether this is so? This would indicate that you are not advised on all radar detections unless they are considered a threat to the UK by the military authorities?

Whilst I have no grounds whatsoever to doubt your honesty, I sincerely trust that you will accept my observation that your statements simply do not fit the facts.

It would seem that your position as a Ministry of Defence spokesman on radar matters is seriously compromised by other organisations.

One wonders whether the NATO Air Defence Ground Environment is more involved in this situation than they would care to admit?

Your comments would be appreciated.

Yours sincerely
Derek Sheffield

The reference to 'the appropriate military authorities' in the main paragraph of this letter from the Ministry of Defence can only mean either the NATO Air Defence Ground Environment (NADGE), or the British military authorities.

The chance of this reference applying to the British military authorities is remote. Mr Pope of the Ministry of Defence states that all UFO reports (and consequently any UFO radar detections) are co-ordinated by him, and therefore *any* advice of a radar detection – from whatever source – by the British military authorities would have had to be passed to the Ministry of Defence.

This reference to 'the appropriate military authorities' can only mean the NATO Air Defence Ground Environment. It implies that NATO decided that their radar detection did not constitute a threat to our national security and did not warrant informing the British military authorities.

It could also mean, of course, that the British military authorities *were* advised by NATO but decided that the radar detection did not warrant further action.

If either of these two instances were followed by NATO or the British armed forces, then one wonders by what premise their decision was made? *It can only mean that for them to have made a decision on an object only six minutes away, they must have been aware of the nature of this phenomenon.*

Consequently I sent the following letter to NATO in Brussels:

20th October 1993

Dear Sirs,

I am an author and am researching a book on the Belgian aerial phenomena of 1989/90.

I have been advised by the Belgian Air Force of a detection by Glons CRC (NADGE) radar on the night of 30th March 1990.

This detection was a major security alert involving aircraft of the Belgian Air Force. The incident lasted for 1 hour.

At 22h 39 an interception occurred during which radar lock-on was achieved by both F-16 interceptors. This lasted for 45.9 seconds.

At this time the unidentified target was travelling on a westerly heading at speeds in excess of 1,000 knots.

In terms of time, this represented a closing period of 6 minutes with British national airspace.

I have no wish to infringe security matters, but I would like to know why the British Ministry of Defence or armed forces were not advised of this matter?

Your co-operation would be appreciated.

Yours faithfully,
Derek Sheffield

No reply was forthcoming within six weeks of sending this letter so I sent a reminder.

29th November 1993

Reference: First reminder of letter sent on 20th October 1993 concerning NADGE detection on 30th March 1990

Dear Sirs,

On the advice of your British office I sent you a letter six weeks ago (on 20th October) requesting non-classified information on a NADGE detection in Belgium on 30th March 1990.

It does not take six weeks to reply to a simple enquiry and I would request a reply at your earliest convenience.

For your information I would advise that my original enquiry, this letter, and any reply that you make will form consecutive pages in the book that I am researching on the Belgian phenomena.

Your immediate co-operation would be appreciated.

Yours faithfully,

Derek Sheffield

There has been no reply from NATO to either of these letters.

CHAPTER TWENTY-ONE

The Penultimate Question

The Ministry of Defence, through Mr N. Pope, replied to my letter, gently informing me that there was little point in pursuing my present line of enquiry . . .

12th November 1993

Dear Mr Sheffield,
    Thank you for your letter dated 23rd October.
    You asked why the Ministry of Defence did not know about the Belgian UFO sightings, and had not seen any official documents relating to them. The simple answer is, as I have explained before, that they did not occur within UK airspace. Although these UFO sightings did indeed occur close to the UK, we would not have been notified unless the Belgians believed there was a threat. For obvious security reasons, I will not enter into any discussions about the range and capabilities of our Air Defences. What I can tell you is that I have sought specialist Air Defence advice when answering your letters, and have been assured that there is nothing that you have described that would be regarded as a threat to the UK.
    Although I would be happy to answer any new questions you may have, I think we have now reached the point where there is little more that I can provide on the questions that you have posed to date.
                   Yours sincerely,
                   N. Pope

By now my European Parliamentary Question was being considered by the Petitions Committee, which I thought might add weight to my case. I decided to press Mr Pope on the question of national security.

20th November 1993

Dear Mr Pope,
    Thank you for your letter dated 12th November.

THE PENULTIMATE QUESTION

I note your observation that we have now reached the point where there is little more that you can provide on the questions that I have posed to date.

I suppose that to a degree you are correct. We have come a long way since your original letter D/Sec (AS) of 24th February 1993 in which you stated 'the key consideration is evidence, without which a threat to national security cannot be judged to exist. Reports of lights or shapes in the sky cannot be classed as evidence, even if the sightings cannot be positively identified.'

Your statement in letter D/Sec(AS)12/3 of the 29th September 1993 that 'radar will only positively detect a radar wavelength of an object of opacity and substance' confirms that the NADGE radar detections in Belgium in 1989/90 by Semmerzake, Glons and Vedem radars were indeed confirmation of unidentified aerial phenomena of opacity and substance. A simple telephone call to NATO would confirm that fact.

Your recent statement in letter D/Sec(AS)12/3 of 12th November 1993, that 'Although these UFO sightings did indeed occur close to the UK', finally qualifies the fact that the Ministry of Defence – when these two statements are taken in conjunction – have now accepted (as have the Belgian government) the authenticity of the Belgian phenomena as being unidentified flying objects that are of opacity and substance.

Having, by a slow process of reason, finally reached this conclusion – and as I am quite sure that this is not a question that would contravene national security – I would ask my penultimate question.

It is simply: *By what premise have your specialist Air Defence advisers reached the conclusion that these phenomena are NOT a threat to national security?*

I would advise that you should inform the Secretary of State for Defence of this correspondence as I have requested Sir Keith Speed, MP, to table this same question to the Minister in the House of Commons.

For your interest: I have been advised by Egon Klepsch, President of the European Parliament, that my report asking for an inquiry into the Belgian phenomena has now been forwarded to the Petitions Committee for their consideration.

Your reply would be appreciated.

Yours sincerely,
Derek Sheffield

UFO: A DEADLY CONCEALMENT

I began to detect a certain amount of impatience with my persistence in Mr Pope's reply . . .

26th November 1993

Dear Mr Sheffield,

Thank you for your letter dated 20th November.

I have to say that the extracts that you quote from my letters are selective; for example, you will recall that I have explained to you on a number of occasions that a radar return does *not* necessarily indicate the presence of a structured craft; radar returns can be caused by clouds, computer error, interference between two radar systems, Anomalous Propagation, or even by flocks of birds.

In view of the above, your assumption that we have accepted the Belgian UFO sightings as being 'unidentified flying objects that are of opacity and substance' is not correct.

In answer to your specific question, Air Defence experts concluded that the Belgian UFO sightings posed no threat to the UK because there was no evidence of any such threat.

Yours sincerely

N. Pope

I felt I should refute the accusations of selectivity in this letter and decided to remind Mr Pope of his previous statements in the numerous letters we had exchanged in our 10-month correspondence, and to press him for a straight answer to the question of a conceived threat to national security and notification of such from the European radar complex.

6th December 1993

Dear Mr Pope,

Thank you for your letter of the 26th November.

I note your observation that I am being selective with quotes from your letters. On the contrary, I would suggest that in your last letter, the selectivity is yours.

Allow me to refresh your memory. Whilst you have previously stated all the reasons quoted in your letter to illustrate that a radar return does not necessarily indicate the presence of a structured craft, you have omitted to say that you qualified these reasons at the conclusion of the paragraph by stating 'it is easy for skilled operators to distinguish between these sort of returns, and the track made by a solid object such as an aircraft'.

As the very first line of your letter states 'I agree that radar will only detect a radar wavelength of an object of opacity and substance', I can hardly be accused of selectivity: these words are yours and not mine.

The detections made by the NATO Air Defence Ground Environment radars at – not *one*, but *five!* – radar stations at Semmerzake, Glons CRC, Bertem and St Hubert in Belgium, and Vedem in Germany, were made by highly skilled operatives well able to distinguish between the anomalies that you quote and true radar reflections. Indeed, two F-16 interceptors of the Belgian Air Force would hardly have been scrambled on fifteen separate occasions if the radar operatives had not been *sure* of their detections (these were also confirmed on 13 occasions by radar lock-on by the pursuing aircraft).

The overwhelming evidence of the NADGE detections proves your point that skilled operators are able to distinguish between false and true returns and must be taken as positive confirmation of the presence of unidentified flying objects of opacity and substance.

In view of the above, I do not understand your consequent retractions, which are not commensurate with the facts.

The fact that these radar detections were confirmed by NATO, the Belgian Minister of Defence and the Belgian Air Force, would prompt me to ask: If NADGE considered the radar detections above Belgium on 30/31st March 1990 to be conclusive proof of objects of opacity and substance and a threat to the national security of the Belgian state, why did your air defence experts conclude that there was no threat to the security of the UK?

In view of the conclusive proof now obtained from the NATO and Belgian agencies, the answer from your Air Defence experts that there was no threat to the UK because there was no evidence of any such threat simply will not suffice. NATO and the Belgians say that there was a threat, and your Air Defence experts say that there was not. I would request a detailed answer that takes into account the NATO and Belgian detections and observations.

Your statement in letter D/Sec(AS)12/3 of the 12th November 1993, 'Although these UFO sightings did indeed occur close to the UK', is your comment and not mine.

I would refer you to the whole context of your letter which discusses why your ministry did not know of the Belgian sightings; it quotes, 'that they did not occur within UK airspace. Although these UFO sightings did indeed occur close to the UK, we would not have been notified unless the Belgians believed there was a threat.'

As stated at the beginning of this letter, the question of selectivity does not arise; I am only able to comment on the words that you have written. The wording of your letter could only be interpreted by the world at large as a clear indication that there was a detection of an entity of opacity and substance in the skies above Belgium; if you now choose to amend them, then that is your prerogative, but this now strongly implies evasion on the point at issue.

Yours sincerely,
Derek Sheffield

It would now seem that the Secretariat (Air Staff) 2a, Room 8245 of the Ministry of Defence, Main Building, Whitehall, London SW1A 2HB, are issuing contradictory statements. It must also now become quite apparent to my reader that their attitude is becoming transparently obvious.

Having first said that radar signals could be many things other than true detections, they then stated that a competent radar operative could easily distinguish between these and returns from a solid object of opacity.

They then stated that there has never been a case within our national boundaries where a radar detection could not be explained by natural phenomena. Evidence from airline pilots shows this to be untrue.

When it was stated that the security of the realm could not be restricted to national boundaries and their comments on the Belgian incidents were requested, they denied any knowledge of these sightings.

When it was pointed out that a major alert was in force because detections by NATO Air Defence Ground Environment radars were confirmed by the Belgian Air Force, that an unidentified object was six minutes from our national boundary and closing at speeds in excess of 1000 knots, their reply was that they would have been advised by the Belgians should there have been any threat to our security.

Apart from the fact that the Belgians at that time were in a full alert situation involving interceptions by their own military F-16 aircraft, we are part of NATO Air Defence Ground Environment – an 80 radar station defence complex that covers all Europe, all stations being interconnected; it is just not possible that we were *not* advised of these incidents.

It is a *deception* to say, as did the Ministry of Defence, that a major alert in Belgium involving positive detections by five main radar stations of our own defence system, confirmed by 15 positive interceptions by military aircraft of the Belgian Air Force, would not have been considered by the Belgians to have been a threat to our national security.

It is a *deception* when the Ministry of Defence state that they had no knowledge of the Belgian detections, yet then state that these UFO sightings did indeed occur close to the UK.

It is a *deception* when the Ministry of Defence state that they had no knowledge of the Belgian sightings, and that air defence experts concluded that the Belgian UFO sightings posed no threat to the UK because there was no evidence of any such threat. Apart from the fact that our own radar defence system and the Belgian military showed quite clearly that there *was* a threat, this is an admission in itself, a direct indication that not only did they know of the Belgian sightings and radar detections, but also they knew what they were.

In view of these facts, all corroborated in the letters contained in this document, I cannot see what possible reply the Ministry of Defence can give to the question: Taking into account the NATO and Belgian detections of these phenomena, if NADGE considered the radar detections above Belgium on 30–31 March 1990 to be conclusive proof of

objects of opacity and substance, and the subsequent interceptions by Belgian Air Force F-16s as proof of their hostile
classification, how was it that UK air defence experts
concluded that there was no threat to the security of the
United Kingdom when they did not know what they were,
and were not advised of them?

Any further comments from the Ministry of Defence will
now only compound their contradictions, and make more
obvious their highly questionable attitude to a perfectly open
question. Any evasions will only point to their involvement.
Their reply was conclusive:

9th December 1993

Dear Mr Sheffield,
    Thank you for your letter of the 6th December.
    I am afraid that there is nothing that can be added to
the replies you have already received on the points that
you have raised.
                Yours sincerely,
                N. Pope

In short, the expected evasion to a simple question, and the
only reply that could be made by a Ministry of Defence in a
confusion of contradictions.

Now I will explain a case of deception and the
involvement of the Ministry of Defence in that deception.

MR NICHOLAS POPE OF THE MINISTRY OF DEFENCE

As will become evident in later chapters, towards the end of
my correspondence with Mr Pope of the MOD, I entered into
a correspondence with Admiral of the Fleet The Lord Hill
Norton, GCB, former Chief of Defence Staff, and a former
senior NATO commander. In a letter to me which is
reproduced on page 217 he states: 'I disregard your letter
from Pope, because he is a very junior civil servant'.

The 2 July 1995 edition of the *Mail on Sunday* carried an
article which was most illuminating. Although the article,
and its accompanying headline, tended to belittle the subject

with mention of *ET*, Mr Spock and pointy ears, and 'little green men', the main point of the article was quite serious. The headline read: 'WHITEHALL SHOCK AS ITS CHIEF ALIEN-WATCHER ADMITS: I BELIEVE IN UFOs'. The article read as follows:

> Nick Pope headed the Secretariat (Air Staff) 2a office, with a brief to deal with inquiries about flying saucers and other unexplained phenomena. It was his calm voice which reassured the many members of the public who called to report strange lights in the sky. . . . But, in possibly the most embarrassing turnaround in Ministry of Defence history, Mr Pope has gone over to the other side. . . . Mr Pope said, 'I came into that job as an open-minded sceptic and I came out a believer.'

It goes on to say:

> he was convinced by the details of a small number of British sightings which have so far defied conventional explanation. 'Probably the best example is the Rendlesham Forest case in December 1980 where some kind of object came down in Suffolk near the RAF bases at Woodbridge and Bentwaters. This is now regarded as the best attested case of a UFO crash outside the US.'

You may remember that in his letter to me of 29 September 1993 (in reference to radar detections) Mr Pope stated:

> The point I was trying to make in my 18th February letter was that we have never detected a structured craft flying in UK airspace, that has remained unidentified.

In my opinion, his statements in the newspaper article and his statements in his correspondence with me are entirely contradictory. If the remarks by Mr Pope in the newspaper article are reported accurately, then the only conclusion possible is that when he made statements in his correspondence to me *he knew them to be untrue*. If this is the case then there can be no doubt that it was a deliberate deception on behalf of the Ministry of Defence.

There is a more sinister scenario which can be drawn from the July 1995 revelations from Mr Pope. I have felt, as more and more information is being fed to the public on this subject, that this is all part of a process by which we are being conditioned to accept the manifestation of the entity on this planet. We are dealing with an intelligence that is far in advance of anything that we could imagine. Is Mr Pope's statement part of this indoctrination?

CHAPTER TWENTY-TWO

A Commons Question

During the protracted correspondence with Mr Pope in the last quarter of 1993, the realization that I was unlikely to get a definitive answer to the main thrust of my enquiries regarding notification of, and reaction to, the Belgian incident of 30–31 March 1990 by the British authorities prompted me to request my Member of Parliament, Sir Keith Speed, to table a question to the Minister of Defence in the House of Commons.

The following letter was sent to Sir Keith Speed at the time of my final letter to the MOD, and Mr Pope was made aware of it at that time.

7th November 1993
Reference: NADGE detection on 30th March 1990

Enclosure: Letter to Robert Ramsay, Directorate-General for the European Parliament. The Director-General. Copies to: The Belgian Prime Minister, Ministry of Defence, Air Force, Gendarmerie

Dear Sir Keith,

I am an author and am researching a book on the Belgian aerial phenomena of 1989/90.

I have been advised by the Belgian Air Force and the Belgian Minister of Defence of a positive detection by Semmerzake (Belgium), Vedem (Germany), and Glons (Belgium) CRC (NADGE) radars on the night of 30th March 1990.

This detection was a major security alert involving interceptor aircraft of the Belgian Air Force. It lasted for 1 hour and 5 minutes.

A total of 13 interceptions were registered. At 22h 39m a positive radar contact was made by two pursuing aircraft, during which radar lock-on was achieved by both F-16 interceptors.

This lasted for 45.9 seconds.

At this time the unidentified target was travelling on a westerly heading towards British airspace at speeds in excess of 1000 knots.

This is a closing time of 6 minutes to the British national boundary. I have no wish to infringe security matters – and the following requests in no way do this – but I would like to table a question to the Minister of Defence in the House of Commons.

Concerning this confirmed radar detection by NATO Air Defence Ground Environment and the imminent intrusion of this detected object into British airspace:

(1) Were the British Ministry of Defence aware of this NADGE detected threat to British airspace?
(2) Did our armed forces or those of NATO deem that there was NO security risk?
(3) If this was so – bearing in mind the existing major alert – by what premise was this decision made?

> Yours sincerely
> Derek Sheffield

Copies of this letter and its enclosure have been requested by Carol Davies of *Adscene*, the reporter who was a main witness to the north Kent sightings, Jeni Balow of the *Kentish Express*, who has covered this story in detail, and the *Kent & Sussex Courier*, which has given this matter much local coverage. Sir Keith's reply was not encouraging . . .

> 16th November 1993

Dear Mr Sheffield,

Thank you for your recent letter about airborne interception of unidentified objects over Belgium.

The questions you pose are not suitable, for technical reasons, to be tabled, and in any event they cannot be tabled before 25th November. I have, however, written to the Minister at the Ministry of Defence, with a copy of your letter, and as soon as I receive a reply I shall be in touch with you again.

> Yours sincerely,
> Lorna Day, CC-Sir Keith Speed

Sir Keith's letter was not clear. I saw no technicalities in tabling my questions. I wrote for clarification . . .

A COMMONS QUESTION

5th December 1993

Dear Sir Keith,

Thank you for your letter of 16th November 1993.

I wonder if you could advise me why the questions that I pose on the Belgian NATO detections in 1990, are not suitable – for technical reasons – to be tabled in the House?

I must confess to some confusion. Your letter states that my questions are not suitable to be tabled, but then implies that they can be tabled after the 25th November 1993.

Your guidance would be appreciated.

Yours sincerely
Derek Sheffield

A reply was received from Sir Keith's private secretary, which once again did not fully answer my questions.

14th December 1993

Dear Mr Sheffield,

Sir Keith has asked me to thank you for your letter of the 5th and to confirm they are not tabled for the reasons he stated earlier and this also applies for after the 25th November. As you know he has taken them up with the Minister and is awaiting a reply; when he hears he will of course be in touch with you.

Yours sincerely,
P. V. Clarke, Private Secretary

I felt that a further letter to Sir Keith was necessary which outlined my reasons for requiring a question to be tabled in the House of Commons, and again requesting clarification of the 'technical reasons' that prevented my questions being tabled.

26th December 1993

Dear Sir Keith,

I apologise for a degree of persistence.

I specifically requested a question to be tabled in the House because I am not satisfied with the obvious evasions that I am getting from the Ministry of Defence.

It is obvious that any answer from the Minister will be as a direct result of consultation with the Ministry of Defence whose answers are not commensurate with the facts.

I attach pages 114/15/16 of a manuscript of a book that I am writing on the Belgian phenomena; this is a copy of a letter written on the 6th December 1993 to the Ministry of Defence.

Their contradictions form part of this book.

I trust they will give you some idea of the complexity of the situation.

If the reply given by the Minister is as indicated, I would then request a tabled question as originally sought.

It is essential in my application to the Petitions Committee of the European Parliament that I obtain a clear and detailed explanation on the positive NADGE major alert in Belgium, and the opinion of the British Ministry of Defence air defence experts that there was no risk to our own national security.

Could you please advise me what the 'technical reasons' are for not raising a question in the House?

Yours sincerely,
Derek Sheffield

A reply was received a few days later which went some way to explaining the situation and requesting my patience.

31st December 1993

Dear Mr Sheffield,

Thank you for your further letter of the 26th December.

While I note the points you make, you do not appear to understand that Parliamentary Questions can be answered, and probably would be, in one or two brief lines, and unless I am very lucky and happen to be in the first ten questions of the day and it is down for an oral answer, I would not have the right of a supplementary. For your information there are normally about 150 questions a day tabled.

I will therefore await a reply from the Minister, to whom I wrote some weeks ago, and will let you have a copy as soon as I receive it. I will then see what needs to be done.

Yours sincerely
Keith Speed

As will become evident in the following chapter, I made contact with a former Chief of Defence Staff who had also been a senior NATO commander. I replied to Sir Keith's letter to inform him of information I had received from that source.

10th January 1994

Dear Sir Keith,

Thank you for your letter of the 31st December. I am not well versed in the intricacies of parliamentary procedures; your letter has explained these with great clarity. I am sure that your approach is the better one.

My concern in making the point was the degree of evasion and contradiction that has been emanating from the MOD. One tends to suspect a degree of covertness in this matter, and associates ministerial delays with this principle.

For your interest, I have now received (from the highest authority in NATO) confirmation of the fact that 'any radar detection by European NADGE would have been passed immediately to UK NADGE. That's how the system works!' My source is unimpeachable, and is in direct contrast to the statement by the Ministry of Defence that they had no knowledge of the Belgian detections.

Thank you for your information.

Yours sincerely,
Derek Sheffield

The delaying tactic was brought to the fore. Having received no further reply by the end of January, the by now familiar reminder was necessary:

27th January 1993

Dear Sir Keith,

Just a gentle reminder: It is now over 10 weeks since I first raised the matter with you of a question to the Minister of Defence on radar detections and airborne interceptions in 1990.

Whilst I appreciate the difficulty of a reply from a Minister on a Ministry of Defence statement which I now suspect to be untrue, it would save undue embarrassment in another place if a reply of some kind could be made with some urgency.

My application to the Petitions Committee of the

European Parliament has now been accepted. I have asked that it be linked with an already approved request on the same subject by Snr Tullio Regge, MEP. It will be seen that this matter will very soon be under discussion by the European Parliament.

The Belgian Minister of Defence, Ministry of Defence, and Air Force, have already provided confirmatory evidence; as has a very senior NATO source. This has provided the link between the Continental radars and our own; and consequently the UK Ministry of Defence. They have denied any knowledge of these detections.

An urgent reply is requested.

Yours sincerely
Derek Sheffield

Keith Speed replied with a brief letter making it clear that there was little point in continuing the correspondence:

31 January 1993

Dear Mr Sheffield,

Thank you for your further letter of the 27th and I agree with you, a reply should have been forthcoming from the Minister by now. I have been and will continue to chase this up, and hope to come back to you very shortly.

Yours sincerely,
Keith Speed

It must now have become very obvious that:

1. Despite pressure at the highest level, a routine question to the Minister of Defence has not been answered for three months.
2. The Ministry of Defence have avoided answering a question repeatedly put to them.
3. NATO have not replied to letters sent to them.
4. There has been no reply from the United Nations headquarters.
5. Mail to America is intercepted before it leaves the country and returned by the Royal Mail.
6. All enquiries on this subject to the USA are directed to the CIA.

7. There have been no replies to a general press release sent to Europe.

8. There has been no reply from an editor at *The Times* newspaper (see Chapter 25).

9. The strong American influence on this subject, with NATO, NADGE and the United Nations, combined with the involvement of the Central Intelligence Agency and the Ministry of Defence, leads one to suspect motives of a clandestine nature.

The evidence indicates that these agencies are conspiring with each other in a deception of massive proportions.

CHAPTER TWENTY-THREE

Rational Deductions

That is as far as things have progressed at present. From the finding of an old newspaper in a wardrobe of a Paris hotel, to a subsequent enquiry to the Central Radar Establishment at West Drayton, we have uncovered a real bag of worms.

After nine letters of evasion from the Ministry of Defence in which they stated that radar detections could not be relied upon, and that unidentified radar detections could be anything *except* material objects, they finally made the grudging admission that radar will only positively detect a radar wavelength of an object of opacity and substance.

This statement finally opened the door on the Belgian incidents, the detection of unidentified flying objects by NATO radar, and the admission by the Ministry of Defence that they had no knowledge of these detections. They said that they can only assume that the appropriate military authorities did not believe that there was any threat to the United Kingdom. This is an admission that decisions for acting on unidentified radar returns, and the reporting of these detections, are at the discretion of NATO, and not the Ministry of Defence.

A direct consequence of this reasoning must be that the Ministry of Defence strongly imply that they are not aware of *all* radar detections because they are not told of them. This can only mean that the Ministry of Defence are not able to give a truthful answer on any question concerning the radar detection of unidentified flying objects, simply because they are not told of them.

I do not believe that when there is a major radar detection by NATO Air Defence Ground Environment, judged to be serious enough to alert two F-16 combat aircraft of the Belgian Air Force on a 65-minute, 13-interception mission, the

Royal Air Force would not have advised the Ministry of Defence had it known about it.

One can only therefore assume that the NATO Air Defence Ground Environment – an American-controlled organization – for reasons of its own did not want the Royal Air Force or the Ministry of Defence to know of this incident.

Being unable to obtain any reply from the Brussels headquarters of NATO (on the question of whether the British Ministry of Defence were advised by NADGE of the Belgian detections in 1989/90), I was at a loss to obtain the information needed to prove deception on the part of the British Ministry of Defence. Admittedly the case was proven that an entity had appeared above Belgium at that time, but what was needed was absolute proof that the Ministry of Defence *knew* of these detections and were concealing their evidence. A connection was needed, establishing that Belgian and German radar stations had informed the British Ministry of Defence of their detections. This would then prove their deception, and, when the reason for their deception was known, would also prove a charge of conspiracy. In short, a definite statement from an unimpeachable source at the top level of NATO.

This came – like manna from heaven – in the form of a newspaper article that mentioned Admiral Lord Hill-Norton. It would seem that this august lord had nailed his colours to the mast by indicating that he suspected governmental secrecy on the subject of these aerial phenomena. While I found this article interesting, it was what came next that made me sit up and take notice. It said simply that not only had Admiral Lord Hill-Norton been a former Chief of Defence Staff, *but he had also been a senior NATO commander.*

One could not ask for a higher authority than that of a lord of the realm who was not only a Chief of Defence Staff but also a senior NATO commander.

I resolved to try to establish a contact.

This proved a simple matter: a telephone call to the House of Lords for an address to which to write, and a telephone enquiry for a number that fitted the name and address.

I telephoned Admiral Hill-Norton.

The Admiral proved to be of great assistance. After explaining who I was, I gave a brief outline of my application to the European Parliament. I explained the unenthusiastic – even obstructive – attitude of the Ministry of Defence, their contradictory statements on this phenomenon, and their denial of any knowledge of the Belgian detections. I said that the fact that NADGE radars had alerted the Belgian Air Force was proof of a major alert. We are part of the NADGE defence system and therefore must have known of this alert. I wanted confirmation from a senior NATO commander that the Ministry of Defence *must* have been advised of this situation. I said that I would understand and respect any reservation on his part should he decline to reply.

Admiral Hill-Norton was engagingly blunt. 'Of course they would have known,' he said. 'The UK Air Defence Ground Environment are part of the European complex, that's how the system works!'

I informed him that I had asked through my Member of Parliament, Sir Keith Speed, for a question to be tabled to the Minister of Defence in the House of Commons, asking whether the Ministry of Defence had been advised by NATO of the Belgian detections. I had emphasized that I would not accept the contradictory statements of his ministry. Sir Keith had replied that Commons questions were usually answered in very brief statements and that more was to be gained by written replies; he advised that we wait for the Minister's reply before passing judgement. I advised Sir Keith that should this be unsatisfactory I would press for a question to be tabled as originally requested.

Admiral Lord Hill-Norton, at this point, suggested that should I have any difficulty in raising a question in the Commons, then, together with the Earl of Clancarty, he would raise a question in the House of Lords. Admiral Lord Hill-Norton expressed an interest in my report and requested that I send him a copy and asked that I keep him informed of any developments. This I have done.

A LETTER TO ADMIRAL LORD HILL-NORTON

9th January 1994

Dear Admiral Hill-Norton,

Thank you for our recent telephone discussion. Having had no reply or even acknowledgement from several letters sent to NATO I seemed to have come to a dead end.

As you know, there is a marked lack of co-operation from the MOD. I have, however, now proven the existence of an entity above Belgium in 1989/90.

The crux of my proof is the positive detection by four radar stations in Belgium and one in Germany. On the detections by these stations, a major alert was instigated and interceptions by the Belgian Air Force were made. These interceptions continued for over 1 hour. At a precise time, this object was on a westerly heading six minutes away from the UK national boundary. Its speed at this time was in excess of 1,000 knots and two F-16 fighters of the Belgian Air Force were in pursuit. All these facts were well substantiated both visually and physically by many thousands of witnesses both civil and military, and confirmed by the Belgian Minister of Defence and armed forces.

The radar stations involved are part of NATO (NADGE), who do not reply to my letters. The MOD state that they have no knowledge of the Belgian detections; they observe that lights or shapes in the sky, even if confirmed by radar, cannot be taken as evidence and must therefore be deemed not to exist. My problem has therefore been to establish that the UK NADGE (and consequently the MOD) *did* have knowledge of these events and are guilty of deception.

Our conversation would seem to confirm this.

As the knowledge of the existence of this entity cannot now be in question – indeed the MOD now state that their air defence experts did not consider the Belgian phenomena to be a risk to UK national security – the penultimate question must be: by what premise did their air defence experts consider that this object was *not* a threat to UK national security?

It is this question that the MOD refuse to answer.

The final question of course will be, why do the United Nations, NATO, the American and British establishments, the armed forces and media of these countries, *all* deny

the existence of a phenomenon that is *known* to exist?
The answer is frightening.

I am an author. For your interest I am at present
compiling a record of this whole issue; this will form
my next book and will be a completely factual record of
events. My application to the European Parliament for an
inquiry into the Belgian sightings will form part of
this story.

I have been informed that my report is now being
considered by the Petitions Committee for submission to
the Parliament. I have asked that my petition (no.
990/93) be linked to the application by Snr Tullio
Regge, MEP, for a centre to be established for the
monitoring of these objects. My reasoning is that one
must first prove the existence of these phenomena, before
progressing further.

I enclose a copy of my report to the European
Parliament. Anticipating problems I prepared six of
these for submission. My apprehensions proved to be
correct.

Two of these disappeared to wrong addresses given by
staff of British MEPs.

I have strong evidence of interception (others for no
apparent reason have gone astray). Luckily the one that
mattered eventually reached the President of the
European Parliament. I have to retain one copy for
publication in my book. I trust that you will return
this copy when you have had chance to consider it.

I will, of course, whatever the outcome, pursue this
matter to the end.

If all doors are ultimately slammed, it will not now
particularly matter. I will publish a detailed account
of the facts and let the public reach their own
conclusions.

Your comments would be appreciated.

Yours sincerely
Derek Sheffield

Admiral Lord Hill-Norton returned a prompt reply to my
letter, informing me of the *Financial Times* report on the EU
observatory for the study of UFOs and requesting copies of
the sections of my report which he felt relevant to him. I noted
his comments on Mr Pope. I found Lord Hill-Norton's letter
very encouraging.

RATIONAL DEDUCTIONS

9th January 1994

Dear Mr Sheffield,

Thank you for your letter, and the copy of your dossier for the European Parliament. I have now had time to read the report but not to study it carefully. I shall send it back to you this week by Recorded Delivery. You are not the first of my UFO correspondents to believe that his mail is tampered with, but I find it very difficult to credit.

Let me say at once that I find the account of the two Belgian sightings entirely convincing. What is unusual is that the Belgian MOD, police, Air Force and politicians have been so forthcoming. This will be useful to your cause. There was a piece in the *Financial Times* on 2.12.93, by the way, stating that the EU was to set up an observatory for the study of UFOs. They may, perhaps, have got wind of your initiative.

I must make my position clear. If NADGE had this object via the Belgian and German radar stations I consider it inconceivable that UK NADGE would not have been aware of it. I also consider it inconceivable that the Operations Division of SHAPE at Mons was not aware of it. I disregard your letter from Pope, because he is a very junior civil servant. . . . No admission will be made by the MOD until they are absolutely forced to it by one means or another. I may feel inclined to table a Written Question, or write directly to Mr Rifkind, rather depending on how you get on. You are right in saying that the question in the fourth paragraph of your letter is the one that matters.

I do not feel inclined to nit-pick my way through various bits of your Report, but I am rather uneasy (simply for verisimilitude) at the claims . . . that the F-16 pilots saw the shape of the object, and its change of shape, on their aircraft radar scopes. I was not aware that this could be seen.

As you want the Report back, would you kindly let me have a copy of Section 6 and Section 8 for my file, in due course?

I hope you will let me know later how you get on with Brussels.

Yours sincerely
Hill-Norton

I replied to Admiral Hill-Norton to thank him for his prompt reply and constructive comments, and to try to clarify some points which his letter had raised. It was gratifying to be in contact with someone of Admiral Hill-Norton's standing who was taking the matter seriously. I gathered from comments in his letter that he had been in contact with others regarding sightings of unidentified objects and thought that he would perhaps assist me with my enquiries if I reached an impasse with the Commons question.

9th January 1994

Dear Admiral Hill-Norton,

Thank you for your prompt reply to my recent letter. Your observations and comments are noted with great interest.

I have received my returned dossier and am pleased to note that your opinions are as mine. Whilst I do not necessarily discount any of the more extreme opinions, I simply believe that one must firstly prove the existence of this phenomenon. All else will then fall into place.

Because the whole American scene has been corrupted by deception and ridicule, I have taken the Belgian sightings of 1989/90 as being purely European incidents and consequently relatively untainted. Whilst this was initially so, there is evidence that the door is being slammed with great haste. Luckily, I already have my evidence from the Belgian MOD and Air Force who - now that I have instigated my request to the European Parliament - have no alternative but to back my request for an enquiry.

My case is simply that the parliamentary statement made by the Belgian Minister of Defence that 'all hypotheses can be excluded, the Minister could not tell what these flying objects were', was inconclusive. In the interests of the security of the member states, the Belgian detections should be investigated further.

I am, however, now concerned at the attitude of the Ministry of Defence, who have denied any knowledge of these detections. This is not commensurate with the facts.

There is conclusive proof of the detection of the phenomena by NADGE radars in Belgium and Germany. We are part of the same radar defensive system. My problem - in the absence of any reply from NATO Headquarters in Brussels – has been to establish a link between the radar systems of Belgium and Germany, and the radar systems of the United Kingdom. Thankfully, you have provided that link.

Your written statement, as a previous Chief of Defence Staff in the Ministry of Defence and a senior NATO commander, that: 'if NADGE had this object via the Belgian and German radar stations I consider it inconceivable that UK NADGE would not have been aware of it', is invaluable; it confirms completely that UK radar *was* aware of the Belgian alert, and as a direct consequence, *so was the Ministry of Defence!*

This connection establishes – beyond all doubt – deception by the Ministry of Defence.

It will be interesting, now that I have advised Sir Keith Speed of my confirmation from the highest authority in NATO 'that any radar detection by European NADGE would have been passed immediately to UK NADGE. That's how the system works!', to see the result that this brings.

As a point of interest, I asked Sir Keith on the 7th November 1993 – over 11 weeks ago – to table a question to the Minister. I suspect that the delay is being caused by confusion within the Ministry as to how to answer the question without admitting their knowledge and involvement in the matter!

I have not disclosed your name – this I would only do with your permission – and I trust that your promotion to the highest authority in NATO will not cause offence, but in the event of being unable to obtain a satisfactory answer from the Minister, I would appreciate the offer from yourself and Earl Clancarty to raise the matter in another place. I would add, that in the event of my application to the European Parliament being blocked in any way, then as an author I will publish this entire story. Should that situation arise, I would appreciate your endorsement of the facts as quoted in your letter.

I note your comment on the claims that the F-16 pilots 'saw the shape of the object, and its change of shape, on their aircraft radar scopes'. It would appear from the statements by the F-16 pilots that the original detections were of an oval-shaped object. When radar lock-on was attempted, the result was a distinct 'diamond image'.

I would agree with you that this is odd, but the
statement by Colonel Wilfrid De Brouwer of the Belgian
Air Force (that this detection could well have been of
an extremely strong electromagnetic force) would
indicate this entity to be a form of light: the only
medium able to traverse the distances of space, and the
phenomenon which I suspect it to be. Radar is a
wavelength akin to light; I suspect that we are dealing
with a completely unknown aspect of light that could
well produce these strange images.

Your observations are well received and constructive.
I enclose various photocopies which are self-
explanatory, and will keep you informed of developments.

Yours sincerely
Derek Sheffield

Towards the end of February I had heard nothing from Sir
Keith Speed regarding his written question to the Minister of
Defence. Being at a loss to know how to proceed I wrote again
to Admiral Hill-Norton to ask his advice and to put to him the
possibility of considering a question in the Lords as he had
suggested in an earlier letter.

20th February 1994

Dear Admiral Hill-Norton,

It is now almost 4 months since I asked Sir Keith
Speed to put a question to the Minister on a subject
that you are familiar with. On the 31st January I
received a letter from Sir Keith in which he agreed that
a reply should have been forthcoming from the Minister
by now.

He said that he has, and will continue, to chase this
up. He said that he hopes to come back to me with a
reply shortly.

It would seem strange that a reply to a question which
contains no element of national security should take
four months to answer. I would consequently request that
some consideration be given by yourself and the Earl of
Clancarty to the wording of a question to be put to the
Minister in the Lords.

It is imperative that this be put in such a manner as
to restrict any connotation of ridicule, or any evasive
answer by the Minister or the Ministry.

It is important that this be a precise question. It must give only the factual information supplied by the Belgian Air Force and the Belgian Minister of Defence, and include NADGE detections by Belgian and German radars. It must contain *no* wording capable of being interpreted in a frivolous way.

This question must be given the deepest thought; your opinions would be appreciated.

> Yours sincerely
> Derek Sheffield

It would appear from the date on the reply which Sir Keith received from the MOD that it was written, or at least signed, at the time I was writing to Admiral Hill-Norton. Sir Keith forwarded to me what he considered to be an unsatisfactory reply at the beginning of March 1994.

Sir Keith Speed's reply to me

1st March 1994

Dear Mr Sheffield,

I have had the enclosed reply from the Minister regarding the UFO sightings over Belgium in 1990.

I should point out that my letter of 31st January was a follow-up to my original letter of 16th November *which went astray in the Ministry of Defence*.

As this reply is not satisfactory, I have written again to the Minister and will come back to you again when I have heard further.

> Yours sincerely,
> Lorna Day (for Sir Keith Speed)

The MOD's reply to Sir Keith Speed

20th February 1994

Dear Keith,

Thank you for your letter of 31 January, enclosing correspondence from your constituent Mr Derek Sheffield of Cherry Tree House, Regent Street, Rolvenden.

Mr Sheffield had asked about a wave of UFO sightings that occurred over Belgium in 1990, and you asked for my views on this.

My officials have already exchanged a number of letters
with Mr Sheffield on this subject over the past year, and
wrote recently to him on 9 December 1993. There really
is little that I can add to this correspondence. While
we are aware that there were some unusual occurrences,
as your constituent says, this is a matter for the
Belgians and not for us. There is no evidence that these
UFO sightings posed any threat to the defence of the UK.
  Furthermore - 9 letters should be enough.
                  Yours ???,
                  Jeremy Hanley

I wrote to Sir Keith to thank him for his reply and the
enclosure from Jeremy Hanley. I pointed out that Hanley had
not answered my question and reiterated the point that
required an answer from the MOD.

                                        5th March 1994
Ref: Your letter 1/3/94 &Enc D/MIN (AF)/94/94
Dear Sir Keith,
  Thank you for your prompt and kind reply and enclosure
from Jeremy Hanley. I am pleased to note that you
consider the reply from Mr Hanley is not satisfactory.
It does not answer the question put in my letter.
Bearing in mind that the Minister has taken four months
to reply, he has not evaluated the situation. As I
implied to you in an earlier letter, it is exactly what
I expected and an evasion of the question.
  The Minister adds that 9 letters from the MOD on this
subject should be enough. To this I would add that most
of these letters were written in trying to obtain
confirmation from the MOD that: (1) radar would only
detect its own reflected wavelength from an object of
substance and opacity, and (2) an operator of any
consequence could easily identify false returns.
  This being so, *I would point out that after four
months, the MOD have still not answered my last
question*:
  'Taking into account the NATO and Belgian detections
of this phenomena, If NADGE considered the radar
detections above Belgium on 30/31st March 1990 to be
conclusive proof of objects of opacity and substance and
a threat to the national security of the Belgian state,
why; at 22h 39m on 30th March 1990, with this phenomenon

only six minutes from UK airspace, did your air defence experts conclude that there was no threat to the security of the UK?'

I would add that Mr Hanley states quite clearly in his letter D/MIN (AF)/94/94 (with reference to the Belgian phenomena): 'While we are aware that there were some unusual occurrences' . . . This is a direct contradiction to the statement by Mr Pope in his letter D/Sec(AS)12/3 of the 13th October 1993 that: 'We have no record that the Belgians (or anybody else) passed us information relating to these sightings.'

I would also refer you to Mr Pope's letter D/Sec(AS)12/3 of 12th November 1993; this stated that: 'Although these UFO sightings did indeed occur close to the UK, we would not have been notified unless the Belgians believed there was a threat'.

Three NADGE radar stations detected these objects and alerted the Belgian Air Force. This was a major security alert. I have confirmation that NADGE informed the MOD of this major alert.

Would the Minister please explain these contradictions and answer the question as above?

Yours sincerely
Derek Sheffield

On 22 March 1994, Sir Keith Speed wrote the following letter to me, enclosing a reply to his written question of 1 March 1994, to the MOD. His letter was written to the MOD four days before I wrote the preceding letter to him.

22nd March 1994

Mr Sheffield

I have now received the enclosed reply from the Minister of State for the Armed Forces about the UFO sightings declared over Belgium some 4$^{1}/_{2}$ years ago. You will note particularly the final sentence of the third paragraph of the Minister's letter, and, having had a brief discussion with the Minister in the Lobby, I am afraid they now regard this matter as closed.

I do not know if you have taken up the suggestion of writing to the Belgian Embassy, but it would seem that this is the remaining step that would be open to you.

Yours sincerely,
Lorna Day, pp Keith Speed

THE SECOND REPLY TO SIR KEITH SPEED FROM THE MOD

14th March 1994

Dear Keith,

Thank you for your letter of 1 March, in which you requested a synopsis of the correspondence between my Department and your constituent Mr Derek Sheffield of Cherry Tree House, Regent Street, Rolvenden.

Mr Sheffield's first letter was forwarded to us in January 1993. He asked what we knew about a wave of UFO sightings that had occurred over Belgium in late 1989 and early 1990. My official explained that our involvement with the subject of UFOs is very limited, our only interest being to ensure that there is no threat to the defence of the UK. They also pointed out that this was, of course, a matter for the Belgians and not for us. In an attempt to be as helpful as possible, it was suggested that Mr Sheffield contact the Belgian Embassy, together with a number of UFO societies who were actively researching these UFO sightings.

Over the next few months Mr Sheffield wrote a steady stream of letters asking about our policy and views on the UFO phenomenon, and again, my officials provided him with full and helpful answers to all his questions. Mr Sheffield continued to focus on the Belgian sightings, and asked a number of questions about radar systems in an attempt to prove that because some of the UFO sightings coincided with some radar returns there must have been some sort of solid object present. My officials explained that there are a number of circumstances such as unusual meteorological conditions or interference between different radar systems, where this is note [sic] necessarily so. Mr Sheffield expressed concern that these sightings were sufficiently close to the UK to pose some sort of threat, but was assured that this was not the case, and was reminded of the effective way in which the RAF detected and intercepted Soviet aircraft probing our defences during the Cold War. Mr Sheffield asked whither [sic] the Belgians informed us about these UFO sightings, and if not, why not. The fact is that the Belgians did not regard these UFO sightings as posing any sort of threat, and for this reason did not notify any other countries.

I can assure you that every effort was made to be as helpful as possible to Mr Sheffield. However, by the time

he wrote his tenth letter in December 1993 it was clear
that no new points were being raised, and he was duly
informed that there was nothing that could usefully be
added to the very comprehensive answers that he had
already received.

Clearly these sightings were very interesting for UFO
researchers. However, given that there was no evidence
of any threat, and given that the sightings occurred
outside the UK, this is not a matter for the Ministry of
Defence.

I hope this is helpful, and has explained the
situation.

Yours ???
Jeremy Hanley MP

At the risk of repeating myself throughout this document, I
would draw attention to Mr Hanley's comment regarding the
effectiveness of the RAF in intercepting Soviet aircraft which
probed the UK air defences during the Cold War. The
implications of this statement are that it is inconceivable that
the UK authorities did not know of the events that were
taking place as the unidentified object over Europe headed
towards the British coast at speeds of up to 1,000 knots being
pursued by two Belgian F-16 interceptors.

The unidentified detection, which had been verified by at
least five European radar stations and locked on to by the
pursuing aircraft's radar, was within six minutes of the
British coast, less than 100 miles away. If the RAF can manage
to get their fighters airborne and fly the distance required to
intercept Soviet aircraft as they enter UK airspace – which I
assume must be somewhere over the sea which surrounds
our islands – it would indicate that either the UK air defence
system can detect the invading aircraft at such a distance as
to allow the RAF to get airborne *or* they must be informed, by
friendly nations, of the approaching threat. I suspect the
former to be the case. I cannot imagine that the British
Ministry of Defence would rely solely on other nations to
inform them of an impending threat that would leave the UK
defences with so little time to take action as to render them
ineffective.

However, let us examine both possibilities, assuming the most basic form of air defence systems. If the UK air defence system can detect activity in the air at distances in excess of 100 miles then it is clear that they would be monitoring the activity in the sky over Belgium on the dates in question. Surely if an 'unidentified' object being pursued by two identifiable 'friendly' interceptor aircraft was detected heading towards UK airspace and came within six minutes of the British coast it must be assumed to be a threat and the RAF must 'scramble' its own interceptors. Most importantly they, and by implication the MOD, *must have been aware of it.* If we take the second possibility, that the UK air defence system is informed by friendly nations of impending violations of UK airspace, then, as I have stated before, given the fact that the Belgians launched their interceptor aircraft to challenge their own unidentified radar detections, then as the object approached the UK, in order to allow time for the RAF to become airborne *they must have informed the UK air defence system.* We know that it was considered a threat by the Belgians – why else would they intercept it?

What other conclusions can be drawn from Jeremy Hanley's boast of the effectiveness of the RAF and the UK air defence system?

- Why did the Ministry of Defence deny any knowledge of these events in their communications to me?
- Why did they later say that the relevant UK authorities did not consider the unidentified detections a threat, when previously they had said that they knew nothing of them?

Depending on the answers to the above questions two points can be raised:

(a) The UK air defence system is dangerously ineffective.

(b) The Ministry of Defence/military authorities knew what the unidentified radar detection was, and, on the basis of that knowledge, did not consider it a threat, unlike the Belgians, who pursued it with tenacity and vigour.

I replied to Sir Keith Speed to explain the reason for the number of letters I had to write to the MOD to break through their evasions in an attempt to get at the truth.

23rd March 1994

Dear Sir Keith,

Thank you for your prompt reply and the enclosed letter D/MIN (AF)/94/94 from the Minister of State for the Armed Forces.

The Minister makes an itemised reply of the 9 letters sent to his Department. He does not comment that his ministry were evasive on the issue of radar detection. Five letters were written before his Department would admit that radar would only positively detect a radar wavelength of an object of opacity and substance. I would suggest that for your interest, you request copies of replies sent to me by the Ministry and form your own conclusions. On the question of false radar signals, the Minister's Department confirmed (D/Sec(AS)12/3 29th September 1993) that skilled radar operatives could easily distinguish between true radar signals and false ones.

Taking both of these facts into account, it would seem that detections by skilled NADGE radar operatives at Semmerzake (Belgium), Glons CRC (Belgium) and Vedem (Germany) were definite detections of objects of opacity and substance.

The Minister states that the Belgians did not consider these sightings as posing any sort of a threat. This is not commensurate with the facts. The Belgian Minister of Defence confirmed Belgian Air Force radar detections, by admitting the presence of flying objects over Liège (Leo Delcroix 9/IM/RT/16 26th May 1993) and stating that 'all hypotheses could be excluded, the Minister could not tell what these flying objects were'.

The ground rules for the Belgian Air Force are quite clear. Visual sightings by individuals of intrusions into Belgian airspace must be confirmed by the state police. These must be confirmed and coordinated by Belgian radar. If positive radar detections are not identified, the detections are classified as hostile. The Belgian Air Force is alerted. I can assure the Minister that two fully armed F-16 interceptor aircraft, vectored to their targets by positive detections of three main

NADGE radar stations, achieving radar lock-on on fifteen occasions over a period of an hour, did indeed constitute a major security threat. It was considered so by the Belgian armed forces.

The Minister's comment that the Belgians did not notify any other countries of these detections would again appear to be wrong. Apart from the fact that German radar at Vedem had also registered these phenomenon, I understand from a NATO source that under the NADGE defensive system, it would have been inconceivable that UK radar would not have been advised of these detections.

Bearing in mind the discrepancies in the Minister's comments, I would once again, for the third time, reiterate the simple question that the Minister and his Department still continue to evade: TAKING INTO ACCOUNT THE NATO AND BELGIAN DETECTIONS OF THIS PHENOMENON, IF NADGE CONSIDERED THE RADAR DETECTIONS ABOVE BELGIUM ON MARCH 30/31st 1990 TO BE CONCLUSIVE PROOF OF OBJECTS OF OPACITY AND SUBSTANCE AND A THREAT TO THE NATIONAL SECURITY OF THE BELGIAN STATE, WHY, AT 22h 39m ON THE 30th MARCH 1990, WITH THIS PHENOMENON ONLY SIX MINUTES FROM UK AIR SPACE, DID YOUR AIR DEFENCE EXPERTS CONCLUDE THAT THERE WAS NO THREAT TO THE SECURITY OF THE UK?

> Yours sincerely,
> Derek Sheffield

Note. I wrote to the Belgian Embassy one year ago. On their advice I contacted the Belgian Air Force. They supplied me with all the information that I have.

Keeping my promise to Admiral Hill-Norton to keep him informed of events, I wrote to him enclosing Jeremy Hanley's letter.

23rd March 1994

Dear Admiral Hill-Norton,

You wished to be kept informed on any developments concerning Sir Keith Speed.

Please find attached photocopies of a letter received from Sir Keith Speed together with a letter he has received from the Minister of State for the Armed Forces.

Sir Keith pointedly refers to the final sentence of the third paragraph of the Minister's letter:

'The fact is that the Belgians did not regard these sightings as posing any sort of a threat, and for this reason did not notify any other countries.'

This is untrue. The Belgians, simply by the action taken, demonstrated their concern for their own national security. I would add that the German radar at Vedem was involved, and that lack of notification is not commensurate with the principles of the NADGE defence system. . . .

Yours sincerely
Derek Sheffield

I wrote a further letter to Admiral Hill-Norton some days later, informing him of impending petitions to government departments in the UK and USA.

5th April 1994

Dear Admiral Hill-Norton,

It has come to my attention that the House of Commons, the Ministry of Defence, and the Pentagon, Washington DC, are all being petitioned by UFO and UFO-related research groups and organizations.

I understand that 650 copies of a six-point document are being delivered to all individually named members of the House of Commons.

These documents will also be presented at the MOD Buildings in Whitehall.

Arrangements have been made for a legal demonstration to take place outside the House of Commons.

These events are due to take place both here and in America, at noon on May 23rd 1994.

The subject of this petition is a request to Congress in the United States and Parliament in Great Britain that the truth to be disclosed on Unidentified Flying Objects.

I would suggest that this would be a very appropriate date for my question to be put to the Minister in the Lords.

Yours sincerely
Derek Sheffield

Admiral Lord Hill-Norton replied to my letter with some interesting information on a forthcoming TV programme and an assurance that he would follow up the matter in parliament in some way.

11 April 1994

Dear Mr Sheffield,

Thank you for your letters of 23 March and 5 April.

I am noted for making quick decisions, but I find it difficult to decide in which way I am most likely to get an answer to your problem. I am sure that an Oral Question in the House will not work, for a number of reasons. I am pretty sure that a letter to Mr Rifkind is the best course, but I have found it difficult to get it into the right form. I shall do something for you, you may be sure.

I gave an interview to Central TV last week which will form part of a programme they are making on UFOs, which will be broadcast on 5 August. I took the opportunity of explaining your problem, and stating my opinion which I have already given to you. I do not know whether this will be included in what actually goes out, or not, but I hope so.

If you get a copy of the document which is being sent to MPs, I should like to have a copy.

Yours sincerely
Hill-Norton

I made enquiries of Central Television and after speaking to Olivia Russell on the telephone, I wrote to her to explain my position.

13th April 1994

Dear Olivia Russell,

To confirm our telephone conversation of today's date.

I understand that Central Television have recently interviewed Admiral of the Fleet Lord Hill-Norton GCB, in connection with a programme due to go out on the 5th August.

Admiral Hill-Norton has informed me that he explained my particular case and stated his comments on this.

I have today received a letter from Ana Miranda de Lage, Vice-Chairman of the Petitions Committee. It states that my 40-page report submitted to the Petitions Committee falls within the sphere of activities of the European Communities. It has been declared admissible, pursuant to rule 156 of the Rules of Procedure of the European Parliament.

The Committee have considered it appropriate that my observations be brought to the attention of the Committee on Energy, Research and Technology of the European Parliament, for further action.

You mentioned the request of Snr Tullio Reggo to the same Committee. I would advise that my appeal is somewhat different. My case is that the statement by the Belgian Minister of Defence that 'all hypotheses had been considered, the Minister did not know what these flying objects were' is inconclusive. As the security of the member states is in question, my request is for a full, in-depth enquiry into these incidents.

My report is an endeavour to prove that a phenomenon of some kind *did* appear above Belgium on 30/31st March 1990. I believe that I have done that. An interesting side issue is a conflict of reports from the MOD that they had *no* knowledge of the Belgian incidents, and from the Minister of Defence that they *did*!

I enclose for your interest the letter from the Petitions Committee, and the last two pages from my report submitted to the European Parliament.

Thank you for your interest
Derek Sheffield

I watched the TV broadcast eagerly but my report was not mentioned in the programme. On the same day of writing to Central Television I wrote to Admiral Lord Hill-Norton to inform him of the acceptance of my report for consideration by the Energy Research and Technology Committee. He replied as follows:

26 April 1994

Dear Mr Sheffield,

Thank you for your letter of 13 April and the enclosure. The latter is a useful step forward in your campaign. I suspect that the Committee probably moves rather slowly, but I also suspect that once they have got their teeth into it they will not let go.

I must confess that I am surprised that you do not know (or have not looked up) my Defence credentials. I was Chief of the Defence Staff 1971–1973 and Chairman of the NATO Military Committee 1974–1977. These are,

respectively, the highest military offices in the United
Kingdom and the Alliance.

Mr Rifkind has more important matters on his mind at
the moment; when I see a lull in the action I will write
to him.

Yours sincerely
Hill-Norton

By this time, Sir Keith Speed had received a further letter
from Jeremy Hanley. This was by now the familiar curt reply
that says nothing new and merely conveys the writer's
irritation.

21 April 1994

Dear Keith,

Thank you for your letter of 2 April, enclosing a
further letter from your constituent Mr Derek Sheffield
of Cherry Tree House, Regent Street, Rolvenden.

The Belgian authorities have advised that since the
sightings took place in the central part of Belgium and
there was no evidence of any threat, reports to other
countries were not made. Our own Air Defence experts
have also confirmed that they do not regard these Belgian
UFO sightings as having posed any sort of threat to the
United Kingdom.

In the circumstances, I am afraid that there is little
else that I can say in this subject.

I really believe this correspondence should end.

Yours ???
Jeremy Hanley MP

I wrote back to my MP to thank him for his efforts on my
behalf and to make a final attempt to explain to him the
contradictions in the various communications I had received
from the Ministry of Defence on this matter.

30th April 1994

Dear Sir Keith,

Thank you for your letter of the 26th April and enclosure from Jeremy Hanley, Minister for the Armed Forces.

Your endeavours on my behalf are much appreciated. Sadly, the reply by the Minister fails completely in its convictions. There are too many glaring anomalies which the Minister has chosen to ignore. His apparent irritation would imply a defence which is not acceptable.

Mr N. G. Pope of the Ministry of Defence stated (Ref: D/Sec(AS)12/3.13/10/93): 'I have yet to see any official documents relating to these sightings. We have no record that the Belgians (or anybody else) passed us information relating to these sightings.'

If the Minister and the Ministry of Defence *had no knowledge of these sightings*, how could the Minister state (Ref: D/MIN/(AF)/94/94.20/2/94): 'While we were aware of some unusual occurrences, this is a matter for the Belgians and not for us.'

I would reiterate the question: 'If, as the Minister and the Ministry of Defence state, they had no knowledge of the Belgian phenomenon and its detection by NADGE radars, how could their air defence experts possibly conclude that this phenomenon did not constitute a threat, *when they had no apparent knowledge of it*?'

I have been advised that my submission to the European Parliament has been considered by the Petitions Committee. They consider the facts contained therein are of direct concern to the Member States of the Community. They have advised that they have forwarded my report to the appropriate section of the European Parliament and recommended that action be taken. I have asked to be present when this is discussed, either as an observer or in a consultative capacity.

I will bring to the attention of the European Parliament the anomalies that appear to exist between the Minister, the Ministry of Defence, and their air defence experts.

Yours sincerely
Derek Sheffield

A promising line of enquiry in the House of Commons had reached an unsatisfactory conclusion. The officials at the

Ministry of Defence refused to give a straight answer to a simple question. I realized that my letter to Sir Keith Speed would probably be an end to the matter as far as he was concerned. I was considering further avenues to explore in an effort to get at the truth when, in mid-May 1994, Admiral of the Fleet, The Lord Hill-Norton, sent me a copy of a written submission he had made to the Rt Hon. Malcolm Rifkind, MP, Secretary of State at the Ministry of Defence. In a letter marked 'Personal', Lord Hill-Norton eloquently pleaded my case . . .

17 May 1994

I have been approached by a Mr Sheffield of Cranbrook, Kent, who has asked me to help him to obtain a satisfactory response from your Ministry to an enquiry he initiated a year or more ago. I enclose a copy of his letter to me dated 16 March 1994, which sets out his request and his complaint. This is a small part of a quite lengthy correspondence.

He had earlier approached his Member, Sir Keith Speed, and I have seen several letters which have been exchanged between Sir Keith and Mr Hanley and also your officials. These letters do not answer Mr Sheffield's enquiries, and he finds them unsatisfactory. I am bound to say that I share that view, in the light of all the circumstances.

There is no need for me to rehearse all that has already been written in these exchanges. In short, detections were made by three NADGE radars in Germany and Belgium in March 1990, air defence aircraft of the Belgian Air Force were scrambled to intercept but although the objects were detected and held on the radar of these aircraft as well, no identification, or visual contact was made. There is no dispute about these facts, which have been confirmed by the Belgian Minister of Defence in public statements, repeated in writing to Mr Sheffield. I have advised Mr Sheffield that, unless the procedure has been changed since I was Chairman of the NATO Military Committee, it is inconceivable that the UK would not be informed (probably automatically) of a possibly hostile, certain unidentified, detection by NADGE radars.

Mr Sheffield has been brushed off with the standard MOD response to all reports (of which I have seen a great many) of UFO activity, which briefly put amount to '. . . no threat was perceived to the UK so no notice was taken or record made of the incident . . .'. In this instance this has, in separate letters, been complicated by written statements by your Ministry that no report of the Belgian detections was ever received in the UK.

Mr Sheffield asks, reasonably enough, '*If, as Ministers assert, they had no knowledge of the Belgian events how could their air defence experts possibly conclude that the phenomenon did not constitute a threat, as they have no knowledge of it?*'

I fear that Mr Sheffield may well make a damaging public uproar about all this. He has already had a petition to the European Parliament upheld, and his dossier has been formally remitted to the relevant Euro Committee. A public demarche, so he tells me, is planned for the MOD, the House of Commons, and simultaneously at the Pentagon on 23 May. At least two television programmes in this country will carry his story within the next few months, and this may well not be the end of it.

I strongly recommend that you should take a personal interest in having the whole matter re-examined, so that a more satisfactory and convincing reply may be given to Mr Sheffield's question, before the matter gets out of hand.

MALCOLM RIFKIND'S REPLY TO LORD HILL-NORTON

11 June 1994

Dear Lord Hill-Norton,

Thank you for your letter dated 17 May concerning the UFO sightings that occurred over Belgium in March 1990.

I am grateful to you for alerting me to this problem, and I am aware that Mr Sheffield may attempt to create a public fuss. However, I am satisfied that correct procedures have been followed, that all relevant information has been passed to Mr Sheffield and that no purpose would be served by continuing the correspondence with him.

You will know that our sole reason for examining reports of UFO sightings is to establish whether or not there is evidence of any threat to the United Kingdom. The Belgian authorities have indicated that they did not notify us of these sightings at the time because there was no evidence of any threat, and because they occurred over the central part of Belgium. I should add that notification of NADGE radar detections is at the discretion of the operators, and does not occur automatically.

We subsequently became aware of these sightings through the UFO literature and through approaches from members of the public such as Mr Sheffield. On the basis of the information now available our own Air Defence experts have confirmed that they would not have been concerned with these UFO reports, and that they saw no reason why the Belgians should have notified any UK authorities. I am sure it goes without saying, however, that any unauthorised penetration of the UK Air Defence Region would be detected by our Air Defenders, and dealt with as appropriate.

It is clear to me from the papers I have seen that the position has been explained in great detail to Mr Sheffield. I am aware of one television programme on the subject, a Central TV production to be shown on 18 October. The MOD desk officer responsible for UFOs was interviewed for this programme and was able to set out the MOD's policy on UFOs. I hope this has explained the situation satisfactorily.

Yours sincerely,
Malcolm Rifkind

Admiral Hill-Norton, in his letter to me which accompanied the copy of Malcolm Rifkind's reply, stated that he thought he had done all that he usefully could do in this matter. However, he expressed a wish to be kept informed of further events with regard to the European Parliament. I wrote to Lord Hill-Norton to thank him for his support. After so many deceptions and disappointments I was beginning to doubt my ability to prove my case and bring this matter to the public's attention. Lord Hill-Norton's contribution had given me a determination to pursue the matter to a conclusion, and, more importantly, had opened the door for me to correspond personally with Malcolm Rifkind, Secretary of State at the

Ministry of Defence – to point out to him the anomalies and apparent deceptions evident within his ministry.

26th June 1994

Dear Mr Rifkind,

Admiral Lord Hill-Norton has advised me of your reply to his letter of the 17th May.

The actual presence of flying objects above Belgium in 1989/90 is not in doubt; neither is the fact that they were unidentified. These facts were confirmed to me by Guy Coëme, the Belgian Minister of Defence at that time, and endorsed by Leo Delcroix, the present Belgian Minister of Defence. This being so – and the actions of the Belgian armed forces would confirm their apprehensions – as they did not know what these flying objects were, how could they possibly state that they did not constitute a threat?

There now also seems to be a subtle alteration to the chronology of these events that I do not understand.

On the 26th November 1993, in a letter Ref D/Sec(AS)12/3, Mr Pope, of the Ministry of Defence, stated in his last paragraph, 'In answer to your specific question, Air Defence experts concluded that the Belgian UFO sightings posed no threat to the UK because there was no evidence of any such threat.' Mr Pope does not say that the reason that there was no evidence of any threat 'was because our Air Defence experts were not aware of these detections at the time'.

Your letter Ref. MO 9/18M of 11th June 1994 to Admiral Hill-Norton confirms this fact by stating that 'our Air Defence experts were not notified at the time of the Belgian radar detections': in fact you state that they only became aware of these sightings through UFO literature and approaches by members of the public'.

This establishes beyond doubt that our Air Defence experts could not possibly have been in any position to ascertain the nature of these phenomena at the actual time of these detections.

Five radar stations (a mixture of array-type and multi-purpose impulsion systems), four in Belgium – Glons, Bertem, Semmerzake, St Hubert – and at Vedem in Germany, all established confirmed radar detections by highly skilled operatives over Wavre, south-east of Brussels. These unidentified detections – possibly

237

hostile – although 100 miles away from our national
boundary, were closing on our airspace at speeds in
excess of 1,000 knots. This represented a contact time
of only six minutes. It is obvious that we do not wait
until an unidentified intruder is only six minutes from
our national boundary to be advised by another country
if they consider this intrusion to be a threat to our
national security! This being so – and the observations
of Admiral Lord Hill-Norton (who held the highest
military office in the UK and NATO) that 'it was
inconceivable that we were *not* informed through NATO of
these radar detections' – I would ask again *why* we were
not advised of these detections and *why* you were not
concerned at this lack of radar detection by our own
radar defence system?

                    Yours sincerely
                    Derek Sheffield

Mr Rifkind passed my letter to T.J.H. Laurence, Commander
Royal Navy, Private Secretary, for reply. I suppose it was
foolish of me to expect Mr Rifkind, an elected Member of
Parliament, to reply to my letter personally. I thought that the
Secretary of State for Defence would wish to know of
apparent deceptions in his ministry and would investigate
the anomalies raised by my questions. However, the reply
from T.J.H. Laurence merely repeated the statements made by
other officials in previous letters. They are statements which,
if compared with information I have received from other
sources – sources of an equal standing and integrity to the
Secretary of State for Defence – are apparently untenable. The
damning factors against the Ministry of Defence are:

- the documented evidence I have received from the
  various sources in the Belgian government;
- the documented evidence from the Belgian Air Force;
- the written statement of the understanding of the
  workings of the NATO air defence system from Admiral
  of the Fleet The Lord Hill-Norton, former Chief of the
  Defence Staff, and former Chairman of the NATO
  Military Committee;
- the mass of circumstantial evidence accumulated on

sightings from the ground by reliable witnesses,
including officers of the Belgian police force;
* the contradictions in the communications to myself from
various officials at the Ministry of Defence.

The letter from T.J.H. Laurence is reproduced below:

14 July 1994

Dear Mr Sheffield,

Thank you for your letter dated 26th June to the
Secretary of State for Defence, concerning UFO sightings
over Belgium. You have asked two specific questions, both
of which have been answered before, however I will try
to answer them again as fully and clearly as possible.

First, why were we not advised of the sightings. It
remains the Ministry of Defence's view that the Belgian
authorities were best placed to make a judgement on
these reported UFO sightings. In view of their location
and the lack of any indication that any threat was
posed, the Belgians decided not to notify any other
countries. It is correct therefore that the UK was not
made aware of these detections. They occurred outside
the UK Air Defence Region and there is no record of
detections having been made on any British system. The
Belgians took the decision that, in the light of the
circumstances, there was no threat to the UK. The
relevant British authorities are content that this
decision was correct.

Second, why are we not concerned at the lack of a
radar detection by our own radar defence system. There
is no evidence that any sightings or radar contacts
occurred within the expected coverage of our own
systems. We would not, therefore, have expected to
detect anything and were neither surprised nor concerned
at the fact that no contacts were detected.

The sequence of events has been explained in previous
letters, and the various questions which you have raised
on this issue have been dealt with at some length. I do
not therefore see any useful purpose in a continuation
of this correspondence.

Yours sincerely
(T.J.H. Laurence)
Commander Royal Navy
Private Secretary

239

MY REPLY TO COMMANDER LAURENCE

18 July 1994

Dear Commander Laurence,

Thank you for your reply to my letter of the 26th June to the Secretary of State for Defence, concerning unidentified NADGE radar detections over Belgium.

I would advise that my letter to the Secretary of State for Defence was simply because he generalizes with platitudes. He does not seem to have taken into account the relative facts which are incontrovertible.

Sadly your letter is in the same vein.

Please do not think me patronizing if I list the following facts.

(1) Radar will only detect its own reflection from an object of opacity and substance.

(2) Radar detections were made by five NADGE radars. Four in Belgium and one in Germany.

(3) These were made by highly skilled operatives who were unable to identify their detections.

(4) When NADGE radar operatives are unable to identify an intruder, it is classified as hostile.

(5) Strict parameters of identification are laid down by the Belgian Air Force before any interception can be attempted.

(6) The final parameter is that if an intrusion is not identified, it is declared hostile.

(7) The NADGE radar operators declared this intrusion hostile.

(8) The Belgian Air Force carried out interceptions for 1 hour and 5 mins on an unidentified radar detection that was deemed hostile.

(9) On the night of March 30/31st 1990 at 22h 39m two F-16 aircraft were in pursuit of this unidentified intruder: many interceptions were made. Radar lock-on was achieved by one aircraft on 13 occasions.

(10) Aircraft were vectored to their target by NADGE radars on all of these occasions.

(11) At 22h 39m, this unidentified radar intruder, which was deemed hostile, was over Wavre - SE of Brussels - and closing on British airspace at 1,000 kts.

(12) Time is the most important factor in terms of national defence. This possible intruder was six minutes from our national boundary.

(13) Our radar is part of NADGE (an 80-station radar complex that covers all Europe).

(14) Admiral of the Fleet, The Lord Hill-Norton who, as former Chief of Defence Staff and Chairman of the NATO Military Committee – the highest military offices in the UK and Alliance – has said that it was inconceivable that we were NOT informed of these detections, or that the Operations Division of SHAPE (at Mons) were not aware of them either!

(15) As the Belgians could not identify their radar detections, it would be impossible for them to assume that they did not constitute a threat.

(16) In view of item 15, the statement by the Ministry of Defence that 'in answer to your specific question, Air Defence experts concluded that the Belgian UFO sightings posed no threat' is completely untenable.

(17) In spite of the fact that we have a radar defence system, five letters were written to the Ministry of Defence before they would admit that radar would only detect its own reflection from an object of opacity and substance.

(18) The Ministry of Defence have stated that there have never been radar detections by our own systems that could not be identified or explained. This is untrue: NADGE is our own system; their detections were not identified.

This evidence cannot be refuted. The statement that the UK was not made aware of these detections is either a censure on our own radar defence systems, or a deception that is highly suspect. Items 15, 16, 17, 18 would strongly indicate deception on the part of the Ministry of Defence. I cannot accept an explanation from the Ministry that is flawed in so many respects; this has been my main reason for a successful appeal to the European Parliament.

Derek Sheffield

Commander Laurence and the Ministry of Defence chose not to reply to this letter. This was not altogether unexpected in view of the final sentence of Commander Laurence's letter.

CHAPTER TWENTY-FOUR

No Luck with Opposition Spokesmen

Having had no success in my efforts to elicit the truth from the UK Ministry of Defence, I began to search for other means of furthering my enquiries.

It is so frustrating to have proven the existence of the Belgian phenomena of 1989 and 1990 – through evidence received from the Belgian authorities and the mass of anecdotal evidence I have accumulated – only to come up against closed doors with every further line of enquiry initiated.

The original purpose of my European Parliamentary Question had been to prove the existence of the objects in the sky over Belgium. The documented evidence I had received from the Belgian authorities and military sources proved this beyond any doubt. What I had not anticipated was the can of worms that opened up as I pursued my enquiries. The intransigence of the Ministry of Defence in the release of information, and their ineptitude in supplying me with contradictory statements from the various sources delegated to deal with my questions, was highly suspect. The only conclusions to be reached from these events are of a frightening collusion between an alliance of nations and an extraterrestrial intelligence, or alternatively a totally inefficient and inept group of men heading an apparently inadequate defence system, which is unable to detect impending violations of UK air space and possible airborne attack, wherever it may originate, when only six minutes from British territory. The evidence of the Belgian Ministry of Defence and the Belgian Air Force indicates an object of opacity and substance that manoeuvred in a manner unthinkable for a manned vehicle of any description that could be manufactured on Earth with the technology available today. I therefore discount any theories of stealth aircraft. The acceleration rates logged by the radar on board the F-16 interceptors would have produced g forces that would have crushed any human body to a pulp. This made me determined not to give in. My problem was, who could I contact to pressurize the Ministry of Defence to issue a comprehensive and truthful statement from a senior official at the MOD? I thought that perhaps a question from the Opposition might provoke some action, bearing in mind Lord Hill-Norton's opinion that the MOD would admit to nothing unless forced to do so. I contacted the House of Commons Information Section for the name of the Opposition Spokesperson on Defence. I sent Dr David Clark, Shadow Secretary of State for Defence, the following letter.

30th June 1994

Dear Dr Clark,

I have been advised by the House of Commons Information Section that you are the Opposition Spokesman on Defence, Disarmament and Arms Control.

An incident has been brought to my attention that occurred on 30/31st March 1990 that has caused me some concern. I have been unable to obtain a satisfactory answer from either Jeremy Hanley or Malcolm Rifkind. This concerned positive detections by highly skilled radar operatives at five NADGE radar stations. These were at Glons, Bertem, Semmerzake, and St Hubert, in Belgium; and Vedem in Germany.

Strict parameters have to be complied with before military action can be taken: witnesses' statements have to be confirmed by the Belgian Police; these in turn have to be confirmed by Belgian radar. If Belgian radar cannot identify the intruder, then the detection is classified as hostile. As all these parameters were met, the detection was classified as hostile and interceptions were ordered by the Belgian Air Force.

At one point, after one hour - involving fifteen confirmed interceptions by the Belgian Air Force - over Wavre (SE of Brussels), this target was on a westerly heading towards the UK at speeds in excess of 1,000 kts. It was being pursued by two F-16 aircraft of the Belgian

Air Force and was *six minutes* from British airspace. All
the above facts have been confirmed by the Belgian
Minister of Defence.

Despite being part of NADGE, the Ministry of Defence
say that they had no knowledge of these incidents at the
time of their occurrence. They say that they would only
have been informed by the Belgians should *they* have
considered this intruder to have been a danger to our
national security. I view this whole matter with
concern. It would seem to indicate a dangerous defect in
our own radar defence system, and a certain naivety in
putting the trust for our own defence in the hands of
another power.

Your comments would be welcomed.

Yours sincerely
Derek Sheffield

Dr David Clark acknowledged my letter on 5 July, and
informed me that he had sent a copy of it to the Military
Attaché at the Belgian Embassy with a request for further
information and a promise to forward a copy of his response
as soon as he received it. I wrote to him with further details of
information I had managed to prise from the Ministry of
Defence in the hope that it would assist him with any replies
he might receive.

The reply from the Belgian Embassy was forwarded to me
on 22 August 1994. This mentions the letter that was allegedly
sent to me in September 1993, which was never received by
me, and has never been traced despite enquiries to the Royal
Mail.

THE BELGIAN EMBASSY'S REPLY TO DR DAVID CLARK

18 August 1994

Dear Dr Clark,

Thank you for your letter dated 5 July 1994 together
with a copy of a letter by Mr Derek Sheffield dated 30
June 1994.

Allow me first to tell you that an official answer was
forwarded to Mr Sheffield by the Belgian Government in
September 93. It read:

'The Belgian Air Force gave a summary on its findings
about the events of 30/31 March 1990 at a press

conference on 11 July 1990. These findings concluded:
   - that it was impossible to determine whether the data
registered by the F-16 radars were originated by either
electromagnetic interferences or by real objects,
   - that no firm correlation could be found between the
visual observations from the ground and the radar
observations, and
   - that the Air Force has found no evidence of either
the origin or the nature of the visual observations.'
   I cannot comment on the last paragraph of Mr
Sheffield's letter but I can assure you that the NADGE
nations are working on the same concept of operations.
Moreover, the Washington Treaty (NATO) is a guarantee
for the security of all the nations concerned.
      Hoping to have shed some light on the issue, I remain
               Yours sincerely
               J. BOUZETTE
               Colonel Defence Attaché

The retractions by the Belgian authorities are confusing.
Initially the information on these incidents was freely
available through press conferences, televised statements,
and statements in the Belgian Parliament by the Minister of
Defence at the time and later by his successor. Indeed, at the
outset of my enquiries the information that was sent to me
was invaluable. Now they talk of electromagnetic
interferences, and you will remember General De Brouwer's
rather testy letter to me stating that a threat to Belgian
national security was never perceived. How does that
account for the thousands of reported sightings, several from
eminent Belgian nationals on the ground? Is it possible that
an electromagnetic interference on a radar-scope is visible
from the ground as a triangular configuration of lights in the
sky? And if no threat was perceived to national security why
were the armed interceptor aircraft launched? So now we
have contradictory statements from the Belgian Ministry of
Defence. It is almost as if the denials from all quarters
originate from one central source. The Belgian official
statements are now in line with statements from the British
Ministry of Defence. One cannot but suspect a conspiracy of
enormous proportions.

I replied to Colonel Bouzette, through the office of Dr David Clark.

23rd August 1994

Dear Dr Clark,

Thank you for your letter and enclosure of the 22nd August. I have several observations to make on the enclosure from Colonel Bouzette.

Although I received confirmatory letters from Guy Coëme, Belgian Minister of Defence at the time of these incidents, and an endorsement by Leo Delcroix, the present Belgian Minister of Defence, at *no time* did I ever receive an official answer from the Belgian government in September 1993. I would very much like to obtain, not only a copy of this letter, but the summary issued at the press conference on 11th July 1990 by the Belgian Air Force, of their findings of the events of 30/31st March 1990. Perhaps Colonel Bouzette could assist me with this.

I had occasion to remind General-Major Schellemans of the Belgian Ministry of Defence of letters which he had not replied to, sent on the 15th July, 29th October and 27th December 1993 and 29th January 1994. General-Major Schellemans informed me that my enquiries had been sent to the Belgian Air Force for their reply.

After a *five-month delay*, I appealed directly to the Belgian Prime Minister for an answer.

General-Major Schellemans' reply stated in effect that because of reorganization and reduction of personnel in the Belgian Air Force, the General Staff were not in a position to answer any questions on this subject. General-Major Schellemans then referred me to Professor Meessen of the Université Catholique de Louvain, who does not reply.

A final letter to General-Major Schellemans of the 17th April is still unanswered.

It would now seem that a reply *was* sent to me by the Belgian government in September 1993 which I did not receive!

Whatever game is General-Major Schellemans playing at? I will advise the European Parliament that his actions are *not* of the co-operation that I have requested from the Belgian Ministry of Defence in the matter now placed as Petition 990/93 before the Committee on Energy,

Research and Technology of the European Parliament.
It would seem by the letter from Colonel Bouzette
that:

(1) It was impossible to determine whether the radar
detections of the F-16 interceptors were of
electromagnetic or real objects.

(2) Whilst there were visual observations of these
objects, there was no firm correlation between these
and ground radar observations; although there was
complete correlation between the five NADGE radars
and the on-board radars of the F-16 interceptors.

(3) The Belgian Air Force was not able to determine the
origin or the nature of the visual observations of
flying objects above Belgium in December 1989 and
March 1990.

As Colonel Bouzette feels that he cannot comment on
the last paragraph of my letter, would he confirm the
following Belgian Air Force procedures as defined by
Flight-Colonel Wilfrid De Brouwer:

'Strict parameters have to be met before the Belgian
Air Force will order an interception: witnesses'
observations have to be confirmed by the Belgian police,
Belgian police observations have to be confirmed by
Belgian radar. If Belgian radar are not able to identify
their detection, the detection is classified as hostile.

'Only then will the Belgian Air Force order an
interception.'

Yours sincerely
Derek Sheffield

Colonel Bouzette has not replied to this letter or confirmed
the Belgian Air Force procedures as defined by Flight-Colonel
Wilfrid De Brouwer. It would seem that when the flimsy and
inadequate responses to uncomplicated questions are
challenged by incontrovertible facts, the strategy is silence;
and presumably a hope that the problem will go away if it is
ignored. The Belgian and the British defence establishments
have both now adopted this tactic. The disturbing factor is, to
whom are they answerable? Clearly not to our elected
representatives. My elected Member of Parliament, Sir Keith
Speed, although initially helpful, received the same
contradictory answers from Jeremy Hanley, and then – for
whatever reason – despite my concise explanation of the facts

in repeated letters to him, decided not to press the matter further. The Opposition defence spokesman, Dr David Clark, although prompt and quite helpful in the initial stages of our correspondence, has declined to reply to at least four letters from me (13 October 1994; 21 October 1994; 13 December 1994; 21 February 1995). These letters requested his assistance in pressing the Belgians and the British Ministry of Defence for explanations of their contradictory and flimsy statements explaining away an apparently serious incident.

The 17 September edition of the *Sunday Express* carried an article by Mark Porter and Tom Utley documenting the events over Belgium five years ago. It contains some interesting quotes.

> Last night a spokesman from the Belgian Ministry of Defence said: 'These incidents were, and still are, being treated with the utmost seriousness. We gave chase but could not begin to keep up in the F-16s. Perhaps we will never fully fathom this mysterious business, but we continue to try.'

This spokesman is clearly not anyone that I have been in communication with at the Belgian Ministry of Defence. I inferred from their final communications with me that there was no threat to national security and the case was closed.
A further quote from the article:

> Labour defence spokesman Dr David Clark told the *Sunday Express* last night that despite 'solid information' from the Belgians, the Ministry of Defence has persistently brushed the matter under the carpet. 'They have official recorded information and our view is the MoD is being far too secretive. They ought to be much more open on this issue. If it wasn't a UFO and was a Stealth bomber then we should be told.'

Where were you when I needed you, Dr Clark? This was clearly not the position held by Dr Clark when he was in correspondence with me. I received no replies to my earlier correspondence. Was he silenced?

CHAPTER TWENTY-FIVE

The Mighty British Press

Towards the end of 1993 I was discussing my investigations into the Belgian incidents with my cousin, Bryan Yates. I was puzzled at the lack of coverage in the British Press at the time of the sightings, and I said to Bryan that I suspected that there might have been some sort of reporting restrictions implemented by the British authorities. He mentioned that an acquaintance from his rugby-playing days, a Mr Dawe, was employed by *The Times*. He considered that he was well-enough acquainted with him to telephone him and ask if he was aware of – or could find out about – any such restrictions.

Bryan telephoned on my behalf and was told that there was no evidence of any reporting restrictions. Mr Dawe expressed an interest in the subject and asked to be kept informed of any developments. I wrote to him at the beginning of December 1993, in the hope that it would open up another avenue of enquiry.

6th December 1993

Dear Mr Dawe,

You may recollect a recent telephone conversation with my cousin, Bryan Yates. The subject concerned investigative journalism with reference to a particular subject. Bryan probably informed you that I have submitted a forty-page report to the European Parliament asking for an enquiry into an event that took place in Belgium in 1990.

For your interest, I have been informed that my application has now been forwarded to the Petitions Committee for their consideration. It would seem that things could now be on their way!.

This whole business came to light when I was researching a book and discovered an event that – although covered in great detail by the Continental

249

media – was not mentioned in the British press.

Further questions at this end – to the Ministry of Defence – led to a blank, but enquiries to the Belgian military agencies (the Belgian Air Force and the Belgian Minister of Defence) opened a Pandora's box beyond belief.

I now have a situation involving the Belgians and NATO, where disclosures have been made that differ greatly from statements made by our own Ministry of Defence. In short, the whole situation is becoming full of evasions.

Bryan said that you would like to be kept in the picture on developments; I enclose a letter sent today to the Ministry of Defence.

Thank you for your interest.

Yours sincerely
Derek Sheffield

Despite a second letter to Tony Dawe of *The Times*, no reply has been forthcoming. I mentioned this in conversation with my cousin. He said that he would be seeing Mr Dawes socially during the next few days. He would give him a gentle reminder.

During the following week I had cause to telephone my cousin. He said that he had raised the point with Mr Dawe.

Mr Dawe said that as there had been implications that my telephone calls were being monitored, he had not known what course to pursue. After some discussion, Mr Dawe said that he would write to me. To date there has been no letter.

It would seem that 'The Thunderer' has gone off like a damp squib!

I have been informed recently that in a book on Kim Philby written by Bruce Page, David Leitch and Phillip Knightley, it was observed that: 'it was no secret in the trade that since the First World War a number of *Times* foreign correspondents had been drawn into British secret-service work'. Also: 'that visits were arranged to *The Times* office in London, so that agents could become familiar with printing machinery'. I suppose that this could imply an involvement with the Ministry of Defence and consequently more confirmation, that even though the press say that there is no obstruction on this particular subject, *there most certainly is!*

I had further dealings with the press in April 1994, when I sent the following Press Release to *The Times*, the *Daily Mail*, Central Television, Reuters and the Press Association.

PRESS RELEASE

On 21 June 1993, I issued a press release stating that a submission had been made in an application to the European Parliament.

This was a request for an enquiry to be instigated into the appearance of a phenomenon above Belgium on the 30/31st March 1990; it took the form of a forty-page report which substantiated the appearance of a phenomenon and the claim by the Belgian Minister of Defence that *All known hypotheses could be excluded. The Minister did not know what these flying objects were.*

There is now a contradiction in the Ministry of Defence. The Ministry of Defence state they had no knowledge of this phenomenon. The Minister of Defence says that they did.

I enclose a letter that has been received today. It is from Ana Miranda de Lage, Vice-Chairman of the Committee on Petitions, The European Parliament. It states that my report has been declared admissible, pursuant to rule 156 of the Rules of Procedure of the European Parliament. It declares that this report is to be brought to the attention of the Committee on Energy, Research and Technology of the European Parliament, for further action.

Bearing in mind the four months' continual coverage by the continental press, and the complete absence of any UK coverage of an event that took place only six minutes from our national boundary, it will be interesting to note whether you will express any interest.

None of the intended recipients in the press replied to either of the press releases so – two months after issuing the second press release – I decided to write to the Press Complaints Commission in an attempt to find out why.

UFO: A DEADLY CONCEALMENT

22 June 1994

Dear Sirs,

I have compiled an investigative document that has been submitted to the European Parliament.

This concerned an event in Belgium covered extensively by the European media – but not apparently by the British press – for a period of four months (from November 1989 to March 1990).

Details of this document were released to the British press and various agencies on 21st June 1993.

This document was passed to the Petitions Committee of the European Parliament for their consideration.

On the 11th April 1994, I received notification from the Vice-Chairman of the Petitions Committee. This states that my document and the issues that it raises fall within the sphere of activities of the European Communities. It has been declared admissible pursuant to Rule 156 of the Rules of Procedure of the European Parliament.

The Committee has considered it appropriate that my observations are brought to the attention of the Committee on Energy, Research and Technology of the European Parliament.

A press release was issued to the British press and various agencies on 14th April 1994 stating this fact.

At no time has there been any apparent press coverage on these releases.

Could you please advise me on this anomaly and inform me if there is any press obstruction to any *serious* investigative research into this subject?

Yours faithfully,

Derek Sheffield

REPLY FROM THE PRESS COMPLAINTS COMMISSION

29 June 1994

Dear Mr Sheffield,

Thank you for your letter dated 22 June 1994.

The Press Complaints Commission is an independent body founded to oversee self-regulation of the Press and charged with upholding a Code of Practice. I regret to have to inform you that the issue which you have raised does not fall within the ambit of this Code or the responsibilities of the Commission.

Press coverage of press releases is a matter for editors and the publication of such at their discretion.

I am sorry that we cannot help you on this occasion but I am enclosing a leaflet explaining the procedures of the Commission when dealing with complaints.

Yours sincerely
Sandra Denis (Ms)
Encl: How to Complain

I studied the leaflet that Sandra Denis had sent to me. I was not aware that I had mentioned the nature of the issue in question. I wrote back to her in the hope that I could persuade the Commission to investigate my case.

30th June 1994

Dear Sirs,

Thank you for your reply to my letter of the 22nd June.

Whilst coverage of press releases is a matter for editors and the publication of such is at their discretion, it would seem that one of the aims of the Complaints Commission is discrimination by newspapers.

It would also seem that section 18 part (iii) of the Code of Practice, is 'Preventing the public from being misled by some statement or organisation'.

Whilst I am probably taking the wording of the Code of Practice out of context, it would seem to me that a block against a serious news item by all the national press and their main agencies on two occasions is more than a coincidence and does amount to a general discrimination by the press.

It would also seem that as a main part of these press releases relates to a possible deception by the Ministry of Defence, this would constitute the public being misled by an organisation.

It would appear that I was incorrect in my assumption as to the aims of the Complaints Commission.

Yours sincerely,
Derek Sheffield

The Press Complaints Commission have chosen not to reply to my letter of 30 June 1994.

It would seem that they did not consider that the omission of press releases (on two occasions) by national newspapers and press agencies, both here and on the Continent, constituted press discrimination.

When this is taken in conjunction with the acceptance by the European Parliament of a document requesting an investigation into an event of such magnitude that the Continental media devoted a total of four months of their time to it; with the strange behaviour of *The Times*; and with a charge of deception by the Ministry of Defence, is not something very odd going on?

CHAPTER TWENTY-SIX

The United Nations

I decided to send a copy of the document I had submitted to the European Parliament to the United Nations. I considered that a co-ordinated investigation by the European Parliament *and* the United Nations, or even a parallel investigation, could only have the effect of shedding more light on the mysteries I had uncovered. I sent the following letter to the United Nations headquarters in New York together with a copy of my report.

Ref: Request for United Nations involvement
in proposed European Parliamentary inquiry

Dear Sir,
I have recently submitted a report to Egon Klepsch, President of the European Parliament.
This has been passed to the Petitions Committee for their consideration for submission to the European Parliament. It is a request for an inquiry to be instigated into the appearance of a phenomenon above Belgium in November 1989 and March 1990. This document has the backing of the Belgian Minister and Ministry of Defence, the Belgian Air Force and the Belgian gendarmerie.
Because of the inconclusive statement by the Belgian Minister of Defence that 'From a military point of view, all relevant hypotheses could be excluded. The Minister could not tell what these flying objects were', and the appearance of the same phenomenon above north Kent in the United Kingdom on the 20th September 1993, the grounds now exist for some co-ordination between the United Nations and the European Parliament in the in-depth investigation of these particular phenomena in relation to NADGE radar detection.
Many years ago a previous Secretary-General of the United Nations, U Thant, stated at a private meeting that 'Apart from the Vietnam war, unidentified flying

objects were the most important problem confronting the United Nations.'

To the best of my knowledge there has been no follow-up to this situation.

In the Belgian sightings there is irrevocable proof – confirmed by radar, the Belgian armed forces and Government – of the appearance of unidentified phenomena above Belgium in 1989/90.

Because of the appearance above north Kent in the United Kingdom in September 1993 of an identical phenomenon, the case for investigation is now of utmost importance.

I would request that my report be considered by the United Nations in conjunction with my application to the European Parliament.

Yours faithfully
Derek Sheffield

I received a most unusual acknowledgement to my letter on United Nations notepaper. It was from the Information Centre at 30 Buckingham Gate, London. It was unsigned and undated. It was non-committal with regard to my request and merely stated that they were replying because they wanted to thank me for my comments . . .

The Secretary-General regrets that, due to the heavy volume of correspondence he receives, he is unable to respond personally to your letter. Your letter has been referred to this office for a reply because we would like to thank you for your comments which have been noted.

Thank you again for writing to the Organisation.

I wrote back to the United Nations on 13 December 1993. I advised them of the many months of research and work that had gone into compiling the report I had sent to New York. I mentioned the involvement of the Belgian authorities and the British Ministry of Defence.

I felt that their reply was at best condescending and at worst indicated another involvement in a clandestine conspiracy.

No reply has been received from the United Nations.

A further episode in the United Nations story came to my notice.

A symposium was arranged to take place at the United Nations Headquarters in New York on 22 October 1993. The principal aim of the meeting was to press for the United Nations to implement decision GA 33/426, which was made on *18 December 1978*. This called for 'the establishment of an agency or a department of the United Nations for undertaking, co-ordinating and disseminating the results of research into unidentified flying objects and related phenomena'. An interesting item on the agenda was that Mr Johnsen Takano, presenting a personal message from the Japanese Deputy Prime Minister, stated that 'the Japanese Government has embarked upon a policy which will change the world forever. They will tell the world all that they know about the UFO.' Mr Johnsen Takano never delivered that message. His contribution was cancelled and as far as I know his revelations have never been heard.

When one bears in mind the statement made by U Thant, Secretary General of the United Nations, at a private meeting that 'Apart from the Vietnam War, unidentified flying objects are the most important problem confronting the United Nations', it is remarkable that after 15 years, this subject has still not been heard.

What is even more remarkable is that on 19 November 1993 a demonstration of some substance was held outside the United Nations building in New York. This received appreciable media coverage. Its purpose? To get the United Nations to implement draft GA 33/426 on research into unidentified flying objects.

Combine these facts with their lack of co-operation with my request to the European Parliament, and something odd is happening in the United Nations.

I was excited by the prospect of the Japanese revealing to the world all that they knew of the UFO situation. When the address was cancelled for 'technical reasons' I decided to write to the Deputy Prime Minister of Japan in the hope that

I could discover what was known by the Japanese and add it to my report to the European Parliament.

21st January 1994

Dear Deputy Prime Minister,

I understand that Mr Johnsen Takano was due to speak at a symposium held at the United Nations Headquarters in New York on 22nd October 1993. He was apparently to tell the symposium of a personal message from the Japanese Deputy Prime Minister concerning the Japanese knowledge of unidentified aerial phenomena. I understand that for technical reasons his address was not given. I am an author. I have researched a series of incidents that happened in Belgium in 1989/90. On the basis of these incidents I have positive proof from the Belgian Minister of Defence and the Belgian Air Force that an entity appeared above Belgium that did not conform to any known hypotheses. On this evidence, I have asked the European Parliament to instigate an official inquiry with a view to confirming the positive existence of these aerial objects. I have been informed that my report is going forward to the Petitions Committee for their consideration.

I have now asked that my request be added to that of Snr Tullio Regge (an Italian MEP), whose recent demand for a centre to be established for the monitoring of unidentified aerial entities is being discussed by the European Parliament.

It would be of great assistance to my request, if you could provide me with any information that would give additional backing to my report.

Yours sincerely
Derek Sheffield

I have never received a reply to this letter.

This was another line of enquiry that led to silence from the officials to whom I directed my questions. It surely cannot be coincidence that every official body with which I have been in contact regarding this matter has either ignored my requests for information; fobbed me off with inconsequential statements which ignored the crucial points of my investigation; stalled for time by continually replying to my questions with the same evasions; denied receipt of my correspondence to them; or simply declined to reply at all. The list is endless. I have exhausted all options in my quest for answers to the mysteries that I have uncovered.

CHAPTER TWENTY-SEVEN

Conclusions

This document has been compiled in the form of the file in which it has developed. It is an absolutely true and factual record of an enquiry that came about as a result of the conclusion of a book entitled *A Question of Reason*, written in 1992.

The publication of this book resulted in an interview on BBC radio, and in my having a discussion with a senior British Airways captain on the subject of unidentified detections by radar, and the evasiveness on this subject by the Ministry of Defence. I was advised that I would find them *apparently* co-operative, but in reality cleverly obstructive. The suggestion was made that I contact the Belgian Air Force.

What has happened since then has been confusing and contradictory. There have been many incidents that I have found difficult to believe; many happenings that have stretched my powers of belief to the limit. I have recorded these exactly as they have happened. The whole point of this document, therefore, is to give an honest, unbiased record of everything that has taken place, so that my readers may form their own opinions and reach their own conclusions.

This, then, is a summary of the relevant points as I see them; there have doubtless been items introduced to misinform, as well as events calculated to induce ridicule – these are included so that my readers may recognize them for what they are. I have included only factual items that are relevant in this summary to the points at issue.

The original reason for this investigation was the discovery, by chance, of two events that occurred in Belgium in November 1989 and March 1990. It did not seem credible that events of such magnitude – which were given six months' continual coverage by the Continental news agencies – were ignored by the British media at that time.

The main crux of these events was the unidentified detections by five radar stations, four Belgian and one German, of the NATO Air Defence Ground Environment (an 80-station radar defence complex that covers Europe), and the military interceptions made by F-16 aircraft of the Belgian Air Force.

Enquiries to the United Kingdom radar establishment at West Drayton as to whether these detections were recorded by our own radar resulted in an immediate reply from the Ministry of Defence in Whitehall. They stated that there had never been a detection by our own radar that had not been identified or explained. They also requested that any further radar enquiries be directed to them, and not to other establishments.

I wrote nine letters to the Ministry of Defence before they would admit (despite the known facts about radar detection) that radar will only detect its own reflection from an object of opacity and substance.

It was at this time that I made contact with sources in the Belgian Air Force. The information I received was considerable. The sheer weight of numbers of reliable public and police witnesses, the mass of data from the radar stations involved, the complexity and detail of the interceptions, the recorded performances of the on-board F-16 radar by the pilots of the Belgian Air Force, when taken in conjunction with the televised press release given by General-Major Wilfrid De Brouwer and the statement by the Belgian Minister of Defence to the Belgian Parliament, prove beyond doubt that unidentified flying objects of some kind were present above Belgium in November 1989, and March 1990.

The opinion was expressed by General-Major Wilfrid De Brouwer that these unidentified detections appeared to be of an extremely powerful electromagnetic force.

It was at this point, owing to the obstructive attitude of the Ministry of Defence and the highly suspect attitude of the British media, that I decided to make an approach to the European Parliament.

It was also because of an anomaly in statements made by

the Minister and the Ministry of Defence that the whole nature of this enquiry began to assume a different aspect; from that of being a simple exercise to establish whether objects of some kind actually did appear above Belgium in 1989/90, to an enquiry into a chain of events that would seem to indicate evasion of a highly suspect nature by the American and British defence establishments.

It was the realization that, although finally admitting the reliability of radar detection, and stating that there had never been an instance where a detection by our radar had never been identified or explained, the Ministry of Defence appeared to have overlooked the fact that the British radar defence system and the radar defence systems of the Belgian and Germans *are one and the same*! We are all part of the 80-station NATO Air Defence Ground Environment radar complex that covers the whole of Europe.

It was also at this time that I made contact with Admiral of the Fleet, the Lord Hill-Norton. Lord Hill-Norton was a former Chief of Defence Staff in the Ministry of Defence, and a senior NATO Commander. Admiral Hill-Norton expressed the opinion that UK radar would almost certainly have been informed of the unidentified Belgian radar detections because 'that is how the system works!' In short, any detection by this radar complex would automatically be notified to the rest of the system.

In a letter to Admiral Hill-Norton, the Secretary of State for Defence, Malcolm Rifkind, stated that we were not advised by the Belgians of their unidentified radar detections because they did not consider them a threat. He stated that notification of unidentified radar detections was at the discretion of the operators, and such detections were not automatically notified to the rest of the NADGE radar system. Malcolm Rifkind did not answer the question put by Admiral Hill-Norton concerning a reply from the Ministry of Defence. They had stated that: 'Our air defence experts did not consider the Belgian detections to be a threat'.

The question was a simple one: If, according to the Secretary of State for Defence, we were *not* advised by the

Belgians of their unidentified radar detections, *how, when our air defence experts did not know of them, could they possibly postulate that they did not constitute a threat?*

One must also consider the irrevocable fact that as we are dealing with the confirmed appearance of a phenomenon – the composition and origins of which are completely unknown – there is no defence ministry, British or Belgian, in any position to postulate whether they constitute a threat or not.

The statements therefore, of Malcolm Rifkind and the Ministry of defence, that the Belgian Ministry of Defence and British air defence experts did not consider these radar detections a threat are not logical and are not commensurate with the facts.

Highly skilled radar operators of the Belgian NATO Air Defence Ground Environment system were not able to identify their positive detections. They were declared *hostile*. Because of this classification they were considered a threat. Interceptions were ordered and made by F-16 aircraft of the Belgian Air Force. At 22h 47m, on the night of 30–31 March 1990, two F-16 aircraft of the Belgian Air Force pursued an unidentified target, moving at radar-recorded speeds well in excess of 1,000 knots, for over 1 hour. After 16 changes of course (all on a westerly heading towards the United Kingdom) contact was lost over Tubize (30 kilometres south-west of Brussels) as the target veered sharply to a south-easterly heading and disappeared after travelling 1½ kilometres on this heading.

At its nearest point, this target, which was classified as hostile, was six minutes from Dover.

The Secretary of State for Defence, in a letter to Admiral The Lord Hill-Norton, stated that notification of radar detections was at the discretion of the radar operators and *did not occur automatically*. A letter from General-Major Wilfrid De Brouwer of the Belgian Air Force has contradicted this, by stating that unidentified detections by the Belgian NATO Air Defence Ground Environment radars *would automatically have been advised* to UK radar at Neatshead in Norfolk. This being so, *particularly in a case involving unidentified radar detections,* it *must* be the case that United Kingdom radar at Neatshead in Norfolk were notified, and consequently *the Minister, and the Ministry of Defence, would have been aware of these detections.*

This proven sequence of events must cast grave doubts on the statements by the Ministry of Defence that there had never been an instance where an unidentified radar detection by our own radar defence system had not been accounted for or explained. It also brings into question the anomaly of the statement by the Secretary of State for Defence, that we were *not* advised by Belgian NATO radars of their unidentified radar detections because the Belgians did not consider them a threat. *If the Belgians had already classified their detections as hostile because they did not know what they were, on what basis could they then make the assumption that they did not consider them a threat?*

General-Major De Brouwer has already stated that unidentified radar detections would automatically have been advised to United Kingdom radar at Neatshead. The classification 'hostile', and consequent ordered interceptions by aircraft of the Belgian Air Force, is proof that the Belgians did consider them a threat.

Because of difficulties with the Ministry of Defence in obtaining any credible information on the Belgian radar detections, I appealed directly to the President of the European Parliament. This resulted in a 36-page submission to the Committee on Petitions, asking for an inquiry to be made into the events that took place in Belgium in 1989/90.

The nature of this submission was that the statement by the Belgian Minister of Defence that there were flying objects of some kind over Belgium in 1989/90, and taking all hypotheses into account, he could not tell what they were, was inconclusive. It was therefore incumbent on the European Parliament, in the interests of the security of the member states, to hold an inquiry to clarify the situation.

On 24/25 February 1994, it was decided that the issues raised by my submission fell within the sphere of activities of the European Committees. It was declared admissible by the

Committee on Petitions pursuant to rule 156 of the Rules of Procedure. It was decided that this petition, now listed as Petition 990/93, should be forwarded to the Committee on Energy, Research and Technology of the European Parliament for their further action.

At the time of its submission, and on its acceptance by the European Parliament, press releases were issued to all the major press agencies on the Continent and in the United Kingdom. None of these agencies deemed it appropriate to allow any coverage whatever to these releases.

I have received an abundance of information from the Belgian Air Force. My initial enquiries to them resulted in a flood of information from several sources and provided me with all the information needed to compile my request for an inquiry by the European Parliament. I assumed from this that I would have the backing of the Belgian establishment.

From the moment that the Belgian Air Force were advised that this report had been submitted, and asked for their assistance in any forthcoming inquiry, sources that had previously been free with their information suddenly stopped. Repeated requests for their support were not replied to.

On 26 January 1995, I sent an appendix to be added to my Petition no. 990/93 to Mr E. Newman, Chairman, Committee on Petitions, Secretariat General, L 2929, Luxembourg. This was to inform the Committee of the contradictory statements by General-Major De Brouwer and the United Kingdom Secretary of State for Defence, concerning the automatic alerting of unidentified radar detections by Belgian and German NATO Air Defence Ground Environment radar stations, to United Kingdom radar at Neatshead in Norfolk. This appendix was also to advise the Committee that the Belgian Minister and Ministry of Defence, the Belgian police and the Belgian Air Force have not replied to my requests for their assistance in any inquiry.

In view of the many documents concerning this matter that have been apparently lost in the post, or not delivered, I had specifically asked Mr Newman for confirmation of receipt of this appendix. Finally, after six reminders and a five-month delay, a copy of this document, sent by a private postal service, reached its destination.

I have asked the Post Office for their assurance that my mail is not being intercepted or tampered with.

The private postal service have provided me with evidence of receipt of delivery, by a Mr Figus of the European Parliament in Luxembourg. The Post Office could only report that delivery was made by the Luxembourg Postal Authorities to the General Post Room of the European Parliament.

I tried to telephone Mr Newman, Chairman of the Petitions Committee, at the European Parliament in Luxembourg. The call was to request confirmation of receipt of the appendix which was to be added to my Petition no. 990/93 sent in January 1995. After an eight-minute delay during which recorded music was played, the call was cut off.

I have now received confirmation from Mr Newman, dated 22 May 1995, that he has received my recent correspondence. He states that when petitions are referred to other committees, it is up to the committee concerned to decide whether or not to take further action. Mr Newman informs me that I may contact the chairman of the relevant committee directly.

The delays involved, the emphasis that further action was at the discretion of the committee, do not fill me with confidence. I have my first apprehensions as to the inclinations of the European Parliament.

This enquiry began, in the first instance, with the intention *not* to speculate as to the material composition of the flying objects that appeared over Belgium, but to establish the fact that something did appear above Belgium in November and March 1990. I believe this document is conclusive proof that this happened.

In the course of my research, certain facts have become obvious by their repetition. This has caused me great concern. From the preceding chapters, it would seem that a policy of evasion and deception is being pursued by the defence, intelligence and media organizations of the American and United Kingdom establishments. It was this that resulted in my appeal to the European Parliament. It has now caused a change in the nature of this enquiry.

It is *not* now an attempt to establish the appearance of these phenomena – this is proven; it is to question *why* such a deception is being carried out.

There are only three possible explanations for the phenomena:

- They are a highly secret military development.
- These objects are a natural phenomenon.
- They are extraterrestrial in origin.

The fact that the first, and subsequent, appearances of these phenomena have caused confusion to all the various national defence organizations involved would indicate that these objects are *not* a secret military development. The Belgian Ministry of Defence stated that all possible hypotheses had been taken into account. This can only mean that these phenomena are neither a highly secret military development, nor a natural phenomenon. If these objects were a natural phenomenon, there would be no need for the intelligence agencies of America and the United Kingdom to pursue such policies of deception and secrecy.

It can only be, therefore, that, as all known hypotheses have been considered and rejected, these phenomena are not of this Earth and are known to the American and British governments.

The point of a deception is to deceive. To deceive is to delude or mislead. A government would mislead either to conceal a fact that it felt – for whatever reason – that it was not in the interest of the public to know, or if it was put in a situation where it had no alternative but to conceal. Either way, whatever form this intelligence has taken, and whatever course it has chosen to follow, its purpose here is suspect. The clandestine actions of the intelligence services would indicate a knowledge, and an involvement, that show that its intentions are not open and honest. It would seem that an infiltration that started in America is penetrating all levels of society: the doors are being slammed in the avenues of power; the cancer is spreading at an alarming rate. The scenario is frightening.

There are two kinds of evidence: the proven physical evidence as in the case of the Belgian detections, and the circumstantial, as generally quoted in this dossier. Provided that the circumstantial evidence is cumulative enough, it can only be regarded as proof that there is a case to be answered.

I have tried to present, without prejudice, a true and accurate record of all the facts, in the form of the letters sent to me by the various agencies involved. It is now up to my readers to carefully consider the evidence in this correspondence, to note the lack of some replies and the transparency of others, and to reach their own conclusions.

The evidence of the correspondence from the following should be noted: the Belgian Air Force; the Belgian Police; two Belgian Ministers of Defence; the Belgian Ministry of Defence; the Belgian Embassy; Professor Meessen, Leuven University; General-Major De Brouwer of the Belgian Air Force; the London office for Members of the European Parliament; three British Members of the European Parliament; Malcolm Rifkind, Secretary of State for Defence; Jeremy Hanley, Minister of State for the Armed Forces; Commander T. J. H. Laurence, Private Secretary to the Secretary of State for Defence; N. Pope, of the Ministry of Defence; Dr David Clark, Shadow Secretary of State for Defence; Admiral of the Fleet the Lord Hill-Norton, GCB; the Rt Hon Sir Keith Speed, RD, MP; the North Atlantic Treaty Organization; the United Nations; the Central Intelligence Agency; *The Times* newspaper; Central Television; Contact International; SOBEPS; Mr Johnsen Tokano, the Japanese Deputy Prime Minister; the General Post Office; Mr E. Newman, Chairman of Petitions, the European Parliament; Mr Neil Fleming; Miss Linda Moulton-Howe; Miss Maria

Ward; the Press Complaints Commission; various letters from senior airline captains; the correspondence from Carol Davis and Mrs B. Ferguson.

The Committee for Energy, Research and Technology of the European Parliament have decided to discuss my application for an inquiry into the Belgian phenomena; to this must now be added a request for an inquiry into a possible international deception, based on the cumulative circumstantial evidence contained in this document.

Now we shall have to wait and see. The crucial question is whether the European Parliament decide to take the necessary action to further an inquiry.

I am able to write this summary before the story reaches its conclusion. If the Committee for Energy, Research and Technology decide not to hold an inquiry, it will indicate an infiltration that has reached the highest levels in the European Parliament, and all will be lost. If they do agree to hold an inquiry, the greatest problem will be in choosing the members to serve on that inquiry.

It would be wise to assume that we are dealing with a vastly superior intelligence that has already arrived here, and whose motives are suspect. If this is so, then the members chosen to serve on such an inquiry must be incorruptible and their integrity absolute.

Whatever the result, the point of this report will have been justified.

Index